The Assembly Of God
Miscellaneous Writings Of
C. H. Mackintosh
Volume III

C. (Charles) H. (Henry) Mackintosh

Alpha Editions

This Edition Published in 2022

ISBN: 9789355891624

Design and Setting By
Alpha Editions
www.alphaedis.com
Email – info@alphaedis.com

TABLE OF CONTENTS

THE MAN OF GOD

The sentence which we have just penned occurs in Paul's second Epistle to his beloved son Timothy—an epistle marked, as we know, by intense individuality. All thoughtful students of Scripture have noticed the striking contrast between the two Epistles of Paul to Timothy. In the first, the Church is presented in its order, and Timothy is instructed as to how he is to behave himself therein. In the second, on the contrary, the Church is presented in its ruin. The house of God has become the great house, in the which there are vessels to dishonor as well as vessels to honor; and where, moreover, errors and evils abound—heretical teachers and false professors, on every hand.

It is in this epistle of individuality, then, that the expression, "The man of God" is used with such obvious force and meaning. It is in times of general declension, of ruin and confusion that the faithfulness, devotedness, and decision of the individual man of God are specially called for. And it is a signal mercy for such an one to know that, spite of the hopeless failure of the Church as a responsible witness for Christ, it is the privilege of the individual to tread as holy a path, to taste as deep communion, and to enjoy as rich blessings, as could be known in the Church's brightest days.

This is a most encouraging and consolatory fact—a fact established by many infallible proofs, and set forth in the very passage from which our heading4 is taken. We shall here quote at length this passage of singular weight and power:

"But continue thou in the things which thou hast learned and hast been assured of, knowing of whom thou hast learned them; and that from a child thou hast known the Holy Scriptures, which are able to make thee wise unto salvation through faith which is in Christ Jesus. All Scripture is given by inspiration of God, and is profitable for doctrine, for reproof, for correction, for instruction in righteousness, that the man of God may be *perfect*, throughly *furnished unto all good works*"[1] (2 Tim. iii. 14-17).

Here we have "the man of God," in the midst of all the ruin and confusion, the heresies and moral pravities of the last days, standing forth in his own distinct individuality, "perfect, thoroughly furnished unto all good works." And, may we not ask, what more could be said in the Church's brightest days? If we go back to the day of Pentecost itself, with all its display of power and glory, have we anything higher, or better, or more solid than that which is set forth in the words "perfect, thoroughly furnished unto all good works?"

And is it not a signal mercy for anyone who desires to stand for God, in a dark and evil day, to be told that, spite of all the darkness, the evil, the error and confusion, he possesses that which can make a child *wise* unto salvation, and make a man *perfect* and thoroughly furnished unto all good works? Assuredly it is; and we have to praise our God for it, with full and overflowing hearts. To have access, in days like these, to the eternal fountain of inspiration, where the child and the man can meet and drink and be satisfied—that fountain so clear that the honest, simple soul can understand; and so deep that you cannot reach the bottom—that peerless, priceless volume which meets the child at his mother's knee, and makes him wise unto salvation; and meets the man in the most advanced stage of his practical career and makes him perfect and fully furnished for the exigence of every hour.

However, we shall have occasion, ere we close this paper, to look more particularly at "the man of God," and to consider what is the special force and meaning of this term. That there is very much more involved in it than is ordinarily understood, we are most fully persuaded.

There are three aspects in which man is presented in Scripture: in the first place, we have *man in nature*; secondly, *a man in Christ*; and, thirdly, we have, *the man of God*. It might perhaps be thought that the second and third are synonymous; but we shall find a very material difference between them. True, I must be a man in Christ before I can be a man of God; but they are by no means interchangeable terms.

Let us then, in the first place, consider

MAN IN NATURE

This is a very comprehensive term indeed. Under this title, we shall find every possible shade of character, temperament, and disposition. Man, on the platform of nature, graduates between two extremes. You may view him at the very highest point of cultivation, or at the very lowest point of degradation. You may see him surrounded with all the advantages, the refinements and the so-called dignities of civilized life; or you may find him sunk in all the shameless and barbarous customs of savage existence. You may view him in the almost numberless grades, ranks, classes, and *castes* into which the human family has distributed itself.

Then again, in the self-same class, or caste, you will find the most vivid contrasts, in the way of character, temper, and disposition. There, for example, is a man of such an atrocious temper that he is the very horror of every one who knows him. He is the plague of his family circle, and a perfect nuisance to society. He can be compared to a porcupine with all his quills perpetually up; and if you meet him once you will not wish to meet him again. There, on the other hand, is a man of the sweetest disposition and most amiable temper. He is just as attractive as the other is repulsive. He is a tender, loving, faithful husband; a kind, affectionate, considerate father; a thoughtful, liberal master; a kindly, genial neighbor; a generous friend, beloved by all, and justly so: the more you know him the more you must like him, and if you meet him once you are sure to wish to meet him again.

Further, you may meet on the platform of nature, a man who is false and deceitful to the very heart's core. He delights in lying, cheating, and deception. He is mean and contemptible in his thoughts, words and ways; a man to whom all who know him would like to give as wide a berth as possible. And, on the other hand, you may meet a man of high principle, frank, honorable, generous, upright; one who would scorn to tell a lie, or do a mean act; whose reputation is unblemished, his character unexceptionable. His word would be taken for any amount; he is one with whom all who know him would be glad to have dealings; an almost perfect natural character; a man of whom it might be said, he lacks but one thing.

Finally, as you pass to and fro on nature's platform, you may meet the atheist who affects to deny the existence of God; the infidel who denies God's revelation; the skeptic and the rationalist who disbelieves everything. And, on the other hand, you will meet the superstitious devotee who spends his time in prayers and fastings, ordinances, and ceremonies; and who feels sure he is earning a place in heaven by a wearisome round of religious observances that actually *un*fit him for the proper functions and responsibilities of domestic and social life. You may meet men of every imaginable shade of religious opinion, high church, low church, broad church, and no church; men who, without a spark of divine life in their souls, are contending for the powerless forms of a traditionary religion.

Now, there is one grand and awfully solemn fact common to all these various classes, castes, grades, shades, and conditions of men who occupy the platform of nature, and that is there is not so much as a single link between them and heaven—there is no link with the Man who sits at the right hand of God—no link with the new creation. They are unconverted, and without Christ. As regards God, and Christ, and eternal life, and heaven, they all—however they may differ morally, socially, and religiously—stand on one common ground; they are far from God—they are out of Christ—they are in their sins—they are in the flesh—they are of the world—they are on their way to hell.

There is really no getting over this, if we are to listen to the voice of Holy Scripture. False teachers may deny it. Infidels may pretend to smile contemptuously at the idea; but Scripture is plain as can be. It speaks in manifold places of a fire that NEVER shall be quenched, and of a worm that shall never die.

It is the very height of folly for anyone to seek to set aside the plain testimony of the word of God on this most solemn and weighty subject. Better far to let that testimony fall, with all its weight and authority, upon the heart and conscience—infinitely better to flee from the wrath to come than to attempt to deny that it is coming, and that, when it does come, it will abide forever—yes, forever, and forever, and forever! Tremendous thought!—over-whelming consideration! May it speak with living power to the soul of the unconverted reader, leading him to cry out in all sincerity, "What is to be done?"

Yes, here is the question, "What must I do to be saved?" The divine answer is wrapped up in the following words which dropped from the lips of two of Christ's very highest and most gifted ambassadors. "Repent and be converted," said Peter to the Jew. "Believe on the Lord Jesus Christ, and thou shalt be saved and thy house," said Paul to the Gentile. And again, the latter of these two blessed messengers, in summing up his own ministry, thus defines the whole matter, "Testifying both to the Jews, and also to the Greeks, repentance toward God, and faith toward our Lord Jesus Christ."

How simple! But how real! How deep! How thoroughly practical! It is not a nominal, national head belief. It is not saying, in mere flippant profession, "I believe." Ah! no; it is something far deeper and more serious than this. It is much to be feared that a large amount of the professed faith of this our day is deplorably superficial, and that many who throng our preaching rooms and lecture halls are, after all, but wayside and stony ground hearers. The plough of conviction and repentance has not passed over them. The fallow ground has never been broken up. The arrow of conviction has never pierced them through and through. They have never been broken down, turned inside out—thoroughly revolutionized. The preaching of the gospel to all such is just like scattering precious seed on the hard pavement or the beaten highway. It does not penetrate. It does not enter into the depths of the soul; the conscience is not reached; the heart is not affected. The seed lies on the surface, it has not taken root, and is soon carried away.

Nor is this all. It is also much to be feared that many of the preachers of the present day, in their efforts to make the gospel simple, lose sight of the abiding necessity of repentance, and the essential necessity of the action of the Holy Ghost, without which so-called faith is a mere human exercise and passes away like the vapors of the morning, leaving the soul still in the region of nature, satisfied with itself, daubed with the untempered mortar of a merely human gospel that cries peace, peace, where there is no peace, but the most imminent danger.

All this is very serious, and should lead the soul into profound exercise. We want the reader to give it his grave and immediate consideration. We would put this pointed question to him, which we entreat him to answer, now, "*Have you got eternal life?*" Say, dear friend, *have you?* "He that believeth on the Son of God hath eternal life." Grand reality! If you have not got this, you have nothing.

You are still on that platform of nature of which we have spoken so much. Yes, you are still there; no matter though you were the very fairest specimen to be found there—amiable, polished, affable, frank, generous, truthful, upright, honorable, attractive, beloved, learned, cultivated, and even pious after a merely human fashion. You may be all this, and yet not have a single pulsation of eternal life in your soul.

This may sound harsh and severe. But it is true; and you will find out its truth sooner or later. We want you to find it out *now*. We want you to see that you are a thorough bankrupt, in the fullest sense of that word. A deed of bankruptcy has been filed against you in the high court of heaven. Here are its terms, "*They that are in the flesh cannot please God.*" Have you ever pondered these words? Have you ever seen their application to yourself? So long as you are unrepentant, unconverted, unbelieving, you cannot do a single thing to please God—not one. "In the flesh" and "on the platform of nature" mean one and the same thing; and so long as you are there, you cannot please God. "You must be born again"—must be renewed in the very deepest springs of your being: unrenewed nature is wholly unable to see, and unfit to enter, the kingdom of God. You must be born of water and of the Spirit—that is by the living word of God, and of the Holy Ghost. There is no other way by which to enter the kingdom. It is not by self-improvement, but by new birth we reach the blessed kingdom of God. "That which is born of the flesh is flesh;" and "the flesh profiteth nothing," for "they that are in the flesh cannot please God."

How distinct is all this! How pointed! How personal! How earnestly we desire that the unawakened or undecided reader should, just now, take it home to himself, as though he were the only individual upon the face of the earth. It will not do to generalize—to rest satisfied with saying, "We are all sinners." No; it is an intensely individual matter. "You *must* be born again." If you again ask, "How?" hear the divine response from the lips of the Master Himself, "As Moses lifted up the serpent in the wilderness, even so must the Son of man be lifted up; that whosoever believeth in Him should not perish, but have eternal life."

Here is the sovereign remedy, for every poor broken-hearted, conscience-smitten, hell-deserving sinner—for every one who owns himself lost—who confesses his sins, and judges himself—for every weary, heavy-laden, sin-burdened soul—here is God's own blessed promise: Jesus died, that you might live. He was condemned, that you might be justified. He drank the cup of wrath, that you might drink the cup of salvation. Behold Him hanging on yonder cross for thee. See what He did for thee. Believe that He satisfied, on your behalf, *all* the claims of justice before the throne of God. See all your sins laid on Him—your guilt imputed to Him—your entire condition represented and disposed of by Him. See His atoning death answering perfectly for all that was or ever could be brought against you. See Him rising from the dead, having accomplished all. See Him ascending into the heavens, bearing in His divine Person the marks of His finished atonement. See Him seated on the throne of God, in the very highest place of power. See Him crowned with glory and honor. Believe in Him, and you will receive remission of sins, the gift of eternal life, the seal of the Holy Ghost. You will pass off the platform of nature—you will be "*A man in Christ.*"

PART II

To all whose eyes have been opened to see their true condition by nature, who have been brought under the convicting power of the Holy Ghost, who know something of the real meaning of a broken heart and a contrite spirit—to all such it must be of the deepest possible interest to know the divine secret of rest and peace. If it be true—and it is true, because God says it—that "they that are *in the flesh* cannot please God," then how is any one to get *out of the flesh*? How can he pass off the platform of nature? How can he reach the blessed position of those to whom the Holy Ghost declares, "Ye are not in the flesh but in the Spirit"?

These are momentous questions, surely. For, be it thoroughly known and ever remembered, that no improvement of our old nature is of any value whatsoever as to our standing before God. It may be all very well, so far as this life is concerned, for a man to improve himself by every means within his reach, to cultivate his mind, furnish his memory, elevate his moral tone, advance his social position. All this is quite true, so true as not to need a moment's argument.

But, admitting in the fullest manner the truth of all this, it leaves wholly untouched the solemn and sweeping statement of the inspired apostle that, "they that are in the flesh cannot please God." There *must* be a new standing altogether, and this new standing cannot be reached by any change in the old nature—by any doings or formalities, feelings, ordinances of religion, prayers, alms or sacraments. Do what you will with nature and it is nature still. "That which is born of the flesh is flesh;" and do what you will with flesh you cannot make it spirit. There must be a new life—a life flowing from the new man, the last Adam, who has become, in resurrection, the Head of a new race.

How is this most precious life to be had? Hear the memorable answer— hear it, anxious reader, hear it and live. "Verily, verily, I say unto you, he that heareth My word, and believeth on Him that sent Me, *hath* everlasting life, and shall not come into judgment; but *is passed* from death unto life" (John v. 24).

Here we have a total change of standing; a passing from death to life; from a position in which there is not so much as a single link with heaven, with the new creation, with the risen Man in glory, into a position in which there is not a single link with the first man, with the old creation, and this present evil world. And all this is through believing on the Son of God—

not *saying* we believe, but really, truly, heartily, believing on the Son of God; not by a mere intellectual faith, but believing with the heart.

Thus only does any one become

A MAN IN CHRIST

Every true believer is a man in Christ. Whether it be the convert of yesterday or the hoary headed saint of fifty or sixty years' standing as a Christian, each stands in precisely the same blessed position—he is in Christ. There can be no difference here. The practical *state* may differ immensely; but the positive standing is one and the same. As on the platform of nature, you may meet with every imaginable shade, class, grade, and condition (though all having one common standing) so on the new, the divine, the heavenly platform, you may meet with every possible variety of practical condition: the greatest possible difference in intelligence, experience, and spiritual power, while all possessing the same standing before God, all being in Christ. There can be no degrees as to standing, whatever there may be as to state. The convert of yesterday, and the hoary headed father in Christ are both alike as to standing. Each is a man in Christ, and there can be no advance upon this. We sometimes hear of, "The higher Christian life:" but, strictly speaking, there is no such thing as a higher or a lower Christian life, inasmuch as Christ is the life of every believer. It may be that those who use the term mean a right thing. They probably refer to the higher stages of the Christian life—greater nearness to God, greater likeness to Christ, greater power in the Spirit, more devotedness, more separation from the world, more entire consecration of heart to Christ. But all these things belong to the question of our *state*, not to our standing. This latter is absolute, settled, unchangeable. It is in Christ—nothing less, nothing more, nothing different. If we are not in Christ, we are in our sins; but if we are in Christ, we cannot possibly be higher, as to standing.

If the reader will turn with us, for a few moments, to I Cor. xv. 45-48, he will find some powerful teaching on this great foundation truth. The apostle speaks here of two men, "The first and the second." And let it be carefully noted that the Second Man is by no means federally connected with the first, but stands in contrast with him—a new, independent, divine, heavenly source of life in Himself. The first man has been entirely set aside, as a ruined, guilty, outcast creature. We speak of Adam federally, as the head of a race. Personally, Adam was saved by grace; but if we look at him from a federal standpoint, we see him a hopeless wreck.

The first man is an irremediable ruin. This is proved by the fact of a *second* Man; for truly we may say of the men as of the covenants, "If the first had been found faultless, then should no place have been sought for the Second." But the very fact of a second Man being introduced demonstrates the hopeless ruin of the first. Why a second, if aught could be made of the first? If our old Adam nature was, in any wise, capable of being improved, there was no need of something new. But "they that are in the flesh cannot please God." "For in Christ Jesus neither circumcision availeth anything, nor uncircumcision, but a new creation" (Rom. viii.: Gal. vi.).

There is immense moral power in all this line of teaching. It sets forth Christianity in vivid and striking contrast with every form of religiousness under the sun. Take Judaism or any other *ism* that ever was known or that now exists in this world, and what do you find it to be? Is it not invariably something designed for the testing, or experimenting for the improvement, or advancement of the first man? Unquestionably.

But what is Christianity? It is something entirely new—heavenly, spiritual, divine. It is based upon the cross of Christ, in the which the first man came to his end, where sin was put away, judgment borne, the old man crucified and put out of God's sight forever, so far as all believers are concerned. The cross closes, for faith, the history of the first man. "I am crucified with Christ," says the apostle. And again, "They that are Christ's have crucified the flesh with its affections and lusts."

Are these mere figures of speech, or do they set forth, in the mighty words of the Holy Ghost, the grand fact of the entire setting aside of the first man, as utterly worthless and condemned? The latter, most assuredly. Christianity starts, as it were, from the open grave of the Second Man, to pursue its bright career onward to eternal glory. It is, emphatically, a new creation in which there is not so much as a single shred of the old thing— for in this "all things are of God." And if "*all things*" are of God, there can be nothing of man.

What rest! What comfort! What strength! What moral elevation! What sweet relief for the poor burdened soul that has been vainly seeking, for years perhaps, to find peace in self-improvement! What deliverance from the wretched thralldom of legality, in all its phases, to find out the precious secret that my guilty, ruined, bankrupt self—the very thing that I have been trying by every means in my power to improve, has been completely and forever set aside—that God is not looking for any amendment in it—that He has condemned it and put it to death in the cross of His Son! What an answer is here to the monk, the ascetic, and the ritualist! Oh, that it were understood in all its emancipating power! This heavenly, this divine, this spiritual Christianity. Surely were it only known in its living power and reality, it would deliver the soul from the thousand and one forms of corrupt religion whereby the arch-enemy and deceiver is ruining the souls of untold millions. We may truly say that Satan's most successful effort against the truth of the gospel, against the Christianity of the New

Testament, is seen in the fact of his leading unconverted people to take and apply to themselves ordinances of the Christian religion, and to profess many of its doctrines. In this way he blinds their eyes to their own true condition, as utterly ruined, guilty, and undone; and strikes a deadly blow at the pure gospel of Christ. The best piece that was ever put upon the "old garment" of man's ruined nature is the profession of Christianity; and, the better the piece, the worse the rent. See Mark ii. 21.

Let us bend an attentive ear to the following weighty words of the greatest teacher and best exponent of true Christianity the world ever saw. "For *I* through the law *am dead* to the law, that I might live to God. *I am crucified* with Christ; nevertheless I live; yet *not I,* but Christ liveth in me." Mark this, "I—not I—but Christ." The old "I"—"crucified." The new "I"—Christ. "And the life which I now live in the flesh, I live by the faith of the Son of God, who loved me and gave Himself for me" (Gal. ii. 19, 20).[2]

This, and nothing else, is Christianity. It is not "the old man," the first man, becoming religious, even though the religion be the profession of the doctrines, and the adopting of the ordinances of Christianity. No; it is the death and burial of the old man—the old I—and becoming a new man in Christ. Every true believer is a new man in Christ. He has passed clean out of the old creation-standing—the old estate of sin and death, guilt and condemnation; and he has passed into a new creation-standing—a new estate of life and righteousness in a risen and glorified Christ, the Head of the new creation, the last Adam.

Such is the position and unalterable standing of the feeblest believer in Christ. There is absolutely no other standing for any Christian. I must either be in the first man or in the Second. There is no *third* man, for the Second Man is the last Adam. There is no middle ground. I am either *in Christ,* or I am *in my sins.* But if I am in Christ, I am as He is before God. "As *He is* so are *we,* in this world." He does not say, "As He *was*" but "as He *is.*" That is, the Christian is viewed by God as one with Christ—the Second Man, in whom He delights. We do not speak of His Deity, of course, which is incommunicable. That blessed One stood in the believer's stead—bore his sins, died his death, paid his penalty, represented him in every respect; took all his guilt, all his liabilities, all that pertained to him as a man in nature, stood as his substitute, in all the verity and reality of that word, and having divinely met his case, and borne his judgment, He rose from the dead, and is now the Head, the Representative, and the only true definition of the believer before God.

To this most glorious and enfranchising truth, Scripture bears the amplest testimony. The passage which we have just quoted from Galatians is a most vivid, powerful, and condensed statement of it. And if the reader will turn to Rom. vi. he will find further evidence. We shall quote some of the weighty sentences.

"What shall we say then? Shall we continue in sin, that grace may abound? Far be the thought. How shall *we that are dead* to sin, live any longer therein? Know ye not, that so many of us as were baptized to Jesus Christ were baptized to His death? Therefore we are buried with Him by baptism unto death; that *like as Christ* was raised up from the dead by the glory of the Father, *even so we also* should walk in newness of life. For if we have been planted together in the likeness of His death, we shall be also of resurrection. Knowing this that *our old man is crucified with Him*, that the body of sin might be destroyed, that henceforth we should not serve sin. For he that is dead is freed from sin. Now if we *be dead with Christ*, we believe that we shall also live with Him. Knowing that Christ being raised from the dead, dieth no more; death hath no more dominion over Him. For in that He died, He died unto sin once; but in that He liveth He liveth unto God. Likewise reckon ye also yourselves to be dead indeed unto sin, but alive unto God, through Jesus Christ our Lord" (Rom. vi. I-11).

Reader, mark especially these words in the foregoing quotation—"We that *are dead*"—"We are buried with Him"—"*Like as Christ* was raised ... *even so* we also"—"Our old man is crucified with Him"—"Dead with Christ"—"Dead indeed unto sin." Do we really understand such utterances? Have we entered into their real force and meaning? Do we, in very deed, perceive their application to ourselves? These are searching questions for the heart, and needful. The real doctrine of Rom. vi. is but little apprehended. There are thousands who profess to believe in the atoning virtue of the death of Christ, but who do not see aught therein beyond the forgiveness of their *sins*. They do not see the crucifixion, death, and burial of the old man—the destruction of the body of sin—the condemnation of sin—the entire setting aside of the old system of things belonging to their first Adam condition—in a word their perfect identification with a dead and risen Christ. Hence it is that we press this grand and all-important line of truth upon the attention of the reader. It lies at the very base of all true Christianity, and forms an integral part of the truth of the gospel.

Let us hearken to further evidence on the point. Hear what the apostle said to the Colossians: "Wherefore, if ye be *dead with Christ* from the rudiments of the world, why, *as though living in the world*, are ye subject to ordinances, after the commandments and doctrines of men, [such as] touch not, taste not, handle not"?—thus it is that human ordinances speak to us, telling us not to touch this, not to taste that, not to handle the other, as if there could possibly be any divine principle involved in such things— "which all are to perish with the using;" and "which, have indeed a show of wisdom in will worship, and humility, and neglecting of the body—not in any honor—to the satisfying of the flesh. If ye then be risen with Christ, seek those things which are above, where Christ sitteth on the right hand of God. Set your mind on things that are above, not on things on the earth. For *ye have died* and your life is hid with Christ in God" (Col. ii., iii. 2).

Here, again, let us inquire how far we enter into the true force, meaning, and application of such words as these—"Why as though *living in the world*," etc.? Are we living in the world or living in heaven—which? The true Christian is one who has died out of this present evil world. He has no more to do with it than Christ. "Like as Christ ... even so we." He is dead to the law—dead to sin: alive in Christ—alive to God—alive in the new creation. He belongs to heaven. He is enrolled as a citizen of heaven. His religion, his politics, his morals are all heavenly. He is a heavenly man walking on the earth, and fulfilling all the duties which belong to the varied relationships in which the hand of God has placed him, and in which the word of God most fully recognizes him, and amply guides him, such as husband, father, master, child, servant, and such like. The Christian is not a monk, an ascetic, or a hermit. He is, we repeat, a heavenly, spiritual man, *in* the world, but not *of* it. He is like a foreigner, so far as his residence here is concerned. He is in the body, as to the fact of his condition; but not in the flesh as to the principle of his standing. He is *a man in Christ.*

Ere closing this article, we should like to call the reader's attention to 2 Cor. xii. In it he will find, at once, the *positive standing* and the *possible state* of the believer. The standing is fixed and unalterable, as set forth in that one comprehensive sentence—"A man in Christ." The state may graduate between the two extremes presented in the opening and closing verses of this chapter. A Christian may be in the third heaven, amid the seraphic visions of that blessed and holy place; or he may, if not watchful, sink down into all the gross and evil things named in vers. 20, 21.

It may be asked, "Is it possible that a true child of God could ever be found in such a low moral condition?" Alas! alas! reader, it is indeed possible. There is no depth of sin and folly into which a Christian is not capable of plunging, if not kept by the grace of God. Even the blessed apostle himself, when he came down from the third heaven, needed "a thorn in the flesh" to keep him from being "exalted above measure." We might suppose that a man who had been up in that bright and blessed region could never again feel the stirrings of pride. But the plain fact is that even the third heavens cannot cure the flesh. It is utterly incorrigible and must be judged and kept under, day by day, hour by hour, moment by moment, else it will cut out plenty of sorrowful work for us.

Still, the believer's standing is in Christ, forever justified, accepted, perfect in Him. And, moreover, he must ever judge his state by his standing, never his standing by his state. To attempt to reach the standing by my state is *legalism*; to refuse to judge my state by the standing is *antinomianism*. Both—though so diverse one from the other—are alike false, alike opposed to the truth of God, alike offensive to the Holy Ghost, alike removed from the divine idea of "A man in Christ."

PART III

Having considered the deeply interesting questions of "a man in nature" and "a man in Christ," it remains for us now to consider, in this third and last Part, the deeply practical subject of the title of this paper, namely,

THE MAN OF GOD

It would be a great mistake to suppose that every Christian is a man of God. Even in Paul's day—in the days of Timothy, there were many who bore the Christian name who were very far indeed from acquitting themselves as men of God, that is, as those who were really God's men, in the midst of the failure and error which, even then, had begun to creep in.

It is the perception of this fact that renders the second Epistle to Timothy so profoundly interesting. In it we have what we may call ample provision for the man of God, in the day in which he is called to live—a dark, evil, and perilous day, most surely, in which all who will live godly must keep the eye steadily fixed on Christ Himself—His name—His person—His Word, if they would make any headway against the tide.

It is hardly possible to read second Timothy without being struck with its intensely individual character. The very opening address is strikingly characteristic. "I thank God, whom I serve from my forefathers with pure conscience, that without ceasing I have remembrance of thee in my prayers night and day."

What glowing words are these! How affecting to harken thus to one man of God pouring the deep and tender feelings of his great, large, loving heart into the heart of another man of God! The dear apostle was beginning to feel the chilling influence that was fast creeping over the professing Church. He was tasting the bitterness of disappointed hopes. He found himself deserted by many who had once professed to be his friends and associates in that glorious work to which he had consecrated all the energies of his great soul. Many were becoming "ashamed of the testimony of our Lord, and of His prisoner." It was not that they altogether ceased to be Christians, or abandoned the Christian profession; but they turned their backs upon Paul, and left him alone in the day of trial.

Now, it is under such circumstances that the heart turns, with peculiar tenderness, to individual faithfulness and affection. If one is surrounded, on all hands, by true-hearted confessors—by a great cloud of witnesses—a large army of good soldiers of Jesus Christ—if the tide of devotedness is flowing around one and bearing him on its bosom, he is not so dependent upon individual sympathy and fellowship.

But, on the other hand, when the general condition of things is low, when the majority prove faithless, when old associates are dropping off, it is then that personal grace and true affection are specially valued. The dark background of general declension throws individual devotedness into beauteous relief.

Thus it is in this exquisite Epistle which now lies open before us. It does the heart good to harken to the breathings of the aged prisoner of Jesus Christ, who can speak of serving God from his forefathers with pure conscience, and of unceasing remembrance of his beloved son and true yoke-fellow.

It is specially interesting to notice that, both in reference to his own history and that of his beloved friend, Paul goes back to facts of very early date—facts in their own individual paths, facts prior to their meeting one another, and prior to what we may call their church associations—important and interesting as these things surely are in their place. Paul had served God, from his forefathers, with pure conscience, before he had known a fellow-Christian. This he could continue to do though deserted by all his Christian companions. So also, in the case of his faithful friend, he says, "I call to remembrance the unfeigned faith that is in thee, which dwelt in thy grandmother Lois, and thy mother Eunice: and I am persuaded that is in thee also."

This is very touching and very beautiful. We cannot but be struck with such references to the previous history of those beloved men of God. The "pure conscience" of the one, and "the unfeigned faith" of the other, indicate two grand moral qualities which all must possess if they would prove true men of God in a dark and evil day. The former has its immediate reference, in all things, to the one living and true God; the latter draws all its springs from Him. That, leads us to walk *before* God; this, enables us to walk *with* Him. Both together are indispensable in forming the character of the true man of God.

It is utterly impossible to over-estimate the importance of keeping a pure conscience before God, in all our ways. It is positively invaluable. It leads us to refer everything to God. It keeps us from being tossed hither and thither by every wave and current of human opinion. It imparts stability and consistency to the entire course and character.

We are all in imminent danger of falling under human influence—of shaping our way according to the thoughts of our fellow-man, adopting his cue, or mounting his hobby.

All this is destructive of the character of the man of God. If you take your tone from your fellow, if you suffer yourself to be formed in a merely human mould, if your faith stands in the wisdom of man, if your object is to please men, then instead of being a man of God, you will become a member of a party or clique. You will lose that lovely freshness and originality so essential to the individual servant of Christ, and become marked by the peculiar and dominant features of a sect.

Let us carefully guard against this. It has ruined many a valuable servant. Many who might have proved really useful workmen in the vineyard, have failed completely through not maintaining the integrity of their individual character and path. They began with God. They started on their course in the exercise of a pure conscience, and in the pursuit of that path which a divine hand had marked out for them. There was a bloom, a freshness, and a verdure about them, most refreshing to all who came in contact with them. They were taught of God. They drew near to the eternal fountain of Holy Scripture and drank for themselves. Perhaps they did not know much; but what they did know was real because they received it from God, and it turned to good account for "there is much food in the tillage of the poor."

But, instead of going on with God, they allowed themselves to get under human influence; they got truth secondhand, and became the vendors of other men's thoughts; instead of drinking at the fountain head, they drank at the streams of human opinion; they lost originality, simplicity, freshness, and power, and became mere copyists, if not miserable caricatures. Instead of giving forth those "rivers of living water" which flow from the true believer in Jesus, they dropped into the barren technicalities and cut and dry common-places of mere systematized religion.

Beloved Christian reader, all this must be sedulously guarded against. We must watch against it, pray against it, believe against it, and live against it. Let us seek to serve God, with a pure conscience. Let us live in His own immediate presence, in the light of His blessed countenance, in the holy intimacy of personal communion with Him, through the power of the Holy Ghost. This, we may rest assured, is the true secret of power for the man of God, at all times, and under all circumstances. We must walk with God, in the deep and cherished sense of our own personal responsibility to Him. This is what we understand by "a pure conscience."

But will this tend, in the smallest degree, to lessen our sense of the value of true fellowship, of holy communion with all those who are true to Christ? By no means; indeed it is the very thing which will impart power, energy, and depth of tone to the fellowship. If every "man in Christ" were only acquitting himself thoroughly as "a man of God," what blessed fellowship there would be! what heart work! what glow and unmistakable power! How different from the dull formalism of a merely nominal assent to certain accredited dogmas of a party, on the one hand, and from the mere *esprit de corps* of cliquism, on the other.

There are few terms in such common use and so little understood as "fellowship." In numberless cases, it merely indicates the fact of a nominal membership in some religious denomination—a fact which furnishes no guarantee whatsoever of living communion with Christ, or personal devotedness to His cause. If all who are nominally "in fellow ship" were acquitting themselves thoroughly as men of God, what a very different condition of things we should be privileged to witness!

But what is fellowship? It is, in its very highest expression, having one common object with God, and taking part in the same portion; and that object, that portion, is Christ—Christ known and enjoyed through the Holy Ghost. This is fellowship with God. What a privilege! What a dignity! What unspeakable blessedness! To be allowed to have a common object and a common portion with God Himself! To delight in the One in whom He delights! There can be nothing higher, nothing better, nothing more precious than this. Not even in heaven itself shall we know aught beyond this. Our own condition will, thank God, be vastly different

We shall be done with a body of sin and death, and be clothed with a body of glory. We shall be done with a sinful, sorrowful, distracting world, where all is directly opposed to God and to us, and we shall breathe the pure, invigorating atmosphere of that bright and blessed world above.

For, in so far as our fellowship is real, it is now as it shall be then, "with the Father and with His Son Jesus Christ"—"in the light," and by the power of the Holy Ghost.

Thus much as to our fellowship with God. And, as regards our fellowship one with another, it is simply as we walk in the light; as we read, "If we walk in the light, as He is in the light, we have fellowship one with another, and the blood of Jesus Christ His Son cleanseth us from all sin" (I John i. 7). We can only have fellowship one with another as we walk in the immediate presence of God. There may be a vast amount of mere intercourse without one particle of divine fellowship. Alas! alas! a great deal of what passes for Christian fellowship is nothing more than the merest religious gossip—the vapid, worthless, soul-withering chit-chat of the religious world, than which nothing can be more miserably unprofitable. True Christian fellowship can only be enjoyed in the light. It is when we are individually walking with God, in the power of personal communion, that we really have fellowship one with another, and this fellowship consists in real heart enjoyment of Christ as our one object, our common portion. It is not heartless traffic in certain favorite doctrines which we receive to hold in common. It is not morbid sympathy with those who think, and see, and feel with us in some favorite theory or dogma. It is something quite different from all this. It is delighting in Christ, in common with all those who are walking in the light. It is attachment to Him, to His person, His name, His Word, His cause, His people. It is joint consecration of heart and soul to that blessed One who loved us and washed us from our sins in His own blood, and brought us into the light of God's presence, there to walk with Him and with one another. This, and nothing less, is Christian fellowship; and where this is really understood it will lead us to pause and consider what we say when we declare, in any given case, "such an one is in fellowship."

But we must proceed with our Epistle, and there see what full provision there is for the man of God, however dark the day may be in which his lot is cast.

We have seen something of the importance—yea, rather, we should say the indispensable necessity of "a pure conscience," and "unfeigned faith," in the moral equipment of God's man. These qualities lie at the very base of the entire edifice of practical godliness which must ever characterize the genuine man of God.

But there is more than this. The edifice must be erected as well as the foundation laid. The man of God has to work on amid all sorts of difficulties, trials, sorrows, disappointments, obstacles, questions and controversies. He has his niche to fill, his path to tread, his work to do. Come what may, he must serve. The enemy may oppose; the world may frown; the Church may be in ruins around him; false brethren may thwart, hinder, and desert; strife, controversy, and division may arise and darken the atmosphere; still the man of God must move on, regardless of all these things, working, serving, testifying, according to the sphere in which the hand of God has placed him, and according to the gift bestowed upon him. How is this to be done? Not only by keeping a pure conscience and the exercise of an unfeigned faith—priceless, indispensable qualities! but, further, he has to harken to the following weighty word of exhortation—"Wherefore I put thee in remembrance that thou stir up the gift of God, which is in thee by the putting on of my hands."

The gift must be stirred up, else it may become useless if allowed to lie dormant. There is great danger of letting the gift drop into disuse through the discouraging influence of surrounding circumstances. A gift unused will soon become useless; whereas, a gift stirred up and diligently used grows and expands. It is not enough to possess a gift, we must wait upon the gift, cultivate it, and exercise it. This is the way to improve it.

And observe the special force of the expression, "the gift of God." In Eph. iv. we read of "the gift of Christ," and there, too, we find all the gifts, from the highest to the lowest range, flowing down from Christ the risen and glorified Head of His body, the Church. But in second Timothy, we have it defined as "the gift of God." True it is—blessed be His holy name!—our Lord Christ is God over all, blessed forever, so that the gift of

Christ is the gift of God. But we may rest assured there is never any distinction in Scripture without a difference; and hence there is some good reason for the expression "gift of God." We doubt not it is in full harmony with the nature and object of the Epistle in which it occurs. It is "the gift of God" communicated to "the man of God" to be used by him notwithstanding the hopeless ruin of the professing Church, and spite of all the difficulty, darkness, and discouragement of the day in which his lot is cast.

The man of God must not allow himself to be hindered in the diligent cultivation and exercise of his gift, though everything seems to look dark and forbidding, for "God hath not given us the spirit of fear; but of power and of love, and of a sound mind." Here we have "God" again introduced to our thoughts, and that, too, in a most gracious manner, as furnishing His man with the very thing he needs to meet the special exigence of his day— "The spirit of power, and of love, and of a sound mind."

Marvelous combination! Truly, an exquisite compound after the art of the apothecary! Power, love, and wisdom! How perfect! Not a single ingredient too much. Not one too little. If it were merely a spirit of power, it might lead one to carry things with a high hand. Were it merely a spirit of love, it might lead one to sacrifice truth for peace' sake; or indolently to tolerate error and evil rather than give offence. But the power is softened by the love; and the love is strengthened by the power; and, moreover, the spirit of wisdom comes in to adjust both the power and the love. In a word, it is a divinely perfect and beautiful provision for the man of God—the very thing he needs for "the last days" so perilous, so difficult, so full of all sorts of perplexing questions and apparent contradictions. If one were to be asked what he would consider most necessary for such days as these? surely he should, at once, say, "power, love, and soundness of mind." Well, blessed be God, these are the very things which He has graciously given to form the character, shape the way, and govern the conduct of the man of God, right on to the end.

But there is further provision and further exhortation for the man of God. "Be not thou therefore ashamed of the testimony of our Lord, nor of me His prisoner; but be thou partaker of the afflictions of the gospel according to the power of God." In pentecostal days, when the rich and mighty tide of divine grace was flowing in, and bearing thousands of ransomed souls upon its bosom; when all were of one heart and one mind; when those outside were overawed by the extraordinary manifestations of divine power, it was rather a question of partaking of the *triumphs* of the gospel, than its afflictions. But in the days contemplated in second Timothy, all is changed. The beloved apostle is a lonely prisoner at Rome; all in Asia had forsaken him; Hymeneus and Philetus are denying the resurrection; all sorts of heresies, errors, and evils are creeping in; the landmarks are in danger of being swept away by the tide of apostasy and corruption.

In the face of all this, the man of God has to brace himself up for the occasion. He has to endure hardness; to hold fast the form of sound words; he has to keep the good thing committed to him; to be strong in the grace that is in Christ Jesus; to keep himself *disentangled*—however he may be *engaged*; he must keep himself free as a soldier; he must cling to God's sure foundation; he must purge himself from the dishonorable vessels in the great house; he must *flee* youthful lusts, and *follow* righteousness, faith, love, peace, with them that call on the Lord out of a pure heart. He must avoid foolish and unlearned questions. He must turn away from formal and heartless professors. He must be thoroughly furnished for all good works, perfectly equipped through a knowledge of the Holy Scriptures. He must preach the Word; be instant in season and out of season. He must watch in all things; endure afflictions; and do the work of an evangelist.

What a category for the man of God! Who is sufficient for these things? Where is the spiritual power to be had for such works? It is to be had at the mercy-seat. It is to be found in earnest, patient, believing, waiting upon the living God, and in no other way. All our springs are in Him. We have only to draw upon Him. He is sufficient for the darkest day. Difficulties are nothing to Him, and they are bread for faith. Yes, beloved reader, difficulties of the most formidable nature are simply bread for faith, and the man of faith will develop and grow strong thereby. Unbelief says, "There is a lion in the way;" but faith slays the lion that roars along the path of the nazarite of God. It is the privilege of the true believer to rise above all the hostile influences which surround him, no matter what they are, or from whence they spring; and, in the calmness and brightness of the divine presence, enjoy as high communion, and taste as rich and rare privileges as ever were known in the Church's brightest days.

Let us remember this—every man of God needs to remember it: there is no comfort, no peace, no strength, no moral power, no true elevation to be derived from looking at the ruins. We must look up out of the ruins to the place where our Lord Christ has taken His seat, at the right hand of the Majesty in the heavens. Or rather, to speak more according to our true position, we should look down from our place in the heavens upon all the ruins of earth. To realize our place in Christ, and to be occupied in heart and soul with Him, is the true secret of power to carry ourselves as men of God. To have Christ ever before us—His work for the conscience, His person for the heart, His Word for the path, is the one grand, sovereign, divine remedy for a ruined self, a ruined world, a ruined Church.

But we close. Very gladly would we linger, in company with the reader, over the contents of this most precious second Timothy. Truly refreshing would it be to dwell upon all its touching allusions, its earnest appeals, its weighty exhortations. But this would demand a volume, and hence we must leave the Christian reader to study the Epistle for himself, praying that the eternal Spirit who indited it may unfold and apply it in living power to his soul, so that he may be enabled to acquit himself as an earnest, faithful, whole-hearted man of God and servant of Christ, in the midst of a scene of hollow profession, and heartless worldly religiousness.

May the good Lord stir us all up to a more thorough consecration of ourselves, in spirit, soul, and body—all we are and all we have—to His service! We think we can really say we long for this—long for it, in the deep sense of our lack of it—long for it, more intensely, as we grow increasingly sick of the unreal condition of things within and around us.

O beloved Christian, let us earnestly, believingly, and perseveringly cry to our own ever gracious God to make us more real, more whole-hearted, more thoroughly devoted to our Lord Jesus Christ in all things.

IN THE FATHER'S HOUSE

"The wanderer no more will roam,The lost one to the fold hath come,The prodigal is welcomed home,O Lamb of God, through Thee!

"Though clothed in rags, by sin defiled,The Father did embrace His child;And I am pardoned, reconciled,O Lamb of God, through Thee!

"It is the Father's joy to bless;His love has found for me a dress,A robe of spotless righteousness,O Lamb of God, in Thee!

"And now my famished soul is fed,A feast of love for me is spread,I feed upon the children's bread,O Lamb of God, in Thee!

"Yea, in the fulness of His grace,God put me in the children's place,Where I may gaze upon His face,O Lamb of God, in Thee!

"Not half His Love can I express,Yet, Lord, with joy my lips confess,This blessed portion I possess,O Lamb of God, in Thee!

"Thy precious name it is I bear,In Thee I am to God brought near,And all the Father's love I share,O Lamb of God, in Thee!"

DECISION FOR CHRIST

In approaching the subject of "Decision for Christ," there are two or three obstacles which lie in our way—two or three difficulties which hang around the question, which we would fain remove, if possible, in order that the reader may be able to view the matter on its own proper ground, and in its own proper bearings.

In the first place, we encounter a serious difficulty in the fact that very few of us, comparatively, are in a condition of soul to appreciate the subject, or to suffer a word of exhortation thereon. We are, for the most part, so occupied with the question of our soul's salvation,—so taken up with matters affecting ourselves, our peace, our liberty, our comfort, our deliverance from the wrath to come, our interest in Christ,—that we have but little heart for aught that purely concerns Christ Himself—His name, His person, His cause, His glory.

There are, we may say, two things which lie at the foundation of all true decision for Christ, namely, a conscience purged by the blood of Jesus, and a heart that bows with reverent submission to the authority of His Word in all things. Now we do not mean to dwell upon these things in this paper; first, because we are anxious to get at once to our immediate theme; and secondly, because we have so often dwelt on the subject of establishing the conscience in the peace of the gospel, and on setting before the heart the paramount claims of the word of God. We merely refer to them here for the purpose of reminding the reader that they are absolutely essential materials in forming the basis of decision for Christ. If my conscience is ill at ease, if I am in doubt as to my salvation, if I am filled with "anxious thought" as to whether I am a child of God or not, decision for Christ is out of the question. I must know that Christ died for me before I can intelligently and happily live for Him.

So, also, if there be any reserve in the heart as to my entire subjection to the authority of Christ as my Lord and Master; if I am keeping some chamber of my heart, be it ever so remote, ever so small, closed against the light of His Word, it must of necessity hinder my whole-hearted decision for Him in this world. In a word, I must know that *Christ is mine* and *I am His* ere my course down here can be one of unswerving, uncompromising decision for Him. If the reader hesitates as to this, if he is still in doubt and darkness, let him pause and turn directly to the cross of the Son of God and hearken to what the Holy Spirit declares as to all those who simply put their trust therein. Let him drink into his inmost soul these words: "Be it known unto you, therefore, that through this Man is preached unto you the forgiveness of sins; and by Him *all* that *believe are* justified from *all* things from which ye could not be justified by the law of Moses." Yes, reader, these are the glad tidings for you. "*All*, from *all*," by faith in a crucified and risen Lord.

But we see another difficulty in the way of our subject. We greatly fear that while we speak of decision for Christ, some of our readers may suppose that we are contending for some notion or set of notions of our own; that we are pressing some peculiar views or principles to which we vainly and foolishly venture to apply the imposing title of "Decision for Christ." All this we do most solemnly disclaim. The words which stand at the head of this paper are the simple expression of our thesis. We do not contend for attachment to sect, party, or denomination; for adherence to the doctrines or commandments of men. We write in the immediate presence of Him who searcheth the hearts and trieth the reins of the children of men, and we distinctly avow that our one object is to urge upon the Christian reader the necessity of decision for Christ. We would not, if we know ourselves, pen a single line to swell the ranks of a party, or draw over adherents to any particular doctrinal creed or any special form of church polity. We are impressed with the conviction that where Christ has His right place in the heart, all will be right; and that where He has not, there will be nothing right. And further, we believe that nothing but plain decision for Christ can effectually preserve the soul from the fatal influences that are at work around us in the professing Church. Mere orthodoxy cannot preserve us. Attachment to religious forms will not avail in the present fearful struggle. It is, we feel persuaded, a simple question of Christ as our *life*, and Christ as our *object*. May the Spirit of God now enable us to ponder aright the subject of "Decision for Christ"!

It is well to bear in mind that there are certain great truths—certain immutable principles—which underlie all the dispensations of God from age to age and which remain untouched by all the failure, the folly and the sin of man. It is on these great moral truths, these foundation principles, that faith lays hold, and in them finds its strength and sustenance. Dispensations change and pass away, men prove unfaithful in their varied positions of stewardship and responsibility, but the word of the Lord endureth forever. It never fails. "Forever, O Lord, Thy word is settled in heaven." And again, "Thou hast magnified Thy word above all Thy name."[3] Nothing can touch the eternal truth of God, and therefore what we want at all times is to give that truth its proper place in our hearts; to let it act on our conscience, form our character, and shape our way. "Thy word have I hid in my heart, that I might not sin against Thee." "Man shall not live by bread alone, but by every word that proceedeth out of the mouth of the Lord." This is true security. Here lies the real secret of decision for

Christ. What God has spoken must govern us in the most absolute manner ere our path can be said to be one of plain decision. There may be tenacious adherence to our own notions, obstinate attachment to the prejudices of the age, a blind devotion to certain doctrines and practices resting on a traditionary foundation, certain opinions which we have received to hold without ever inquiring as to whether or not there be any authority whatever for such opinions in Holy Scripture. There may be all this and much more, and yet not one atom of genuine decision for Christ.

Now we feel we cannot do better than furnish our readers with an example or two drawn from the page of inspired history, which will do more to illustrate and enforce our theme than aught that we could possibly advance. And first, then, let us turn to the book of Esther, and there contemplate for a few moments the instructive history of

"MORDECAI THE JEW"

This very remarkable man lived at a time in which the Jewish economy had failed through the unfaithfulness and disobedience of the Jewish people. The Gentile was in power. The relationship between Jehovah and Israel could no longer be publicly acknowledged. The faithful Jew had but to hang his harp on the willows and sigh over the faded light of other days. The chosen seed was in exile; the city and temple where their fathers worshiped were in ruins, and the vessels of the Lord's house were in a strange land. Such was the outward condition of things in the day in which Mordecai's lot was cast. But in addition to this there was a man very near the throne occupying only the second place in the empire, sitting beside the very fountain-head of authority, possessing princely wealth, and wielding almost boundless influence. To this great man, strange to say, the poor exiled Jew sternly refuses to bow. Nothing will induce him to yield a single mark of respect to the second man in the kingdom. He will save the life of Ahasuerus, but he will not bow to Haman.

Reader, why was this? Was this blind obstinacy, or bold decision—which? In order to determine this we must inquire as to the real root or principle of Mordecai's acting. If, indeed, there was no authority for his conduct in the law of God, then must we at once pronounce it to have been blind obstinacy, foolish pride, or, it may have been, envy of a man in power. But if, on the other hand, there be within the covers of the five inspired books of Moses a plain authority for Mordecai's deportment in this matter, then must we, without hesitation, pronounce his conduct to have been the rare and exquisite fruit of attachment to the law of his God, and uncompromising decision for Him and His holy authority.

This makes all the difference. If it be merely a matter of private opinion,—a question concerning which each one may lawfully adopt his own view,—then, verily, might such a line of conduct be justly termed the most narrow-minded bigotry. We hear a great deal now-a-days about narrow-mindedness on the one hand, and large-heartedness on the other. But as a Roman orator, over two thousand years ago, exclaimed in the senate-house of Rome, "Conscript fathers: long since, indeed, we have lost the true names of things," so may we, in the bosom of the professing Church, at the close of the nineteenth century, repeat, with far greater force, "Long since we have lost the true names of things." For what do men now call bigotry and narrow-mindedness? A faithful clinging to and carrying out of "Thus saith the Lord." And what do they designate large-heartedness? A readiness to sacrifice truth on the altar of politeness and civility.

Reader, be thou fully assured that thus it is at this solemn moment. We do not want to be sour or cynical, morose or gloomy; but we must speak the truth if we are to speak at all. We desire that the tongue may be hushed in silence, and the pen may drop from the hand, if we could basely cushion the plain, bold, unvarnished truth through fear of scattering our readers, or to avoid the sneer of the infidel. We cannot shut our eyes to the solemn fact that God's truth is being trampled in the dust—that the name of Jesus is despised and rejected. We have only to pass from city to city, and from town to town, of highly-favored England, and read upon the walls the melancholy proofs of the truth of our assertions. Truth is flung aside, in cold contempt. The name of Jesus is little set by. On> the other hand, man is exalted, his reason deified, his will indulged. Where must all this end? "In' the blackness of darkness forever."

How refreshing, in the face of all this, to ponder the history of Mordecai the Jew! It is very plain that he knew little and cared less about the thoughts of men on the question of narrow-mindedness. He obeyed the word of the Lord; and this we must be allowed to call real breadth of mind, true largeness of heart. For what, after all, is a narrow mind? A narrow mind we hold to be a mind which refuses to open itself to admit the truth of God. And what, on the contrary, is a large and liberal heart? A heart expanded by the truth and grace of God. Let us not be scared away from decision in the path of obedience by the scornful epithets which men have bestowed upon that path. It is a path of peace and purity, a path where the light of an approving conscience is enjoyed, and upon which the beams of divine favor ever pour themselves in undimmed lustre.

But why did Mordecai refuse to bow to Haman? Was there any great principle at stake? Was it merely a whim of his own? Had he a "Thus saith the Lord" for his warrant in refusing a single nod of the head to the proud Amalekite? Yes. Let us turn to the seventeenth chapter of the book of Exodus, and there we read, "And the Lord said unto Moses, Write this for a memorial in a book, and rehearse it in the ears of Joshua: for I will utterly put out the remembrance of Amalek from under heaven. And Moses built an altar, and called the name of it Jehovah-nissi; for he said, Because the Lord hath sworn that the Lord will have war with Amalek from generation to generation.[4]

Here, then, was Mordecai's authority for not bowing to Haman the Agagite. A faithful Jew could not do reverence to one with whom Jehovah was at war. The heart might plead a thousand excuses and urge a thousand reasons. It might seek an easy path for itself on the plea that the Jewish system was in ruins and the Amalekite in power, and that therefore it was worse than useless, yea, it was positively absurd, to maintain such lofty ground when the glory of Israel was gone and the Amalekite was in the place of authority. "Of what use," it might be argued, "can it be to uphold the standard when all is gone to pieces? You are only making your degradation more remarkable by the pertinacious refusal to bow your head. Would it not be better to give just one nod? That will settle the matter. Haman will be satisfied, and you and your people will be safe. Do not be obstinate. Show a tendency to be courteous. Do not stand up in that dogged way for a thing so manifestly non-essential. Besides, you should remember that the command in Exodus xvii. was only to be rehearsed in the ears of Joshua, and only had its true application in his bright and palmy days. It was never meant for the ears of an exile, never intended to apply in the days of Israel's desolation."

All this, and much beside, might have been urged on Mordecai; but ah, the answer was simple: "God hath spoken. This is enough for me. True, we are a scattered people; but the word of the Lord is not scattered. He has not reversed His word about Amalek, nor entered into a treaty of peace with him. Jehovah and Amalek are still at war, and Amalek stands before me in the person of this haughty Agagite. How can I bow to one with whom Jehovah is at war? How can I do homage to a man whom the faithful Samuel would hew in pieces before the Lord?" "Well, then," it might be further urged upon this devoted Jew, "you will all be destroyed. You must either bow or perish." The answer is still most simple: "I have nothing to do with consequences. They are in the hand of God. Obedience is my path, the results are with Him. It is better to die with a good conscience than live with a bad one. It is better to go to heaven with an uncondemning heart than remain upon earth with a heart that would make me a coward. God has spoken. I can do no otherwise. May the Lord help me! Amen."

Oh, how well we can understand the mode in which this faithful Jew would be assaulted by the enemy. Nothing but the grace of God can ever enable any one to maintain a deportment of unflinching decision at a moment in which everything within and around is against us. True it is, we know that it is better to suffer anything than deny our Lord or fly in the face of His commandments; but yet how little are some of us prepared to endure a single sneer, a single scornful look, a single contemptuous expression, for Christ's sake. And perhaps there are few things harder, for some of us at least, to bear than to be reproached on the ground of narrow-mindedness and bigotry. We naturally like to be thought large-hearted and liberal. We like to be accounted men of enlightened mind, sound judgment, and comprehensive grasp. But we must remember that we have no right to be liberal at our Master's expense. We have simply to obey.

Thus it was with Mordecai. He stood like a rock, and allowed the whole tide of difficulty and opposition to roll over him. He would not bow to the Amalekite, let the consequence be what it might. Obedience was his path. The results were with God. And look at the result! In one moment the tide was turned. The proud Amalekite fell from his lofty eminence, and the exiled Jew was lifted from his sackcloth and ashes and placed next the throne. Haman exchanged his wealth and dignities for a gallows; Mordecai exchanged his sackcloth for a royal robe.

Now it may not always happen that the reward of simple obedience will be as speedy and as signal as in Mordecai's case. And moreover, we may say that we are not Mordecais, nor are we placed in his position. But the principle holds good, whoever and wherever we are. There is not one of us, however obscure or insignificant, that has not a sphere within which our influence is felt for good or for evil. And besides, independent altogether of our circumstances and the apparent results of our conduct, we are called upon to obey implicitly the word of the Lord—to have His word hidden in our hearts—to refuse with unswerving decision, to do or say aught that the word of the living God condemns. "How can I do this great wickedness, and sin against God?" This should be the language, whether it be the question of a child tempted to steal a lump of sugar, or the most momentous step in evil that one can be tempted to take. The strength and moral security of Mordecai's position lay in this fact, that he had the word of God for his authority. Had it not been so, his conduct would have been senseless in the extreme. To have refused the usual expression of respect to one in high authority, without some weighty reason, could only be regarded as the most unmeaning obstinacy. But the moment you introduce a "Thus saith the Lord," the matter is entirely changed. The word of the Lord endureth forever. The divine testimonies do not fade away or change with the times and seasons. Heaven and earth shall pass away, but one jot or tittle of what our God hath spoken shall never pass away. Hence, what had been rehearsed in the ears of Joshua, as he rested in triumph under the banner of Jehovah, was designed to govern the conduct of Mordecai, though clothed in sackcloth as an exile, in the city of Shushan. Ages and generations had passed away; the days of the Judges and the days of the Kings had run their course; but the commandment of the Lord with respect to Amalek had lost—could lose—none of its force. "The Lord *hath sworn* that the Lord will have war with Amalek," not merely in the days of Joshua, nor in the days of the Judges, nor in the days of the Kings, but "from generation to generation." Such was the record—the imperishable and immutable record of God; and such was the plain, solid and unquestionable foundation of Mordecai's conduct.

And here let us say a few words as to the immense importance of entire submission to the word of God. We live in a day which is plainly marked by strong self-will. Man's reason, man's will and man's interest are working together, with appalling success, to ignore the authority of Holy Scripture. So long as the statements of the word of God chime in with man's reason, so long as they do not run counter to his will, and are not subversive of his interests, so long will he tolerate them; or, it may be, he will quote them with a measure of respect, or at least with self-complacency; but the moment it becomes a question of Scripture *versus* reason, will or interest, the former is either silently ignored or contemptuously rejected. This is a very marked and solemn feature of the days that are now passing over our heads. It behooves Christians to be aware of it, and to be on their watch-tower. We fear that very few, comparatively, are truly alive to the real state of the moral atmosphere which enwraps the religious world. We do not refer here so much to the bold attacks of infidel writers. To these we have alluded elsewhere. What we have now before us is rather the cool indifference on the part of professing Christians as to Scripture; the little power which pure truth wields over the conscience; the way in which the edge of Scripture is blunted or turned aside. You quote passage after passage from the inspired volume, but it seems like the pattering of rain upon the window: the *reason* is at work, the *will* is dominant, *interest* is at stake, human opinions bear sway, God's truth is practically, if not in so many words, set aside.

All this is deeply solemn. We know of few things more dangerous than intellectual familiarity with the letter of Scripture where the spirit of it does not govern the conscience, form the character, and shape the way. We want to tremble at the word of God, to bow down in reverential submission to its holy authority in all things. A single line of Scripture ought to be sufficient for our souls on any point, even though, in carrying it out, we should have to move athwart the opinions of the highest and best of men. May the Lord raise up many faithful and true-hearted witnesses in these last days,—men like the faithful Mordecai,—who would rather ascend a gallows than bow to an Amalekite!

For the further illustration of our theme, we shall ask the reader to turn to the sixth chapter of the book of Daniel. There is a special charm and interest in the history of these living examples presented to us in the Holy Scriptures. They tell us how the truth of God was acted upon, in other days, by men of like passions with ourselves; they prove to us that in every age there have been men who so prized the truth, so reverenced the word of the living God, that they would rather face death, in its most appalling forms, than to depart one hair's breadth from the narrow line laid down by the authoritative voice of their Lord and Master. It is healthful to be brought into contact with such men—healthful at all times, but peculiarly so in days like the present, when there is so much laxity and easy-going profession—so much of mere theory—when every one is allowed to go his own way, and hold his own opinion, provided always that he does not interfere with the opinions of his neighbor—when the commandments of God seem to have so little weight, so little power over the heart and conscience. Tradition will get a hearing; public opinion will be respected; anything and everything, in short, but the plain and positive statements of the word of God, will get a place in the thoughts and opinions of men. At such a time, it is, we repeat, at once healthful and edifying to muse over the history of men like Mordecai the Jew, and Daniel the prophet, and scores of others, in whose estimation a single line of Holy Scripture rose far above all the thoughts of men, the decrees of governors, and the statutes of kings, and who declared plainly that they had nothing whatever to do with consequences where the word of the Lord was concerned. Absolute submission to the divine command is that which alone becomes the creature.

It is not, be it observed and well remembered, that any man or any number of men have any right to demand subjection to their decisions or decrees. No man has any right to enforce his opinions upon his fellow. This is plain enough, and we have to bless God for the inestimable privilege of civil and religious liberty, as enjoyed under this government. But what we urge upon our readers, just now, is plain decision for Christ, and implicit subjection to His authority, irrespective of everything, and regardless of consequences. This is what we do most earnestly desire for ourselves and for all the people of God in these last days. We long for that condition of soul, that attitude of heart, that quality of conscience, which shall lead us to bow down in implicit subjection to the commandments of our Lord and Saviour Jesus Christ. No doubt there are difficulties, stumbling blocks, and hostile influences to be encountered. It may be said, for instance, that "It is very difficult for one, now-a-days, to know what is really true and right. There are so many opinions and so many ways, and good men differ so in judgment about the simplest and plainest matters, and yet they all profess to own the Bible as the only standard of appeal; and, moreover, all declare that their one desire is to do what is right, and to serve the Lord, in their day and generation. How, then, is one to know what is true or what is false, seeing that you will find the very best of men ranged on opposite sides of the same question?"

The answer to all this is very simple. "If thine eye be single thy whole body shall be full of light." But, most assuredly, my eye is not single if I am looking at men, and reasoning on what I see in them. A single eye rests simply on the Lord and His Word. Men differ, no doubt—they have differed, and they ever will differ, but I am to harken to the voice of my Lord and do His will. His Word is to be my light and my authority, the girdle of my loins in action, the strength of my heart in service, my only warrant for moving hither and thither, the stable foundation of all my ways. If I were to attempt to shape my way according to the thoughts of men, where should I be? How uncertain and unsatisfactory would my course be! If I really want to be guided aright, my God will surely guide me; but if I am looking to men, if I am governed by mixed motives, if I am seeking my own ends and interests, if I am seeking to please my fellows, then, undoubtedly, my body shall be full of darkness, heavy clouds shall settle down upon my pathway, and uncertainty mark all my goings.

Christian reader, think of these things. Think deeply of them. Depend upon it they have a just claim upon your attention. Do you earnestly desire to follow your Lord? Do you really aim at something beyond mere empty profession, cold orthodoxy, or mechanical religiousness? Do you sigh for reality, depth, energy, fervor, and whole-heartedness? Then make Christ your one object, His Word your rule, His glory your aim. May the blessed Spirit be pleased to use for the furtherance of these ends our meditation on the interesting narrative of

"DANIEL THE PROPHET"

"It pleased Darius to set over the kingdom a hundred and twenty princes, which should be over the whole kingdom; and over these, three presidents, of whom Daniel was first; that the princes might give accounts unto them, and the king should have no damage. Then this Daniel was preferred above the presidents and princes, because an excellent spirit was in him; and the king thought to set him over the whole realm. Then the presidents and princes sought to find occasion against Daniel concerning the kingdom; but they could find none occasion or fault; forasmuch as he was faithful, neither was there any error or fault found in him" (Dan. vi. I-4).

What a testimony! How truly refreshing to the heart! "No error or fault!" Even his most bitter enemies could not put their finger upon a single blemish in his character, or a flaw in his practical career. Truly this was a rare and admirable character—a bright witness for the God of Israel, even in the dark days of the Babylonish captivity—an unanswerable proof of the fact that no matter where we are situated, or how we are circumstanced, no matter how unfavorable our position, or how dark the day in which our lot is cast, it is our happy privilege so to carry ourselves, in all the details of daily life, as to give no occasion to the enemy to speak reproachfully.

How sad when it is otherwise! How humiliating when those who make a high profession are found constantly breaking down in the most commonplace affairs of domestic and commercial life! There are few things which more tend to discourage the heart than that.

No doubt worldly people are only too ready to find occasion against those who profess the name of Jesus; and, further, we have to remember that there are two sides to every question, and that, very frequently, a broad margin must be left for exaggeration, high coloring, and false impressions. But still, it is the Christian's plain duty so to walk in every position and relationship of life, as that "no error or fault" may be found in him. We should not make any excuses for ourselves. The duties of our situation, whatever it may happen to be, should be scrupulously performed. A careless manner, a slovenly habit, an unprincipled mode of acting, on the part of the Christian, is a serious damage to the cause of Christ, and a dishonor to His holy name. And, on the other hand, diligence, earnestness, punctuality, and fidelity, bring glory to that name. And this should ever be the Christian's object. He should not aim at his own interest, his own reputation, or his own advancement, in seeking to carry himself aright in his family and in his calling in life. True, it will promote his interest, establish his reputation, and further his progress, to be upright and diligent in all his ways; but none of these things should ever be his motive. He is to be ever and only governed by the one thing, namely, to please and honor his Lord and Master. The standard which the Holy Ghost has set before us, as to all these things, is furnished in the words of the apostle to the Philippians, "That ye may be blameless and harmless, the sons of God without rebuke in the midst of a crooked and perverse nation, among whom ye shine as lights in the world." We should not be satisfied with anything less than this. "They could find none occasion nor fault, forasmuch as he was faithful, neither was there any error or fault found in him." Noble testimony! Would that it were more called forth, in this our day, by the deportment, the habits, the temper, and ways of all those who call themselves Christians.

But there was one point in which Daniel's enemies felt they could lay hold of him. "Then said these men, We shall not find any occasion against this Daniel, except we find it against him concerning *the law of his God.*" Here was a something in the which occasion might be found to ruin this beloved and honored servant of God. It appears that Daniel had been in the habit of praying three times a day with his windows open toward Jerusalem.

This fact was well known, and was speedily laid hold of, and turned to account. "Then these presidents and princes assembled together to the king, and said thus unto him, King Darius, live for ever. All the presidents of the kingdom, the governors, and the princes, the counsellors, and the captains, have consulted together to establish a royal statute, and to make a firm decree, that whosoever shall ask a petition of any god or man for thirty days, save of thee, O king, he shall be cast into the den of lions. Now, O king, establish the decree, and sign the writing, that it be not changed, according to the law of the Medes and Persians, which altereth not. Wherefore king Darius signed the writing and the decree."

Here, then, was a deep plot, a subtle snare, laid for the blameless and harmless Daniel. How would he act in the face of all this? Would he not feel it right to lower the standard? Well, if the standard was something of his own, he might surely lower it, and perhaps he ought. But if it were something divine—if his conduct was based upon the truth of God, then clearly it was his place to hold it up as high as ever, regardless of statutes, decrees, and writings established, signed, and countersigned. The whole question hinged upon this. Just as in the case of Mordecai the Jew, the question hinged upon the one point of whether he had any divine warrant for refusing to bow to Haman; so, in the case of Daniel the prophet, the question was, had he any divine authority for praying toward Jerusalem. It certainly seemed strange and odd. Many might have felt disposed to say to him, "Why persist in this practice? What need is there for opening your windows and praying toward Jerusalem, in such a public manner? Can you not wait until night has drawn her sable curtain around you, and your closet door has shut you in, and then pour out your heart to your God? This would be prudent, judicious, and expedient. And, surely, your God does not exact this of you. He does not regard time, place, or attitude. All times and places are alike to Him. Are you wise—are you right, in persisting in such a line of action under such circumstances? It was all well enough before this decree was signed, when you could pray when and as you thought right; but now it does seem like the most culpable fatuity and blind obstinacy to persevere; it is as though you really courted martyrdom."

All this, and much more, we may easily conceive, might be suggested to the mind of the faithful Jew; but still the grand question remained, "What saith the Scripture?" Was there any divine reason for Daniel's praying toward Jerusalem? Assuredly there was! In the first place, Jehovah had said to Solomon, in reference to the temple at Jerusalem, "Mine eyes and My heart shall be there perpetually." Jerusalem was God's earthly centre. It was, it is, and ever shall be. True, it was in ruins—the temple was in ruins; but God's word was not in ruins; and here is faith's simple but solid warrant. King Solomon had said, at the dedication of the temple, hundreds of years before Daniel's time, "If Thy people sin against Thee, (for there is no man that sinneth not,) and Thou be angry with them, and deliver them over before their enemies, and they carry them away captive unto a land far off or near. Yet if they bethink themselves in the land whither they are carried captive, and turn and pray unto Thee, in the land of their captivity, saying, We have sinned, we have done amiss, and have dealt wickedly; if they return to Thee with all their heart and with all their soul in the land of their captivity, whither they have carried them captive, and pray toward their land, which Thou gavest unto their fathers, and toward the city which Thou hast chosen, and toward the house which I have built for Thy name: then hear Thou from the heavens, even from Thy dwelling-place, their prayer and their supplications, and maintain their cause, and forgive Thy people which have sinned against Thee" (2 Chron. vi. 36-39).

Now this was precisely what Daniel was doing—this was the ground he took. He was a captive exile, but his heart was at Jerusalem, and his eyes followed his heart. If he could not sing the songs of Zion, he could at least breathe his prayers toward Zion's hill. If his harp was on the willows at Babylon, his fond affections turned toward the city of God, now a heap of ruins, but ere long to be an eternal excellency, "the joy of the whole earth." It mattered not to him that a decree had been signed by earth's greatest monarch, forbidding him to pray toward the city of his fathers and to his father's God. It mattered not to him that the lion's den was yawning to receive him, and the lion's jaws ready to devour him. Like his brother Mordecai, he had nothing to do with consequences. Mordecai would rather mount the gallows than bow to Haman, and Daniel would rather descend to the lion's den than cease to pray to Jehovah. These, surely, were the worthies. They were men whose hearts and consciences were governed absolutely by the word of God. The world may dub them bigots and fools; but, oh! how the heart does long for such bigots and fools, in these days of false liberality and wisdom!

It might have been said to Mordecai and Daniel that they were contending for mere trifles—for things wholly indifferent and non-essential. This is an argument often used; but, oh! it has no weight with an honest and devoted heart. Indeed, there is nothing more contemptible, in the judgment of every true lover of Jesus, than the principle that regulates the standard as to essentials and non-essentials. For, what is it? Simply this, "All that concerns my salvation is essential; all that merely affects the glory of Christ is non-essential." How terrible is this! Reader, dost thou not utterly abhor it? What! shall we accept salvation as the fruit of our Lord's death, and deem aught that concerns Him non-essential? God forbid. Yea; rather let us entirely reverse the matter, and regard all that concerns the honor and glory of the name of Jesus, the truth of His Word, and the integrity of His cause, as vital, essential, and fundamental; and all that merely concerns ourselves as non-essential and indifferent. May God grant us this mind! May nothing be deemed trivial by us which has for its foundation the word of the living God!

Thus it was with those devoted men whose history we have been glancing at. Mordecai would not bow his head, and Daniel would not close his window. Blessed men! The Lord be praised for such, and for the inspired record of their actings. Mordecai would rather surrender life than diverge from the truth of God, and Daniel would rather do the same than turn away from God's centre. Jehovah had said that He would have war with Amalek from generation to generation, and therefore Mordecai would not bow. Jehovah had said of Jerusalem, "Mine eyes and My heart shall be there perpetually;" therefore Daniel would not cease to pray toward that blessed centre. The word of the Lord endureth forever, and faith takes its stand on that imperishable foundation. There is an eternal freshness about every word that has come forth from the Lord. His truth holds good throughout all generations; its bloom can never be brushed away, its light can never fade, its edge can never be blunted. All praise be to His holy name!

But let us look for a moment at the result of Daniel's faithfulness. The king was plunged into the deepest grief when he discovered his mistake. "He was sore displeased with himself." So well he might. He had fallen into a snare; but Daniel was in good keeping. It was all right with him. "The name of the Lord is a strong tower, the righteous runneth into it, and is safe." It matters not whether it be a lion's den at Babylon or a prison at Philippi; faith and a good conscience can make a man happy in either. We question if Daniel ever spent a happier night on this earth, than the night he spent in the lion's den. He was there for God, and God was there with him. He was there with an approving conscience and an uncondemning heart. He could look up from the very bottom of that den straight into heaven: yea, that den was heaven upon earth to his happy spirit. Who would not rather be Daniel in the den than Darius in the palace? The one happy in God; the other "sore displeased with himself." Darius would have every one pray to him; Daniel would pray to none but God. Darius was bound by his own rash decree; Daniel was bound only by the word of the living God. What a contrast!

And then see in the end what signal honor was put upon Daniel. He stood publicly identified with the one living and true God. "O Daniel," cried the king, "servant of the living God." Truly he had earned this title for himself. He was, unquestionably, a faithful servant of God. He had seen his three brethren cast into a furnace because they would worship *only* the true God, and he had been cast into the lion's den because he would pray *only* to Him; but the Lord had appeared for them and him, and given them a glorious triumph. He had allowed them to realize that precious promise made of old to their fathers, that they should be the head and their enemies the tail; that they should be above and their enemies below. Nothing could be more marked—nothing could more forcibly illustrate the value which God puts upon plain decision and true-hearted devotedness, no matter where, when, or by whom exhibited.

Oh! for an earnest heart in this day of lukewarmness! O Lord, revive Thy work!

How gentle God's commands!How kind His precepts are!We'll cast our burdens on the Lord,And trust His constant care.

Beneath His watchful eyeHis saints securely dwell:The hand that bears all nature up,Will guard His children well.

Why should an anxious loadPress down our weary mind?We haste, O Father, to Thy throne,And sweet refreshment find.

Thy goodness stands approved--Unchanged from day to day:We drop our burdens at Thy feet,To bear a song away!

—Philip Doddrige.

PRAYER,
IN ITS PROPER PLACE

There is a strong tendency in the human mind to take a one-sided view of things. This should be carefully guarded against. It would ever be our wisdom to view things as God presents them to us, in His holy Word. We should put things where He puts them, and leave them there. Were this more faithfully attended to, the truth would be much more clearly understood, and souls much better instructed. There is a divinely appointed place for everything, and we should avoid putting right things in wrong places, just as carefully as we would avoid setting them aside altogether. The one may do as much damage as the other. Let any divine institution be taken out of its divinely-appointed place, and it must necessarily fail of its divinely-appointed end. This, I imagine, will hardly be questioned by any enlightened or well-regulated mind. It will be admitted, on all hands, to be wrong to put things in any place but just where God intended them to be.

And in proportion to the importance of a right thing is the importance of having it in its right place. This remark holds good, in a special manner, with respect to the hallowed and most precious exercise of prayer. It is hard to imagine how any one, with the word of God in his hand, could presume to detract from the value of prayer. It is one of the very highest functions, and most important privileges of the Christian life. No sooner has the new nature been communicated by the Holy Ghost, through faith in Christ, than it expresses itself in the sweet accents of prayer. Prayer is the earnest breathing of the new man, drawn forth by the operation of the Holy Ghost, who dwells in all true believers. Hence, to find any one praying is to find him manifesting divine life in one of its most touching and beauteous characteristics, namely, dependence. There may be a vast amount of ignorance displayed in the prayer, both in its character and object; but the *spirit* of prayer is, unquestionably, divine. A child may ask for a great many foolish things; but, clearly, he could not ask for any thing if he had not life. The ability and desire to ask are the infallible proofs of life. No sooner had Saul of Tarsus passed from death unto life, than the Lord says of him, "*Behold he prayeth!*" (Acts ix.) Doubtless he had, as "a Pharisee of the Pharisees," said many "long prayers;" but not until he "saw that Just One, and heard the voice of His mouth," could it be said of him, "behold, *he prayeth.*"

Saying prayers and praying, are two totally different things. A self-righteous Pharisee may excel in the former; none but a converted soul can enjoy the latter. The spirit of prayer is the spirit of the new man; the language of prayer is the distinct utterance of the new life. The moment a spiritual babe is born into the new creation, it sends up its cry of dependence and of trust toward the Source of its birth. Who would dare to hush or hinder that cry? Let the babe be gently satisfied and encouraged, not ignorantly hindered or rudely silenced. The very cry which ignorance would seek to stifle, falls like sweetest music on the parent's ear. It is the proof of life. It evidences the existence of a new object around which the affections of a parent's heart may entwine themselves.

All this is plain enough. It commends itself to every renewed mind. The man who could think of hushing the accents of prayer must be wholly ignorant of the precious and beautiful mysteries of the new creation. The understanding of the praying one may need to be instructed; but oh! let not the spirit of prayer be quenched. Let the beams of divine revelation, in all their emancipating power, shine in upon the struggling conscience, but let not the breathings of the new life be interrupted. The newly-converted soul may be in great darkness. The chilling mists of legalism may enwrap his spirit. He may not, as yet, be able to rest fully in Christ and His accomplished work. His awakened conscience may not, as yet, have found its peace-giving answer in the precious blood of Jesus. Doubts and fears may sorely beset him. He may not know about the important doctrine of the two natures, and the continual conflict between them. He is bowed down beneath the humiliating sense of indwelling sin, and sees not, as yet, the ample provision which redeeming love has made for that very thing, in the sacrifice and priesthood—the blood and advocacy of the Lord Jesus Christ. The joyous emotions which attended upon the first moments of his conversion may have passed away. The beams of the Sun of Righteousness may be hidden by the heavy clouds which arise from within and around him. It is not with him as in days past. He marvels at the sad change which has come over him, and well nigh doubts if he were ever converted at all.

Need we wonder that such an one should cry mightily to God? Yea, the wonder would be if he could do aught else. How, then, should we treat him? Should we teach him not to pray? God forbid. This would be to do the work of Satan, who, assuredly, hates prayer most cordially. To drop a syllable which could even be understood as making little of an exercise so entirely divine, would be to fly in the face of the entire book of God, to deny the very example of Christ, and hinder the utterance of the Holy Ghost in the new-born soul. The Old and New Testament Scriptures literally teem with exhortations and encouragements to pray. To quote the passages would fill a volume. The blessed Master Himself has left His people an example as to the unceasing exercise of a spirit of prayer. He both prayed Himself and taught His disciples to pray. The same is true of the Holy Ghost in the apostles. (See the following passages; Luke iii. 21; vi.

12; ix. 28, 29; xi. I-13; xviii. I-8; Acts i. 14; iv. 31; Rom. xii. 12; xv. 30; Eph. vi. 18; Phil. iv. 6; Col. iv. 2-4; I Thess. v. 17; 2 Thess. iii. I, 2; I Tim. ii. I-3; Heb. xiii. 18; James v. 14, 15.)

If my reader will look out and ponder the foregoing passages, he will have a just view of the place which prayer occupies in the Christian economy. He will see that disciples are exhorted to pray; and that it is only disciples who are so exhorted. He will see that prayer is a grand prominent exercise of the household of God, and that he must be of that household to engage in it. He will see that prayer is the undoubted utterance of the new life; and that the life therefore must be there to utter itself. He will see that prayer is an important part of the Christian's privilege; and that it enters in no wise in the foundation of the Christian's peace.

Thus, he will be able to put prayer in its proper place; and how important it is that it should be so put! How important it is that the anxious inquirer should see that the deep and solid foundations of his present and everlasting peace were laid in the work of the Cross, nineteen centuries ago! How important that the blood of Jesus should stand out before the soul in clear and bold relief, in its solitary grandeur, as the alone foundation of the sinner's rest! A soul may be earnestly seeking and crying for salvation, and all the while be ignorant of the great fact that it is ready to his hand—that he is actually commanded to accept a free, full, present, personal, and eternal salvation—that Christ has done all—that a brimming cup of salvation is set before him, which faith has only to take and drink for its everlasting satisfaction. The gospel of God's free grace points to the rent vail—the empty tomb—the occupied throne above. (Matt. xxviii; Heb. i. and x.) What do these things declare? What do they utter in the anxious sinner's ear? Salvation! salvation! The rent vail, the empty tomb, the occupied throne, all cry out, salvation!

Reader, do you really want salvation? Then why not take it, as God's free gift? Are you looking to your own heart or to Christ's finished work for salvation? Is it needful, think you, to wait that God should do something more for your salvation? If so, then Christ's work were not finished; the ransom were not paid. But Christ said "*It is finished*," and God says, "I have found a ransom" (Job xxxiii. John xix.). And if *you* have to do, say, or think aught, to complete the work of salvation, then Christ would not be a whole, a perfect Saviour. And, further, it would be a plain denial of Rom. iv. 5, which says, "To him that *worketh not*, but believeth on Him that *justifieth the ungodly*, his faith is counted for righteousness." Take heed that you are not mixing up your poor prayers with the glorious work of redemption, completed by the Lamb of God on the cross. Prayer is most precious; but, remember, "without faith it is impossible to please God" (Heb. xi. 6); and if you have faith, you have Christ; and having Christ, you have ALL. If you say you are crying for mercy, the word of God points you to mercy's copious stream flowing from the finished sacrifice. You have all your anxious heart can want in Jesus, and He is God's free gift to you just as you are, where you are, *now*. If you had *to be* aught else but what you are, or *to go* anywhere else from where you are, then salvation would not be "by grace, through faith" (Eph. ii. 8). If you are anxious to get salvation, and God desires you should have it, why need you be another moment without it? It is all ready. Christ died and rose again. The Holy Ghost testifies. The word is plain. "*Only believe.*"

Oh, may the Spirit of God lead any anxious soul to find settled repose in Jesus. May He lead you to look away from all besides, straight to an all-sufficient atonement. May He give clearness of apprehension, and simplicity of faith to all; and may He especially endow all who stand up to teach and preach with the ability "rightly to divide the word of truth," so that they may not apply to the unregenerate sinner, or the anxious inquirer, such passages of Scripture as refer only to the established believer. Very serious damage is done both to the truth of God, and to the souls of men, by an unskilful division and application of the Word. There must be spiritual life, before there can be spiritual action; and the *only* way to get spiritual life is by *believing* on the name of the Son of God[5] (John i. 12, 13; iii. 14-16, 36; v. 24; xx. 31). If, therefore, the precepts of God's word be applied to persons who have not the spiritual life to act in them, confusion must be the result. The precious privileges of the Christian are turned into a heavy yoke for the unconverted. A strange system of half-law half-gospel is propounded, whereby true Christianity is robbed of its characteristic glory, and the souls of men are plunged in mist and perplexity. There is urgent need for clearness in setting forth the true ground of a sinner's peace. When souls are convicted of sin, and have life, but not liberty, they want a full, clear, unclouded gospel. The claims of a divinely-awakened conscience can only be answered by the blood of the Cross. If anything, no matter what, be added to the finished work of Christ, the soul must be filled with doubt and darkness.

May God grant us to know more fully the true place and value of simple faith in the Lord Jesus Christ, and of earnest prayer in the Holy Ghost.

C. H. M.

"GILGAL"
JOSHUA V

"Whatsoever things were written aforetime were written for our learning, that we through patience and comfort of the Scriptures might have hope" (Rom. xv. 4). These few words furnish a title, distinct and unquestionable, for the Christian to range through the wide and magnificent field of Old Testament Scripture, and gather therein instruction and comfort, according to the measure of his capacity and the character or depth of his spiritual need. And were any further warrant needed, we have it with equal clearness in the words of another inspired epistle: "Now all these things happened unto them (Israel) for ensamples; and they are written for our admonition, upon whom the ends of the world are come" (I Cor. x. 11).

No doubt, in reading the Old Testament, as in reading the New, there is constant need of watchfulness—need of self-emptiness, of dependence upon the direct teaching of the Holy Spirit, by whom all Scripture has been indited. The imagination must be checked, lest it lead us into crude notions and fanciful interpretations, which tend to no profit, but rather to the weakening of the power of Scripture over the soul, and hindering our growth in the divine life.

Still, we must never lose sight of the divine charter made out for us in Rom. xv. 4—never forget for a single moment that "whatsoever things were written aforetime were written for our learning." It is in the strength of these words that we invite the reader to accompany us back to the opening of the book of Joshua, that we may together contemplate the striking and instructive scenes presented there, and seek to gather up some of the precious "learning" there unfolded. If we mistake not, we shall learn some fine lessons on the banks of the Jordan, and find the air of Gilgal most healthful and bracing for the spiritual constitution.

We have all been accustomed to look at Jordan as the figure of death— the death of the believer—his leaving this world and going to heaven. Doubtless the believer has often read and heard these lines:

"Could we but stand where Moses stood,And view the landscape o'er,Not Jordan's stream nor death's cold floodCould fright us from the shore."

But all this line of thought, feeling and experience is very far below the mark of true Christianity. A moment's reflection in the true light which Scripture pours upon our souls would be sufficient to show how utterly deficient is the popular religious thought as to Jordan. For instance, when a be dies and goes to heaven, is he called to fight? Surely not. All is rest and peace up yonder—ineffable, eternal peace. Not a ripple on that ocean. No sound of alarm throughout that pure and holy region. No conflict there. No need of armor. We shall want no girdle, because our garments may flow loosely around us. We shall not need a breast-plate of righteousness, for divine righteousness has there its eternal abode. We shall have no need of sandals, for there will be no rough or thorny places in that fair and blissful region. No shield called for there, inasmuch as there will be no fiery darts flying. No helmet of salvation, for the divine and eternal results of God's salvation shall then be reached. No sword, inasmuch as there will be neither enemy nor evil occurrent throughout all that blissful, sunny region.

Hence, therefore, Jordan cannot mean the death of the believer and his going to heaven, for the simplest of all reasons, that it was when Israel crossed the Jordan that their fighting, properly speaking, began. True they had fought with Amalek in the wilderness; but it was in Canaan that their real war commenced. The careful reader of the Scriptures will readily see this.

But does not Jordan represent death? Most surely it does. And must not the believer cross it? Yes; but he finds it dry, because the Prince of Life has gone down into its deepest depths, and opened up a pathway for His people, by the which they pass over into their heavenly inheritance.

Moses, from Pisgah's top, gazed upon the promised land. *Personally*, under the governmental dealings of God, he was prevented from going over Jordan. But looking at him *officially*, we know that the law could not possibly bring the people into Canaan; so Moses' course must end there, for he represents the law.

But Christ, the true Joshua, has crossed the Jordan, and not only crossed it, but turned it into a pathway by which the ransomed host can pass over dry-shod into the heavenly Canaan. The Christian is not called to stand shivering on the brink of the river of death, as one in doubt as to how it may go with him. That river is dried up for faith. Its power is gone. Our adorable Lord "has abolished death, and brought life and incorruptibility to light by the gospel." Faith can now, therefore, sing triumphantly, O death, where is thy sting? O grave, where is thy victory? The sting of death is sin; and the strength of sin is the law; but thanks be to God, which giveth us the victory through our Lord Jesus Christ" (I Cor. xv. 55-57).

Glorious, enfranchising fact! Let us praise Him for it. Let all our ransomed powers adore Him. Let our whole moral being be stirred up to chant the praises of Him who has taken the sting from death, and destroyed him who had the power of death, that is, the devil, and conducted us into a sphere which is pervaded throughout with life, light, incorruptibility, and glory. May our entire practical career be to His glory!

We shall now proceed to examine more particularly the teaching of Scripture on this great subject, and may the Holy Spirit Himself be our immediate instructor!

"And Joshua rose early in the morning; and they removed from Shittim, and came to Jordan, he and all the children of Israel, and lodged there before they passed over. And it came to pass after three days, that the officers went through the host; and they commanded the people, saying, When ye see the ark of the covenant of the Lord your God, and the priests, the Levites, bearing it, then ye shall remove from your place, and go after it. *Yet there shall be a space between you and it*, about two thousand cubits by measure: come not near unto it, *that ye may know the way by which ye must go: for ye have not passed this way heretofore*" (Josh. iii. I-4).

There are three deeply important points in Israel's history which the reader would do well to ponder. There is, first, the blood-stained lintel, in the land of Egypt; secondly, the Red Sea; thirdly, the river Jordan.

Now in each of these we have a type of the death of Christ, in some one or other of its grand aspects—for, as we know, that precious death has many and various aspects, and nothing can be more profitable for the Christian, and nothing, surely, ought to be more attractive, than the study of the profound mystery of the death of Christ. There are depths and heights in that mystery which eternity alone will unfold; and it should be our delight now, under the powerful ministry of the Holy Ghost, through the perfect light of Holy Scripture, to search into these things for the strength, comfort and refreshment of the inward man.

Looking, then, at the death of Christ, as typified by the blood of the paschal lamb, we see in it that which screens us from the judgment of God. "I will pass through the land of Egypt this night, and will smite all the firstborn in the land of Egypt, both man and beast; and against all the gods of Egypt I will execute judgment; I am the Lord. And the blood shall be to you for a token upon the houses where ye are; and when I see the blood, I will pass over you, and the plague shall not be upon you to destroy you, when I smite the land of Egypt" (Ex. xii.).

Now, we need hardly say, it is of the deepest moment for the exercised, consciously guilty soul, to know that God has provided a shelter from wrath and judgment to come. No right-minded person would think for a moment of undervaluing this aspect of the death of Christ. "When I see the blood, I will pass over you." Israel's safety rested upon God's estimate of the blood. He does not say, "When *you* see the blood." The Judge saw the blood, knew its value, and passed over the house. Israel was screened by the blood of the lamb—by God's estimate of that blood, not by their own. Precious fact!

How prone we are to be occupied with our thoughts about the blood of Christ, instead of with God's thoughts! We feel we do not value that precious blood as we ought—who ever did, or ever could? and then we begin to question if we are safe, seeing we so sadly fail in our estimate of Christ's work and in our love to His person.

Now if our *safety* depends in the smallest degree upon our estimate of Christ's work, or our love to His person, we are in more imminent danger than if it depended upon our keeping the law. True it is,—most true—who could think of denying it?—we ought to value Christ's work, and we ought to love Himself. But if all this be put upon the footing of a righteous claim, and if our safety rests upon our answering to that claim, then are we in greater danger and more justly condemned than if we stood on the ground of a broken law. For just in proportion as the claims of Christ are higher than the claims of Moses, and in proportion as Christianity is higher than the legal system, so are we worse off, in greater danger, farther from peace, if our safety depends upon our response to those higher claims.

Mark, it is not that we ought not to answer to such claims; we most certainly ought. But who among us does? and hence, so far as we are concerned, our ruin and guilt are only made more manifest, and our condemnation more righteous, if we stand upon the claims of Christ, because we have not answered to them. If we are to be saved by our estimate of Christ, by our response to His claims, by our appreciation of His love, we are worse off by far than if we were placed under the claims of the law of Moses.

But, blessed be God, it is not so. We are saved by grace,—free, sovereign, divine and eternal grace,—not by our sense of grace. We are sheltered by the blood, not by our estimate of the blood. Jehovah did not say, on that awful night, "When *you* see the blood, and estimate it as you ought, I will pass over you." Nothing of the kind. This is not the way of our God. He wanted to shelter His people, and to let them know that they were sheltered,—perfectly, because divinely sheltered,—and therefore He places the matter wholly upon a divine basis; He takes it entirely out of their hands, by assuring them that their safety rested simply and entirely upon the blood, and upon His estimate thereof. He gives them to understand that they had nothing whatever to do with providing the shelter. It was His to *provide*. It was theirs to *enjoy*.

Thus it stood between Jehovah and His Israel in that memorable night; and thus it stands between Him and the soul that simply trusts in Jesus now. We are not saved by *our* love, or *our* estimate, or *our* anything. We are saved by the blood behind which faith has fled for refuge, and by God's estimate of it, which faith apprehends. And just as Israel, within that blood-stained lintel screened from judgment,—safe from the sword of the destroyer,—could feed upon the roasted lamb, so may the believer, perfectly sheltered from the wrath to come,—sweetly secure from all danger, screened from judgment,—feed upon Christ in all the preciousness of what He is.

But more of this by and by.

We are specially anxious that the reader should weigh the point on which we have been dwelling, if he be one who has not yet found peace, even as to the question of safety from judgment to come, which, as we shall see (if God permit) ere we close this paper, is but a part, though an ineffably precious part, of what the death of Christ has procured for us.

We have very little idea indeed of how much of the leaven of self-righteousness cleaves to us, even after our conversion, and how immensely it interferes with our peace, our enjoyment of grace, and our consequent progress in the divine life. It may be we fancy we have done with self-righteousness when we have given up all thought of being saved by our works; but alas, it is not so, for the evil takes new forms; and of all these, none is more subtle than the feeling that we do not value the blood as we ought, and the doubting our safety on that ground. All this is the fruit of self-righteousness. We have not done with *self*. True, we are not, it may be, making a saviour of our *doings*, but we are of our *feelings*. We are seeking, unknown to ourselves perhaps, to find some sort of title in our love to God or our appreciation of Christ.

Now all this must be given up. We must rest simply on the blood of Christ, and upon God's testimony to that blood. He sees the blood. He values it as it deserves. He is satisfied. This ought to satisfy us. He did not say to Israel, When I see how you behave yourselves; when I see the unleavened bread, the bitter herbs, the girded loins, the shod feet, I will pass over you.

No doubt all these things had their proper place; but that proper place was not as the ground of safety, but as the secret of communion. They were called to behave themselves—called to keep the feast; but it was as *being*, not *in order to be*, a sheltered people. This made all the difference. It was because they were divinely screened from judgment that they could keep the feast. They had the authority of the word of God to assure them that there was no judgment for them; and if they believed that word, they could celebrate the feast in peace and safety. "Through faith he kept the passover, and the sprinkling of blood, lest He that destroyed the firstborn should touch them" (Heb. xi. 28).

Here lies the deep and precious secret of the whole matter. It was by faith he kept the passover. God had said, "When I see the blood, I will pass over you," and He could not deny Himself. It would have been a denial of His very nature and character, and an ignoring of His own blessed remedy, had a single hair of an Israelite's head been touched on that deeply solemn night. It was not, we repeat, in anywise a question of Israel's state or Israel's deservings. It was simply and entirely a question of the value of the blood *in God's sight*, and of the truth and authority of His own word.

What stability is here!—what peace and rest! What a solid ground of confidence! The blood of Christ! the word of God! True, divinely true—let it never be forgotten or lost sight of—it is only by the grace of the Holy Spirit that the word of God can be received, or the blood of Christ relied upon. Still, it is the word of God and the blood of Christ, and nothing else, which give peace to the heart as regards all question of coming judgment. There can be no judgment for the believer. And why? Because the blood is on the mercy-seat, as the perfect proof that judgment has been already executed.

"He bore on the tree the sentence for me,And now both the Surety and sinner are free."

Yet, all praise to His name, thus it stands as to every soul that simply takes God at His word, and rests in the precious blood of Christ. It is as impossible that such an one can come into judgment, as that Christ Himself can. All who are sheltered by the blood are as safe as the word of God is sure—as safe as Christ Himself. It seems perfectly wonderful for any poor sinful mortal to be able to pen such words; but the blessed fact is, it is either this or nothing. If there is any question as to the believer's safety, then the blood of Christ is not on the mercy-seat, or it is of no account in the judgment of God. If it be a question of the believer's state, of his worthiness, of his feelings, of his experience, of his walk, of his love, of his devotedness, of his appreciation of Christ, then would there be no force, no value, no truth in that glorious sentence, "When I see the blood, I will pass over;" for in that case the form of speech should be entirely changed, and a dark and chilling shade be cast over its heavenly lustre. It should then be, "When I see the blood, and———"

But no, beloved, anxious reader, it is not, and it never can be, thus. Nothing must ever be added—not the weight of a feather, to that precious blood which has perfectly satisfied God as a Judge, and which perfectly shelters every soul that has fled for safety behind it. If the righteous Judge has declared Himself satisfied, surely the guilty culprit may well be satisfied also. God is satisfied with the blood of Jesus; and when the soul is satisfied likewise, all is settled, and there is peace as regards the question of judgment. "There is no condemnation to them that are in Christ Jesus." How can there be, seeing He has borne the condemnation in their stead? To doubt the believer's exemption from judgment is to make God a liar, and to make the blood of Christ of none effect.

The reader will note that thus far we have been occupied only with the question of deliverance from judgment—a most weighty question surely. But, as we shall see in the course of this series of papers, there is far more secured for us by the death of Christ than freedom from judgment and wrath, blessed as that is. That peerless sacrifice does a great deal more for us than keep God out as a Judge.

But for the present we pause, and shall close this paper with a solemn and earnest question to the reader, *Art thou sheltered by the blood of Jesus?* Do not rest, beloved, until you can answer with a clear and unhesitating "Yes." Remember, you are either sheltered by the blood, or exposed to the horrors of eternal judgment.

PART II

In our last paper we had before us Israel under the shelter of the blood. A grand reality, most surely: who could duly estimate it? What human language could suitably unfold the deep blessedness of being screened from the judgment of God by the blood of the Lamb—of being within that hallowed circle where wrath and judgment can never come? Who can speak aright of the privilege of feeding in perfect safety on the Lamb whose precious blood has forever averted from us the wrath of a sin-hating God?

But blessed as all this is, there is much more than this. There is far more comprehended in the salvation of God than deliverance from judgment and wrath. We may have the fullest assurance that our sins are forgiven, that God will never enter into judgment with us on account of our sins, and yet be very far indeed from the enjoyment of the true Christian position. We may be filled with all manner of fears about ourselves—fears occasioned by the consciousness of indwelling sin, the power of Satan, the influence of the world. All these things may crop up before us, and fill us with the gravest apprehensions.

Thus, for example, when we turn to Ex. xiv., we find Israel in the deepest distress, and almost overwhelmed with fear. It would seem as if they had for the moment lost sight of the fact that they had been under the cover of the blood.

Let us look at the passage.

"And the Lord spake unto Moses, saying, Speak unto the children of Israel, that they turn and encamp before Pi-hahiroth, between Migdol and the sea, over against Baal-zephon: before it shall ye encamp by the sea. For Pharaoh will say of the children of Israel, They are entangled in the land, the wilderness hath shut them in. And I will harden Pharaoh's heart, that he shall follow after them: and I will be honored upon Pharaoh, and upon all his host; that the Egyptians may know that I am the Lord. And they did so. And it was told the king of Egypt that the people fled: and the heart of Pharaoh and of his servants was turned against the people, and they said, Why have we done this, *that we have let Israel go from serving us?*"—mark these words:—"And he made ready his chariot, and took his people with him. And he took six hundred chosen chariots, and all the chariots of Egypt, and captains over every one of them. And the Lord hardened the heart of Pharaoh king of Egypt, and he pursued after the children of Israel: and the children of Israel went out with a high hand. But the Egyptians pursued after them, all the horses and chariots of Pharaoh, and his horsemen, and his army, and overtook them, encamping by the sea, beside Pi-hahiroth, before Baal-zephon. And when Pharaoh drew nigh, the children of Israel lifted up their eyes, and, behold, the Egyptians marched after them; and they were *sore afraid*: and the children of Israel *cried out* unto the Lord."

Now, we may feel disposed to ask, Are these the people whom we have seen so recently feeding, in perfect safety, under the cover of the blood? The very same. Whence, then, these fears, this intense alarm, this agonizing cry? Did they really think that Jehovah was going to judge and destroy them, after all? Not exactly. Of what, then, were they afraid? Of perishing in the wilderness after all. "And they said unto Moses, Because there were no graves in Egypt, hast thou taken us away to die in the wilderness? Wherefore hast thou dealt thus with us, to carry us forth out of Egypt? Is not this the word that we did tell thee in Egypt, saying, Let us alone, that we may serve the Egyptians! For it had been better for us to serve the Egyptians, than that we should die in the wilderness."

All this was most gloomy and depressing. Their poor hearts seem to fluctuate between "graves in Egypt" and death in the wilderness. There is no sense of deliverance; no adequate knowledge either of God's purposes or of God's salvation. All seems utter darkness, almost bordering upon hopeless despair. They are thoroughly hemmed in and "shut up." They seem in a worse plight than ever. They heartily wish themselves back again amid the brick-kilns and stubble fields of Egypt. Deserts sands on either side of them; the sea in front; Pharaoh and all his terrific hosts behind!

The case seemed perfectly hopeless; and hopeless it was, so far as they were concerned. They were utterly powerless, and they were being made to realize it, and this is a very painful process to go through; but very wholesome and valuable, yea, most necessary for all. We must all, in one way or another, learn the force, meaning, and depth of that phrase, "without strength." It is exactly in proportion as we find out what it is to be without strength, that we are prepared to appreciate God's "due time."

But, we may here inquire, "Is there aught in the history of God's people now answering to Israel's experience at the Red Sea?" Doubtless there is; for we are told that the things which happened unto Israel are our ensamples, or types. And, most surely, the scene at the Red Sea is full of instruction for us. How often do we find the children of God plunged in the very depths of distress and darkness as to their state and prospects! It is not that they question the love of God, or the efficacy of the blood of Jesus, nor yet that God will reckon their sins to them, or enter into judgment with them. But still, they have no sense of full deliverance. They do not see the application of the death of Christ to their *evil nature*. They do not realize the glorious truth that by that death they are completely delivered from this present evil world, from the dominion of sin, and from the power of Satan. They see that the blood of Jesus screens them from the judgment of God; but they do not see that *they* are "dead to sin;" that their "old man is crucified with Christ;" that not only have their sins been put upon Christ at the cross, but *they themselves*, as sinful children of Adam, have been, by the act of God, identified with Christ in His death; that God pronounces them *dead and risen with Christ*. (See Col. iii. I-4 and the sixth chapter of Romans.) But if this precious truth is not apprehended, by faith, there is no bright, happy, emancipating sense of full and everlasting salvation. They are, to speak according to our type, at Egypt's side of the Red Sea, and in danger of falling into the hands of the prince of this world. They do not see "*all* their enemies dead on the sea-shore." They cannot sing the song of redemption. No one can sing it, until he stands by faith on the wilderness side of the Red Sea, or, in other words, until he sees his complete deliverance from sin, the world, and Satan—the great foes of every child of God.

Thus, in contemplating the facts of Israel's history, as recorded in the first fifteen chapters of Exodus, we observe that they did not raise a single note of praise until they had passed through the Red Sea. We hear the cry of sore distress under the cruel lash of Pharaoh's task-masters, and amid the grievous toil of Egypt's brick-kilns. And we hear the cry of terror when they stood "between Migdol and the sea." All this we hear; but not one note of praise, not a single accent of triumph, until the waters of the Red Sea rolled between them and the land of bondage and of death, and they saw all the power of the enemy broken and gone. "Thus the Lord saved Israel that day out of the hand of the Egyptians; and Israel saw the Egyptians dead upon the sea-shore. And *Israel saw that great work which the Lord did* upon the Egyptians: and the people feared the Lord and His servant Moses. *Then sang* Moses and the children of Israel."

Now, what is the simple application of all this to us as Christians? What grand lesson are we to learn from the scenes on the shores of the Red Sea? In a word, of what is the Red Sea a type? And what is the difference between the blood-stained lintel and the divided sea?

The Red Sea is the type of the death of Christ, in its application to all our spiritual enemies, sin, the world, and Satan. By the death of Christ the believer is completely and forever delivered from the *power* of sin. He is, alas! conscious of the *presence* of sin; but its power is gone. He has died to sin, in the death of Christ; and what power has sin over a dead man? It is the privilege of the Christian to reckon himself as much delivered from the dominion of sin as a man lying dead on the floor. What power has sin over such an one? None whatever. No more has it over the Christian. Sin *dwells* in the believer, and will do so to the end of the chapter; but its *rule* is gone.

Christ has wrested the sceptre from the grasp of our old master, and shivered it to atoms. It is not merely that His blood has purged our *sins*; but His death has broken the power of *sin*.

It is one thing to know that our sins are forgiven, and another thing altogether to know that "the body of sin is destroyed"—its rule ended—its dominion gone. Many will tell you that they do not question the forgiveness of their past sins, but they do not know what to say as to indwelling sin. They fear lest, after all, that may come against them, and bring them into judgment. Such persons are, to use the figure, "between Migdol and the sea." They have not learnt the doctrine of Rom. vi. They have not as yet, in their spiritual intelligence and apprehension, reached the resurrection side of the Red Sea. They do not know what it is to be dead unto sin, and alive unto God through Jesus Christ our Lord.

And let the reader particularly note the force of the apostle's word, "*reckon*." How very different it is, in every way, from our word, "*realize*!" This latter word may do very well where natural or human things are concerned. We can realize physical or material facts; but where a spiritual truth is involved, it is not a question of realizing, but of reckoning. How can I realize that I am dead to sin? All my own experience, my own feelings, my inward self-consciousness seems to offer a flat contradiction to the truth. I cannot realize that I am dead; but God tells me I am. He assures me that He counts me to have died to sin when Christ died. I believe it; not because I feel it, but because God says it. I reckon myself to be what God tells me I am. If I were sinless, if I had no sin in me, I should never be told to reckon myself dead to sin; neither should I ever be called to listen to such words as, "Let not sin, therefore, *reign* in your mortal body." But it is just because I have sin dwelling in me, and in order to give me full practical deliverance from its reigning power, that I am taught the grand enfranchising truth, that the dominion of sin is broken by the death of Christ in which I also died.

How do I know this? Is it because I feel it? Certainly not. How could I feel it? How could I realize it? How could I ever have the self-consciousness of it, while in the body? Impossible. But God tells me I have died in the death of Christ. I believe it. I do not reason about it. I do not stagger at it because I cannot find any evidence of its truth in myself. I take God at His word. I reckon myself to be what He tells me I am. I do not endeavor to struggle, and strive, and work myself into a sinless state which is impossible. Neither do I imagine myself to be in it, which were a deceit and a delusion; but by a simple, childlike faith, I take the blessed ground which faith assigns me, in association with a dead Christ. I look at Christ there, and see in Him, according to God's word, the true expression of where I am, in the Divine Presence. I do not reason from myself upwards, but I reason from God downwards. This makes all the difference. It is just the difference between unbelief and faith,—between law and grace—between human religion and divine Christianity. If I reason from self, how can I have any right thought of what is in the heart of God?—all my conclusions must be utterly false. But if, on the other hand, I listen to God and believe His Word, my conclusions are divinely sound. Abraham did not look at himself and the improbability, nay, the impossibility of having a son in his old age; but he believed God and gave glory to Him. And it was counted to Him for righteousness.

It is an unspeakable mercy to get done with self, in all its phases and in all its workings, and to be brought to rest, in all simplicity, on the written Word, and on the Christ which that written Word presents to our souls. Self-occupation is a deathblow to fellowship, and a great barrier to the soul's rest and progress. It is impossible for any one to enjoy settled peace so long as he is occupied with himself. He must cease from self, and harken to God's Word, and rest, without a single question, on its pure, precious, and everlasting record. God's Word never changes. I change; my frames, my feelings, my experience, my circumstances, change continually; but God's Word is the same yesterday, and to-day, and forever.

Furthermore, it is a grand and essential point for the soul to apprehend that Christ is the only definition of the believer's place before God. This gives immense power, liberty, and blessing. "As He is, so are we, in this world" (I John iv. 17). This is something perfectly wonderful! Let us ponder it: let us think of a poor, wretched, guilty slave of sin, a bondslave of Satan, a votary of the world, exposed to an eternal hell—such an one taken up by sovereign grace, delivered completely from the grasp of Satan, the dominion of sin, the power of this present evil world—pardoned, washed, justified, brought nigh to God, accepted in Christ, and perfectly and forever identified with Him, so that the Holy Ghost can say, as Christ is, so is he in this world!

All this seems too good to be true; and, most assuredly, it is too good for us to get; but, blessed be the God of all grace, and blessed be the Christ of God! it is not too good for Him to give. God gives like Himself. He will be God, spite of our unworthiness and Satan's opposition. He will act in a way worthy of Himself, and worthy of the Son of His love. Were it a question of our deservings, we could only think of the deepest and darkest pit of hell. But seeing it is a question of what is worthy of God to give, and that He gives according to His estimate of the worthiness of Christ, then, verily, we can think of the very highest place in heaven. The glory of God, and the worthiness of His Son, are involved in His dealings with us; and hence everything that could possibly stand in the way of our eternal blessedness, has been disposed of in such a manner as to secure the divine glory, and furnish a triumphant answer to every plea of the enemy. Is it a question of trespass? "He has forgiven us all trespasses." Is it a question of sin? He has condemned sin at the cross, and thus put it away. Is it a question of guilt? It is canceled by the blood of the cross. Is it a question of death? He has taken away its sting, and actually made it part of our property. Is it a question of Satan? He has destroyed him, by annulling all his power. Is it a question of the world? He has delivered us from it, and snapped every link which connected us with it.

Thus, beloved Christian reader, it stands with us if we are to be taught by Scripture, if we are to take God at His word, if we are to believe what He says. And we may add, if it be not thus, we are in our sins; under the power of sin; in the grasp of Satan; obnoxious to death; part and parcel of an evil, Christless, Godless world, and exposed to the unmitigated wrath of God—the vengeance of eternal fire.

Oh that the blessed Spirit may open the eyes of God's people, and give them to see their proper place, their full and eternal deliverance in association with Christ who died for them, and *in whom they have died*, and *thus* passed out of the power of all their enemies!

PART III

Having glanced at two of the leading points in our subject, namely, Israel freed from guilt under the shelter of the blood, and Israel freed from all their enemies in the passage of the Red Sea, we have now to contemplate for a few moments Israel crossing the Jordan, and celebrating the paschal feast at Gilgal, in which they represent the risen position of Christians now.

The Christian is one who is not only sheltered from judgment by the blood of the Lamb, not only delivered from the power of all his enemies by the death of Christ, but is also associated with Him where He now is, at the right hand of God; he is, with Christ, passed out of death, in resurrection, and is blessed with all spiritual blessings, in the heavenlies, in Christ. He is thus a heavenly man, and, as such, is called to walk in this world in all the varied relationships and responsibilities in which the good hand of God has placed him. He is not a monk, or an ascetic, or a man living in the clouds, fit neither for earth or heaven. He is not one who lives in a dreamy, misty, unpractical region; but, on the contrary, one whose happy privilege it is, from day to day, to reflect, amid the scenes and circumstances of earth, the graces and virtues of Christ, with whom, through infinite grace, and on the solid ground of accomplished redemption, he is linked in the power of the Holy Ghost.

Such is the Christian, according to the teaching of the New Testament. Let the reader see that he understands it. It is very real, very definite, very positive, very practical. A child may know it, and realize it, and exhibit it. A Christian is one whose sins are forgiven, who possesses eternal life, and knows it; in whom the Holy Ghost dwells; he is accepted in and associated with a risen and glorified Christ; he has broken with the world, is dead to sin and the law, and finds his object and his delight, and his spiritual sustenance, in the Christ who loved him and gave Himself for him, and for whose coming he waits every day of his life.

This, we repeat, is the New Testament description of a Christian. How immensely it differs from the ordinary type of Christian profession around us we need not say. But let the reader measure himself by the divine standard, and see wherein he comes short; for of this he may rest assured, that there is no reason whatsoever, so far as the love of God, or the work of Christ, or the testimony of the Holy Ghost, is concerned, why he should not be in the full enjoyment of all the rich and rare spiritual blessings which appertain to the true Christian position. Dark unbelief, fed by legality, bad teaching, and spurious religiousness, rob many of God's dear children of their proper place and portion. And not only so, but, from want of a thorough break with the world, many are sadly hindered from the clear perception and full realization of their position and privileges as heavenly men.

But we are rather anticipating the instruction unfolded to us in the typical history of Israel, in Josh. iii.-v., to which we shall now turn. "And Joshua rose early in the morning; and they removed from Shittim, and came to Jordan, he and all the children of Israel, and lodged there before they passed over. And it came to pass, after three days, that the officers went through the host. And they commanded the people, saying, When ye see the ark of the covenant of the Lord your God, and the priests the Levites bearing it, then ye shall remove from your place, and go after it. *Yet there shall be a space between you and it,* about two thousand cubits by measure: *come not near unto it, that ye may know the way by which ye must go; for ye have not passed this way heretofore*" (Josh. iii. I-4).

It is most desirable that the reader should, with all simplicity and clearness, seize the true spiritual import of the river Jordan. It typifies the death of Christ in one of its grand aspects, just as the Red Sea typifies it in another. When the children of Israel stood on the wilderness side of the Red Sea, they sang the song of redemption. They were a delivered people—delivered from Egypt and the power of Pharaoh. They saw all their enemies dead on the sea-shore. They could even anticipate, in glowing accents, their triumphal entrance into the promised land. "Thou in Thy mercy hast led forth the people which Thou hast redeemed; Thou hast guided them in Thy strength unto Thy holy habitation. The people shall hear, and be afraid: sorrow shall take hold on the inhabitants of Palestina. Then the dukes of Edom shall be amazed; the mighty men of Moab, trembling shall take hold upon them: all the inhabitants of Canaan shall melt away. Fear and dread shall fall upon them: by the greatness of Thine arm they shall be still as a stone; till Thy people pass over, O Lord, till the people pass over which Thou hast purchased. Thou shalt bring them in, and plant them in the mountain of Thine inheritance, in the place, O Lord, which Thou hast made for Thee to dwell in; in the sanctuary, O Lord, which Thy hands have established. The Lord shall reign for ever and ever."

All this was perfectly magnificent, and divinely true. But they were not yet in Canaan. Jordan—of which, most surely, there is no mention in their glorious song of victory—lay between them and the promised land. True, in the purpose of God and in the judgment of faith, the land was theirs; but they had to traverse the wilderness, cross the Jordan, and take possession.

How constantly we see all this exemplified in the history of souls! When first converted, there is nothing but joy and victory and praise. They know their sins forgiven; they are filled with wonder, love, and praise. Being justified by faith, they have peace with God, and they can rejoice in hope of His glory, yea, and joy in Himself through Jesus Christ our Lord. They are in Rom. v. I-11; and, in one sense, there can be nothing higher. Even in heaven itself we shall have nothing higher or better than "joy in God." Persons sometimes speak of Rom. viii. being higher than Rom. v.: but what can be higher than "joy in God"? If we are brought to God, we have reached the most exalted point to which any soul can come. To know Him as our portion, our rest, our stay, our object, our all; to have all our springs in Him, and know Him as a perfect covering for our eyes, at all times, and in all places, and under all circumstances—this is heaven itself to the believer.

But there is this difference between Rom. v. and viii., that vi. and vii. lie between; and when the soul has traveled practically through these latter, and learns how to apply their profound and precious teaching to the great questions of indwelling sin and the law, then it is in a better state, though, most assuredly, not in a higher standing.

We repeat, and with emphasis, the words "*traveled practically*." For it must be even so, if we would really enter into these holy mysteries according to God. It is easy to talk about being "dead to sin" and "dead to the law"—easy to see these things written in Rom. vi. and vii.—easy to grasp, in the intellect, the mere theory of these things. But the question is, have we made them our own—have they been applied practically to our souls by the power of the Holy Ghost? Are they livingly exhibited in our ways to the glory of Him who, at such a cost to Himself, has brought us into such a marvelous place of blessing and privilege?

It is much to be feared that there is a vast amount of merely intellectual traffic in these deep and precious mysteries of our most holy faith, which, if only laid hold of in spiritual power, would produce wonderful results in practice.

But we must return to our theme; and in doing so, we would ask the reader if he really understands the true spiritual import of the river Jordan? What does it really mean? We have said that it typifies the death of Christ. But in what aspect? for that precious death, as we are now considering, has many and various aspects. We believe the Jordan sets forth the death of our Lord Jesus Christ as that by which we are introduced into the inheritance He has obtained for us. The Red Sea *delivered Israel from* Egypt and the power of Pharaoh. Jordan *brought them into* the land of Canaan.

We find both in the death of Christ. He, blessed be His name, has, by His death on the cross—His death for us—delivered us from our sins, from their guilt and condemnation, from Satan's power, and from this present evil world.

But more than this: He has, by the same infinitely precious work, brought us *now* into an entirely new position, in resurrection and in living union and association with Himself, where He is at God's right hand. Such is the distinct teaching of Eph. ii. "But God, who is rich in mercy, for His great love wherewith He loved us, even when we were dead in sins, *hath quickened us together with Christ*, (by grace ye are saved;) and *hath raised us up together*, and made us *sit together in the heavenlies* in Christ Jesus" (vers. 4-6).

Note the little word "*hath*." He is not speaking of what God *will* do, but of what He *hath* done—done for us, and with us, in Christ Jesus. The believer has not to wait till he passes out of this life to enjoy his inheritance in heaven. In the person of his living and glorified Head, through faith, by the Spirit, he belongs there now, and is free to all that God has given to all His own.[6]

Is all this real and true? Yes! As real and true as that Christ hung on the cross and lay in the grave; as real and true as that we were dead in trespasses and sins; as real and true as the truth of God can make it; as real and true as the indwelling of the Holy Spirit in the body of every true believer.

Mark, reader, we are not now speaking of the practical working-out of all this glorious truth in the life of Christians from day to day. This is another thing altogether. Alas, alas! if our only idea of true Christian position were to be drawn from the practical career of professing Christians, we might give up Christianity as a myth or a sham.

But, thank God, it is not so. We must learn what true Christianity is from the pages of the New Testament, and, having learnt it there, judge ourselves, our ways, our surroundings, by its heavenly light. In this way, while we shall ever have to confess and mourn our shortcomings, our hearts shall ever, more and more, be filled with praise to Him whose infinite grace has brought us into such a glorious position, in union and fellowship with His own Son—a position, blessed be God, in nowise dependent upon our personal state, but which, if really apprehended, must exert a powerful influence upon our entire course, conduct, and character.

PART IV

The more deeply we ponder the typical instruction presented in the river Jordan, the more clearly we must see that the whole Christian position is involved in the standpoint from which we view it. Jordan means death, but, for the believer, a death that is *past*—the death we have gone through as identified with Christ, and which, through resurrection, has brought us on the other side—the Canaan side—where He is now. He, typified by the ark, has passed over before us into Jordan, to stem its torrent for us, and make it a dry path for our feet, so that we might pass clean over into our heavenly inheritance. The Prince of life has destroyed, on our behalf, him that had the power of death. He has taken the sting from death; yea, He has made death itself the very means by which we reach, even now, in spirit and by faith, the true heavenly Canaan.

Let us see how all this is unfolded in our type. Mark particularly the commandment given by the officers of the host. "When ye see the ark of the covenant of the Lord your God, and the priests the Levites bearing it, then ye shall remove from your place, and go after it." The ark must go first. They dared not to move one inch along that mysterious way, until the symbol of the divine Presence had gone before.

"Yet there shall be a space between you and it, about two thousand cubits by measure: *come not near unto it that ye may know the way by which ye must go*; for ye have *not passed this way heretofore.*" It was an awful flood ahead of them. No mortal could tread it with impunity. Death and destruction are linked together. "It is appointed unto men once to die; but after this the judgment" (Heb. ix.) Who can stand before the king of terrors? Who can face that grim and terrible foe? Who can encounter the swellings of Jordan? Who, except the Ark go first, can face death and judgment? Poor Peter thought he could; but he was sadly mistaken. He said unto Jesus, "Lord, whither goest thou? Jesus answered him, Whither I go, *thou canst not follow Me now*, but thou shalt follow Me afterwards."

How fully these words explain the import of that mystic "space" between Israel and the ark. Peter did not understand that space. He had not studied aright Josh. iii. 4. He knew nothing of that terrible pathway which his blessed Master was about to enter upon. "Peter said unto Him, Lord, why cannot I follow Thee now? I will lay down my life for Thy sake."

Poor dear Peter! How little he knew of himself, or of that which he was—sincerely, no doubt, though ignorantly—undertaking to do! How little did he imagine that the very sound of death's dark river, heard even in the distance, would be sufficient so to terrify him, as to make him curse and swear that he did not know his Master! "Jesus answered him, Wilt thou lay down thy life for My sake? Verily, verily, I say unto thee, the cock shall not crow till thou hast denied Me thrice."

"Yet there shall be a space between you and it." How needful! How absolutely essential! Truly there was a space between Peter and his Lord. Jesus had to go before. He had to meet death in its most terrific form. He had to tread that rough path in profound solitude—for who could accompany Him? "There shall be a space between you and it: come not near to it, that ye may know the way by which ye must go; for ye have not passed this way heretofore."

"Thou canst not follow Me *now;* but thou shalt follow me *afterwards.*" Blessed Master! He would not suffer His poor feeble servant to enter upon that terrible path, until He Himself had gone before, and so entirely changed its character, that the pathway of death should be lighted up with the beams of life and the light of God's face. Our Jesus has "abolished death, and brought life and incorruptibility to light by the gospel."

Thus death is no longer death to the believer. It was death to Jesus, in all its intensity, in all its horrors, in all its reality. He met it as the power which Satan wields over the soul of man. He met it as the penalty due to sin. He met it as the just judgment of God against sin—against us. There was not a single feature, not a single ingredient, not a single circumstance, which could possibly render death formidable which did not enter into the death of Christ. He met all; and, blessed be God, *we are accounted as having gone through all in and by Him.* We died in Him, so that death has no further claim upon us, or power over us. Its claims are disposed of, its power broken and gone for all believers. The whole scene is cleared completely of death, and filled with life and incorruptibility.

And hence, in Peter's case, we find our Lord, in the last chapter of John, most graciously meeting the desire of His servant's heart—a desire in which he was perfectly sincere—the desire to follow his beloved Lord. "Verily, verily, I say unto thee, When thou wast young, thou girdest thyself, and walkedst whither thou wouldest; but when thou shalt be old, thou shalt stretch forth thy hands, and another shall gird thee, and carry thee whither thou wouldest not. This spake He signifying by what death he should glorify God." Thus death, instead of being the judgment of God to overwhelm Peter, was turned into a means by which Peter could glorify God.

What a glorious change! What a stupendous mystery! How it magnifies the cross, or rather the One who hung thereon! What a mighty revolution, when a poor sinful man can, by death, glorify God! So completely has death been robbed of its sting, so thoroughly has its character been changed that, instead of shrinking from it with terror, we can meet it, if it does come, and go through it with song of victory; and instead of its being to us the wages of sin, it is a means by which we can glorify God. All praise to Him who has so wrought for us! to Him who has gone down into Jordan's deepest depths for us, and made there a highway by which His ransomed people can pass over into their heavenly inheritance! May our hearts adore Him! May all our powers be stirred up to magnify His holy name! May our whole life be devoted to His praise! May we appreciate the grace and lay hold of the inheritance.

But we must proceed with our type.

"And Joshua spake unto the priests, saying, Take up the ark of the covenant, and pass over before the people. And they took up the ark of the covenant, and went before the people. And the Lord said unto Joshua, This day will I begin to magnify thee in the sight of all Israel, that they may know that as I was with Moses, so I will be with thee." Joshua stands before us as a type of the risen Christ, leading His people, in the power of the Holy Ghost, into their heavenly inheritance. The priests bearing the ark into the midst of Jordan typify Christ going down into death for us, and destroying completely its power. "He passed through death's dark raging flood, to make our rest secure;" and not only to make it secure, but to lead us into it, in association with Himself, now, in spirit and by faith; by-and-by, in actual fact.

"And Joshua said unto the children of Israel, Come hither, and hear the words of the Lord your God. And Joshua said, Hereby ye shall know that the *living* God is among you, and that He will without fail drive out from before you the Canaanites.... Behold, the ark of the covenant of the Lord of all the earth passeth over before you into Jordan."

The passage of the ark into Jordan proved two things, namely, the presence of the living God in the midst of His people; and that He would most surely drive out all their enemies from before them. The death of Christ is the basis and the guarantee of everything to faith. Grant us but this, that Christ has gone down into death for us, and we argue, with all possible confidence, that, in this one great fact, all is secured. God is with us, and God is for us. "He that spared not His own Son, but delivered Him up for us all, how shall He not with Him also freely give us all things?" The difficulty of unbelief is, "How shall He?" The difficulty of faith is, "How shall He *not*?"

Israel might wonder how all the hosts of Canaan could ever be expelled from before them: let them gaze on the ark in the midst of Jordan, and cease to wonder, cease to doubt. The less is included in the greater. And hence we can say, What may we not expect, seeing that Christ has died for us? There is nothing too good, nothing too great, nothing too glorious, for God to do for us, and in us, and with us, seeing He has not spared His only-begotten Son, but delivered Him up for us all. Everything is secured for us by the precious death of Christ. It has opened up the everlasting flood-gates of the love of God, so that the rich streams thereof might flow down into the very depths of our souls. It fills us with the sweetest assurance that the One who could bruise His only-begotten Son, on the cursed tree, for us, will meet our every need, carry us through all our difficulties, and lead us into the full possession and enjoyment of all that His eternal purpose of grace has in store for us. Having given us such a proof of His love, even when we were yet sinners, what may we not expect at His hands now that He views us in association with that blessed One who glorified Him in death—the death that He died for us? When Israel saw the ark in the midst of Jordan, they were entitled to consider that all was secured. As our Lord also said to His disciples before leaving them, "Be of good cheer, I have overcome the world;" and, in view of His cross, He could say, "Now is the prince of this world cast out." True, Israel had, as we know, to take possession: they had to plant their feet upon the inheritance; but the power that could stem death's dark waters, could also drive out every foe from before them, and put them in peaceful possession of all that God had promised.

PART V

In closing this series of brief papers on Gilgal, we must turn our thoughts to the practical application of that which has been engaging our attention. If it be true—and it is true—that Jesus died for us, it is equally true that we have died in Him; as one of our own poets has sweetly put it:

"For me, Lord Jesus, Thou hast diedAnd I have died in Thee:Thou'rt risen--my bands are all untied,And now Thou livest in me.The Father's face of radiant graceShines now in light on me."

Now this is a great practical truth—none more so. It lies at the very foundation of all true Christianity. If Christ has died for us, then, in very deed, He has taken us completely out of our old condition, with all that appertained to it, and placed us upon an entirely new footing. We can look back from resurrection-ground on which we now stand, into the dark river of death, and see there, in its deepest depths, the memorial of the victory gained for us by the Prince of Life. We do not look forward to death; we look back at it. We can truly say, "The bitterness of death is past."

Jesus met death for us in its most terrible form. Just as the river of Jordan was divided when it presented its most formidable appearance— "for Jordan overfloweth all its banks all the time of harvest"—so our Jesus encountered our last great enemy, vanquished him in his most fearful form, and left behind, in the very centre of death's dark domain, the imperishable record of His glorious victory. All praise, homage, and adoration to His peerless name! It is our privilege, by faith and in spirit, to stand on Canaan's side of Jordan, and erect our memorial of what the Saviour, the true Joshua, has done for us.

"And it came to pass, when all the people were clean passed over Jordan, that the Lord spake unto Joshua, saying, Take you twelve men out of the people, *out of every tribe a man*. And command ye them, saying, Take you hence out of the midst of Jordan, *out of the place where the priests' feet stood firm*, twelve stones; and ye shall carry them over with you, and leave them in the lodging-place where ye shall lodge this night. Then Joshua called the twelve men whom he had prepared of the children of Israel, *out of every tribe a man*. And Joshua said unto them, Pass over before the ark of the Lord your God, into the midst of Jordan, and take you up *every man of you* a stone upon his shoulder, according unto the number of the tribes of the children of Israel: that this may be a sign among you, that when your children ask their fathers in time to come, saying, What mean ye by these stones? then ye shall answer them, That the waters of Jordan were cut off before the ark of the covenant of the Lord; when it passed over Jordan, the waters of Jordan were cut off: and these stones shall be *for a memorial* unto the children of Israel for ever" (Josh. iv: I-7).

The great fact was to be seized, and practically carried out by the whole assembly, "of every tribe a man"—"every man of you a stone upon his shoulder," a stone taken from the very spot where the priests' feet stood firm. All were to be brought into living personal contact with the great mysterious fact that the waters of Jordan were cut off. All were to engage in erecting such a memorial of this fact as should elicit inquiry from their children as to what it meant. It was never to be forgotten.

What a lesson is here for us! Are we erecting our memorial? Are we giving evidence—such evidence as may strike even the mind of a child—of the fact that our Jesus has vanquished the power of death for us? Are we affording any practical proof in daily life that Christ has died for us, and that we have died in Him? Is there aught in our actual history, from day to day, answering to the figure set forth in the passage just quoted—"every man of you a stone upon his shoulder"? Are we declaring plainly that we have passed clean over Jordan—that we belong to heaven—that we are not in the flesh, but in the Spirit? Do our children see aught in our habits and ways, in our spirit and deportment, in our whole character and manner of life, leading them to inquire, "What mean ye by these things?" Are we living as those who are dead with Christ—dead to sin—dead to the world?

Are we practically freed from the world—letting go our hold of present things, in the power of communion with a risen Christ?

These are searching questions for the soul, beloved Christian reader. Let us seek to meet them honestly, as in the divine presence. We profess these things, we hold them in theory. We say we believe that Jesus died for us, and that we died in Him. Where is the proof—where the abiding memorial—where the stone on the shoulder? Let us judge ourselves honestly before God. Let us no longer rest satisfied with anything short of the thorough, practical, habitual carrying out of the great truth that "we are dead, and our life is hid with Christ in God." Mere profession is worthless. We want the living power—the true result—the proper fruit.

"And the people came up out of Jordan on the tenth day of the first month, and encamped in Gilgal, in the east border of Jericho. And *those twelve stones which they took out of Jordan*"—stones of peculiar import—no other stones could tell such a tale, teach such a lesson, or symbolize such a stupendous fact—no other stones like them—"those twelve stones did Joshua pitch in Gilgal. And he spake unto the children of Israel, saying, When your children shall ask their fathers in time to come, saying, What mean these stones? then ye shall let your children know, saying, *Israel came over this Jordan on dry land*. For the Lord your God dried up the waters of Jordan from before you, until ye were passed over, as the Lord your God did to the Red Sea, which He dried up from before us, until we were gone over: that all the people of the earth might know the hand of the Lord, that it is mighty: that ye might fear the Lord your God forever."

Here, then, we see Israel at Gilgal. "Everything was finished that the Lord commanded Joshua to speak unto the people, according to all that Moses commanded Joshua." Every member of the host had passed clean over Jordan—not one had been suffered to feel the slightest touch of the river of death. Grace had brought them all safely over into the inheritance promised to their fathers. They were not only separated from Egypt by the Red Sea, but actually brought into Canaan across the dry bed of the Jordan, and encamped in Gilgal, in the plains of Jericho.

And now mark what follows. "And it came to pass, when all the kings of the Amorites which were on the side of Jordan westward, and all the kings of the Canaanites which were by the sea, heard that the Lord had dried up the waters of Jordan from before the children of Israel, until we were passed over, that their heart melted, neither was there spirit in them any more, because of the children of Israel. *At that time*"—note the words!—when all the nations were paralyzed with terror at the very thought of this people—"at that time the Lord said unto Joshua, Make thee *sharp knives*, and circumcise again the children of Israel the second time."

How deeply significant is this: How suggestive are these "sharp knives"! How needful! If Israel are about to bring the sword upon the Canaanites, Israel must have the sharp knife applied to themselves. They had never been circumcised in the wilderness. The reproach of Egypt had never been rolled away from them. And ere they could celebrate the passover, and eat of the old corn of the land of Canaan, they must have the sentence of death written upon them. No doubt this was aught but agreeable to nature; but it must be done. How could they take possession of Canaan with the reproach of Egypt resting upon them? How could uncircumcised people dispossess the Canaanites? Impossible! The sharp knives had to do their work throughout the camp of Israel ere they could eat of Canaan's food or prosecute the warfare which of necessity belongs to it.

"And Joshua made him sharp knives, and circumcised the children of Israel at the hill of the foreskins. And this is the cause why Joshua did circumcise. All the people that came out of Egypt that were males, even all the men of war, died in the wilderness by the way, after they came out of Egypt.... And their children, whom he raised up in their stead, them Joshua circumcised: for they were uncircumcised, because they had not circumcised them by the way.... And the Lord said unto Joshua, This day have I rolled away the reproach of Egypt from off you. Wherefore the name of the place is called Gilgal ("rolling") unto this day. And the children of Israel encamped in Gilgal, and kept the passover on the fourteenth day of the month, at even, in the plains of Jericho. And they did eat of the old corn of the land on the morrow after the passover, unleavened cakes and parched corn, in the self-same day. And the manna ceased on the morrow after they had eaten of the old corn of the land; neither had the children of Israel manna any more; but they did eat of the fruit of the land of Canaan that year."

Here, then, we have a type of the full Christian position. The Christian is a heavenly man, dead to the world, crucified with Christ, associated with Him where He now is, and, while waiting for His appearing, occupied in heart with Him, feeding by faith upon Him as the proper nourishment of the new man.

Such is the Christian's position—such his portion. But in order to enter fully into the enjoyment thereof, there must be the application of the "sharp knife" to all that belongs to mere nature. There must be the sentence of death written upon that which Scripture designates as "the old man."

All this must be really and practically entered into if we would maintain our position or enjoy our proper portion as heavenly men. If we are indulging nature; if we are living in a low, worldly atmosphere; if we are going in for this world's pursuits, its pleasures, its politics, its riches, its honors, its fashions, and its distinctions—then, verily, it is impossible that we can be enjoying fellowship with our risen Head and Lord.[7] Christ is in heaven, and to enjoy Him we must be living, in spirit and by faith, where He is. He is not of this world; and if we are of it, we cannot be enjoying fellowship with Him. "If we say that we have fellowship with Him, and walk in darkness, we lie, and do not the truth" (I John i. 6).

This is most solemn. If I am living in and of the world, I am walking in darkness, and I can have no fellowship with a heavenly Christ. "Wherefore," says the blessed apostle, "if ye be dead with Christ from the rudiments of the world, why, *as though living in the world*, are ye subject to ordinances?" Do we really understand these words? Have we weighed the full force of the expression, "living in the world"? Is the Christian not to be as one living in the world? Clearly not. He is to live, in spirit, where Christ is. As to fact, he is obviously on this earth, moving up and down, and in and out, in the varied relations of life, and in the varied spheres of action in which the hand of God has set him. But his home is in heaven. His life is there. His object, his rest, his proper *all*, is in heaven. He does not belong to earth. His citizenship is in heaven; and in order to make this good in practice from day to day, there must be the denial of self, the mortification of our members.

All this comes vividly out in Col. iii. Indeed, it would be impossible to give a more striking exposition of the entire subject of "Gilgal" than that presented in the following lines: "If ye then be risen with Christ, seek those things which are above, where Christ sitteth on the right hand of God. Set your affections on things above, not on things on the earth. For ye have died, and your life is hid with Christ in God. When Christ our life shall appear, then shall ye also appear with Him in glory." And now comes the true spiritual import and application of "Gilgal" and its "sharp knives"— "Mortify, therefore, your members which are upon the earth."

May the Holy Spirit lead us into a deeper and fuller understanding of our place, portion and practice as Christians. Would to God that we better knew what it is to feed upon the old corn of the land, at the true spiritual Gilgal, that thus we might be better fitted for the conflict and service to which we are called!

THOUGHTS ON
THE CONFIRMATION VOWS

"All that the Lord hath spoken we will do." Such were the memorable words with which the people of Israel virtually abandoned the ground on which the blessed God had just been setting them, and on which, too, He had dealt with them in bringing them up out of the land of Egypt. "Ye have seen," said He, "what I did unto the Egyptians, and how I bare you on eagles' wings, and brought you unto Myself." All this was grace—pure, perfect, divine grace. He heard the groans and beheld the sorrows of the people amid the darkness and degradation of Egyptian bondage, and in His unmingled mercy He came down to deliver them. He sought not their aid, He looked not for aught from them. "His own arm brought salvation." He acted *for* them, *with* them, and *in* them; and that, too, in the solitariness and sovereignty of His own unfailing grace. He said to Moses at the opening of the book of Exodus, "*I am come down to deliver them.*" This was absolute and unqualified grace. There was no "if," no "but," no condition, no vow, no resolve. It was FREE GRACE, founded upon God's eternal counsels, and righteously displayed in immediate connection with "the blood of the Lamb." Hence, from first to last, the word to Israel was, "*stand still, and see the salvation of Jehovah.*" They were not called to "resolve," or to "vow," or to "do." God was acting for them—He was doing ALL: He placed Himself between them and every enemy, and every evil. He spread forth the shield of His salvation that they might hide themselves behind its impenetrable defences, and abide there in peace.

But, alas, Israel made a vow—a strange, a singular vow indeed. Not satisfied with God's doings, they would fain talk of their own. They would be doing, as if God's salvation were incomplete; and in lamentable ignorance of their own weakness and nothingness, they said, "All that the Lord hath spoken we will do." This was taking a bold stand, a high ground. For a poor worm to make such a vow proved how little grace was really understood, or nature's true condition apprehended.

However, Israel having undertaken to "*do,*" they were put to the test, and the most cursory view of Ex. xix. will be sufficient to show what a marked change took place the moment they had uttered the words "we will do." The Lord had just reminded them of how He "bare them on eagles' wings, and brought them unto Himself;" but now He says, "Set bounds unto the people round about, saying, Take heed to yourselves, that ye go not up into the mount, or touch the border of it: whosoever toucheth the mount shall be surely put to death." This was a very different aspect of things. And let my reader remember, it was the simple result of man's having said, "I will do." There is far more involved in those words than many might imagine. If we take our eyes off from God's actings, and fix them on our own, the consequences must be disastrous in the extreme. But we shall see this more fully ere we close this paper. Let us now inquire how the house of Israel fulfilled their singular vow. We shall see that it ended like human vows in every age.[8]

Did they do "*all*" that the Lord commanded? Did they "continue in all things which are written in the book of the law, to do them?" Alas, no. On the contrary, we find that ere the tables of testimony were given, they had broken the very first commandment in the Decalogue, by making a golden calf, and bowing down thereto. This was the earliest fruit of their broken vow; and then, onward they went, from stage to stage, dishonoring the name of the Lord—breaking His laws, despising His judgments, trampling under foot His sacred institutions. Then followed the stoning of His messengers whom, in patient grace and long-suffering, He sent unto them. Finally, when the only-begotten Son came forth from the bosom of the Father, they with wicked hearts rejected and with wicked hands crucified Him. Thus we pass from Sinai to Calvary: at the former we hear man undertaking to do all the Lord's commandments, and at the latter see him crucifying the Lord Himself. So much for man's vows, so much for man's "*I will do.*" The fragments of the tables of testimony scattered beneath the fiery mount told the first melancholy tale of the failure of man's audacious resolution: nor was there any real break in the narrative, which has its closing scene around the cross of Calvary. All was failure—gross, unmitigated failure. Thus it must ever be when man presumes to vow or resolve in the presence of God.

Now there is a very striking resemblance between Israel's vow at the foot of mount Sinai and the Confirmation Vow of the Establishment. We have rapidly glanced at the former; let us now refer to the latter.

In "the ministration of public baptism of infants," after various prayers and the reading of the Gospel, the minister addresses the godfathers and godmothers on this wise: "Dearly beloved, ye have brought this child here to be baptized; ye have prayed that our Lord Jesus Christ would vouchsafe to receive him, to release him of his sins, to sanctify him with the Holy Ghost, to give him the kingdom of heaven and everlasting life. Ye have heard also that our Lord Jesus Christ hath promised in His gospel to grant all these things that ye have prayed for: which promise He, for His part, will most surely keep and perform. Wherefore, after this promise made by Christ, this infant must also faithfully, for his part, promise by you that are his sureties (until he come of age to take it upon himself), that *he will renounce* the devil and all his works, and constantly believe God's holy word and *obediently keep His commandments.* I demand, therefore, Dost thou, in the name of this child, renounce the devil and all his works, the vain pomp and glory of the world, with all covetous desires of the same, and the carnal desires of the flesh, so that thou wilt not follow nor be led by them? *Answer.* I RENOUNCE THEM ALL." Again: "Wilt thou obediently keep God's holy will and commandments, and walk in the same all the days of thy life? *Answer.* I WILL

Both the above vows the children, when come to years of discretion, deliberately and solemnly take upon themselves, as may be seen by reference to "The Order of Confirmation." Thus we have, in the first place, people vowing and resolving, on behalf of unconscious infants, to "renounce the world, the flesh, and the devil," and to keep all God's commandments, all the days of their life; and, in the second place, we find those children, in due time, placing themselves under the weight of those awful vows; and all this, moreover, as a necessary condition to the fulfilment of Christ's promise. That is to say, if they allow aught of the world, the flesh or the devil to adhere to them; or if they fail in the faithful keeping of *all* God's commandments, then they cannot be saved, but must, so far as they are concerned, inevitably be condemned. In short, salvation is here made to depend on a covenant to which man makes himself a party. Christ is represented as willing to do His part, provided always that man accomplishes his; but not otherwise. In other words, there is an "*if*" in the matter, and, as a consequence, there never is, and never can be, the certainty of salvation; yea, there can only be the constant terror of eternal condemnation hanging over the soul; that is, if there is any thought about the matter at all.

If the heart is not perfectly assured of the fact that Christ has in very deed done all; that He has put away our sin; that He has forever canceled our debt; that He has settled, by His perfect sacrifice, every question that could possibly arise, whether it be the charges of conscience, the accusings of Satan, or the claims of divine justice; that He has not left a cloud on the prospect; that all is perfectly done—in a word, that we stand before God in the power of divine righteousness, and in the same favor with His own Son; if, I say, there be any doubt in the soul as to the eternal truth of all these things—then there cannot be settled peace. And that there is not this settled peace in the case of those who have taken on themselves the above tremendous vows is but too evident from the clouds and darkness which hang around their spirits as they tread the next stage of their ecclesiastical journey.

We could hardly expect that persons who boldly vow to renounce all evil, and perfectly to fulfil all good, could approach the Lord's table with any other acknowledgment than the following, namely: "The burden of our sins is intolerable." It would need an obtuse conscience to be able to shake off the conviction that those vows have been unfulfilled; and then, assuredly, the burden must be intolerable. If I have taken vows upon me, they will, without doubt, prove in the sequel to be dishonored vows; and thus the whole matter of my salvation comes to the ground, and I find myself, according to the terms of my own self-chosen covenant, righteously exposed to the curses of a broken law. I have undertaken to do everything; and yet I have in reality done nothing. Hence I am "cursed; for the word is, "Cursed is every one that continueth not in all things which are written in the book of the law, to do them."

Nor will it at all alter the matter to say that those extraordinary vows are entered into in dependence upon divine grace; for there cannot be such a thing as dependence upon *grace* when people are placing themselves directly under the *law*. No two things can be more opposite than law and grace. They are put in direct contrast in Paul's epistles to the Romans and Galatians. "Whosoever of you are justified by the law ([Greek: en nomô]),[9] ye are fallen from grace" (Gal. v. 4). Hence, to think of depending upon grace when putting myself under law is precisely the same as if I were to look to God for grace to enable me to subvert the entire gospel of His Son Jesus Christ. "As many as are of works of law ([Greek: ergôn nomou])[9] are under the curse." Could I depend upon God's grace to enable me to abide under the curse? The thought is preposterous in the extreme. And be it observed that the apostle, in the last-quoted passage, does not merely say, "As many as fail to keep the law are under the curse." This he distinctly teaches, no doubt; but the special point is, that as many as attempt to stand before God on the ground of "works of law," are of necessity under the curse, for the simplest of all reasons, that they are not able to satisfy His claims. In order for man to satisfy God's claims, he must be what in himself he cannot be; that is, without sin. The law demands, as its right, perfect obedience; and those who take upon them the Confirmation Vows promise perfect obedience. They promise to renounce all evil, and to fulfil all good, in the most absolute manner; and moreover, they make their salvation to depend upon their fulfilment of those vows; else why make them at all?

This, when looked at in the light of the apostolic teaching in Romans and Galatians, is the most complete denial of all the fundamental truths of the gospel. In the first place, it is a denial of man's total ruin, of his condition as one "dead in trespasses and sins," "alienated from the life of God," "without strength," "ungodly," "enmity against God." If I can undertake to renounce all evil, and to do all God's commandments, then, assuredly, I do not know myself to be a lost, ruined, helpless creature; and, as a consequence, I do not need a Saviour. If I can boldly undertake to "*renounce*" and to "*do*," to "keep" and to "walk," I am manifestly not lost, and hence I do not want salvation; I am not dead, and hence I do not want life; I am not "without strength," and hence I do not want the energy of that new, that divine life which is imparted by the Holy Ghost to all who, by His grace, believe in the Son of God. If I am capable of doing for myself, I do not want another, even the Lord Jesus Christ, to do all for me.

Again, as flowing out of what has already been stated, those vows do entirely set aside the essential glories, divine dignities and sacred virtues of the cross of Christ. If I can get a godfather and godmother to take vows on them on my behalf until I am capable of taking them on myself, then it is evident I cannot possibly know the deep blessedness of having all my vows, all my responsibilities and liabilities as a lost sinner, all my sins and shortcomings,—everything, in short,—fully and eternally answered in the Cross. If there is anything in my case which has not been perfectly settled in the Cross, then I must inevitably perish. I may make vows and resolutions, but they are as the morning cloud that passeth away. I may get a sponsor to renounce the devil on my behalf, and I may in due time talk of renouncing him for myself; but what if the devil all the while has fast hold of both my sponsor and myself? He will not renounce me, unless the chain by which he binds me has been snapped asunder by the Cross.

Again, I may get a sponsor to undertake to keep all God's commandments for me, and, in due time, I may undertake to keep them for myself; but what if neither my sponsor nor I really understand the true nature or spirituality, the majesty or stringency, of that law? Yea, more. What if both he and I are, by our very vows, made debtors to do the whole law, and thus shut up under its terrible curse? What then becomes of all our vows and resolutions? Is it not plain that I am throwing overboard the cross? Truly so. That cross must either be everything or nothing to me. If it is anything it must be everything; and if it is not everything it is nothing. Thus it stands, my beloved reader. The gospel of the grace of God sets forth Christ as the great Sponsor and Surety of His people. The Confirmation Service sets one sinner to stand sponsor for another, or for himself. The gospel sets forth One, who is possessed of "unsearchable riches," as the security for His people; the Confirmation Service sets one bankrupt to stand security for another or for himself. What avails such security? Who would accept of it? It is perfectly valueless to God and man. If I am a bankrupt, I cannot promise to pay anything, and if I could promise, no one would accept of it—yea, it would be justly regarded in the light of an empty formality. The promissory note of a bankrupt is little worth; and truly the vows and resolutions of a poor ruined sinner are not merely an empty formality, but a solemn mockery, in the presence of Almighty God. No one who knows himself would presume to vow, or resolve, to keep all God's commandments—such an one would have the full conviction that he could never do anything of the kind.

But, as a further reply to the statement that those Confirmation Vows are made in entire dependence upon the grace of God, I would observe that grace can only be known or trusted by those who are His. "They that know Thy name will put their trust in Thee," and none else. Now, the word of God connects eternal life with the knowledge of Him. "This is life eternal, that they might know Thee, the only true God, and Jesus Christ, whom Thou hast sent" (John xvii. 3). If, therefore, I have eternal life, I need not make vows to get it. If I am eternally saved, I need not make vows to get salvation. If my sins are all canceled by the precious blood of the Lamb, I need not make vows to get them canceled. Neither baptismal vows, confirmation vows, sacramental vows, nor any other vows are necessary for one who has found life, righteousness, wisdom, sanctification, redemption—yea, all things in Christ.

The comfort and peace of the feeblest believer are based upon the fact that Christ took all his vows, all his liabilities, all his sins, all his iniquities entirely upon Himself, and, by His death upon the cross, gloriously discharged them all. This sets him entirely free. Hence, it follows that if I am not a child of God, I cannot keep vows; and if I am, I need not make them. In either case, I deny man's fallen condition, and set aside the true glories of the Cross. It may be in ignorance—it may be with the most sincere intention—no doubt; but the most profound ignorance and the purest sincerity cannot alter the real principle which lies at the root of all manner of vows, promises, and resolutions. There is, beyond all question, involved therein a plain denial of the great foundation-truths of the Christian religion. A vow assumes the competency to fulfil. Well, then, if I vow to keep all God's commandments perfectly, all the days of my life, I am not lost or without strength. I must have strength, else I could not undertake such a ponderous responsibility.

And, my reader, remark further the strange anomaly involved in this system of vows; that while it denies my lost estate, it robs me of everything approaching to a certainty of ever being saved. If I resolve to keep God's commandments as a necessary condition of my salvation, I never can be sure of being saved until I have fulfilled the condition; but inasmuch as I never can fulfil it, I, therefore, never can be sure of my salvation; and thus I travel on, from stage to stage, from baptism to confirmation, from confirmation to communion, and from communion to the death-bed, in a state of miserable doubt and torturing uncertainty. This is not the gospel. It is "a different gospel which is not another." The immediate effect of the work of Christ, when laid hold of by faith, is to give settled peace to the conscience; the effect of the system of vows, is to keep the heart in constant doubt and heaviness. How many have approached the ordinance of confirmation with trembling hearts, at the thought of having to take upon their own shoulders the solemn vows which, from the period of their baptism, had rested on their godfathers and godmothers. How could it be otherwise with an honest mind? If I am really sincere, the thought of having to take on myself those solemn baptismal vows, must fill me with horror. Some, alas! go through these things with thoughtless hearts and frivolous minds; but it is evident the confirmation service was never framed for such. It was designed for thoughtful, serious, earnest spirits; and all such must, assuredly, retire from the ceremony, with troubled hearts and burdened consciences.

With what different feelings we gaze upon the cross of the Son of God! There, in good truth, Satan was renounced, and his works destroyed. There the law of God was magnified and made honorable, vindicated, and established. There the justice of God was fully answered. There Satan was vanquished; there conscience gets its full answer; there the cup of God's unmingled wrath against sin was drained to the dregs by His blessed Son. Where is the proof of all this? Not in the unaccomplished, dishonored vows of poor frail mortals; but in a risen, ascended, glorified Christ, seated at the right hand of the Majesty in the heavens.

Who that knows aught of the pure and most excellent grace of God, or that has tasted aught of the true blessedness of divinely-accomplished redemption, could tolerate such language as, "CHRIST FOR HIS PART" and "THIS INFANT FOR HIS PART?" Who that has listened, by faith, to those words, "It is finished," issuing, as they do, from amid the solemn scenes of Calvary, could endure a sinful mortal's "*I do*," or "*I will*?" What a total setting aside of grace! What a tarnishing of the brightness of God's salvation! What an insult to the righteousness of God, which is by faith, and without works! What a manifest return to a religion of ordinances and the poor works of man! Christ and an infant, or the infant's sureties, are placed on the same platform to work out salvation. Is it not so? If not, what mean the words, "Christ for His part, and this infant for his part?" Is it not plain that salvation is made to depend upon something or some one besides Christ? Unquestionably. The vows must be fulfilled, or there is no salvation! Miserable condition! Christ's accomplished work abandoned for a sinner's unaccomplishable vows and resolutions! Man's "I do" substituted for Christ's "I have finished!"

My reader, can you own such a fearful surrender of the truth of God? Are you content with such a sandy foundation? Whither, think you, will such a system lead you? To heaven, or to Rome? Which? Be honest. Take the New Testament, search it from cover to cover, and see if you can find such a thing as infants making vows by proxy, to renounce the world, the flesh, and the devil, and to keep all God's commandments, in order to salvation. There is not so much as a shadow of a foundation for such an idea. "By works of law shall no flesh living be justified." "But now the righteousness of God, without law, is manifested, being witnessed by the law and the prophets." "To him that worketh not, but believeth on Him that justified the ungodly, his faith is counted to him for righteousness." "For by grace are ye saved, through faith; and that not of yourselves it is the gift of God: not of works, lest any man should boast." "Not by works of righteousness which we have done, but according to His mercy He saved us." (See Rom. iii. 20-28; iv. 4, 5; Eph. ii. 8, 9; Titus iii. 5-7.)

These are but a very few of the numerous passages which might be adduced in proof of the fact that the Confirmation Vows are diametrically opposed to the truth of God—totally subversive of the grace of God. If my vows mean anything I must be miserable, because I am in imminent danger of being lost forever, inasmuch as I have *not* kept them, and never could keep them.

Oh! what sweet relief for the wearied heart and sin-burdened conscience in the atoning blood of Jesus! What full deliverance from my worthless and worse than worthless vows! *Christ has done all.* He has put away sin—made peace—brought in everlasting righteousness—brought life and immortality to light. In Him may you, my beloved reader, find abiding peace, unfading joy, and everlasting glory. To Him and His perfect work I now most affectionately commend you, body, soul, and spirit, fully assuring you my object in this paper is not to attack the prejudices, or wound the feelings of any, but simply to take occasion to show how the perfect work of the Lord Jesus Christ is thrown into full and blessed relief by being looked at in contrast with the "Confirmation Vows."

THOUGHTS

ON

THE LORD'S SUPPER

DESIGNED FOR THE HELP OF CHRISTIANS IN THIS
DAY OF DIFFICULTY.

NEW EDITION, REVISED.

PREFACE

The institution of the Lord's Supper must be regarded, by every spiritual mind, as a peculiarly touching proof of the Lord's gracious care and considerate love for His Church. From the time of its appointment until the present hour, it has been a steady, though silent, witness to a truth which the enemy, by every means in his power, has sought to corrupt and set aside, namely, that redemption is an accomplished fact to be enjoyed by the weakest believer in Jesus. Eighteen centuries have rolled away since the Lord Jesus appointed "the bread and the cup" in the Eucharist as the significant symbols of His broken body and His blood shed for us; and notwithstanding all the heresy, all the schism, all the controversy and strife, the war of principles and prejudices which the blotted page of ecclesiastical history records, this most expressive institution has been observed by the saints of God in every age. True, the enemy has succeeded, throughout a vast section of the professing Church, in wrapping it up in a shroud of dark superstition; in presenting it in such a way as actually to hide from the view of the communicant the grand and eternal reality of which it is the memorial; in displacing Christ and His accomplished sacrifice by a powerless ordinance—an ordinance, moreover, which by the very mode of its administration proves its utter worthlessness and opposition to the truth. (See note to page 29.) Yet, notwithstanding Rome's deadly error in reference to the ordinance of the Lord's Supper, it still speaks to every circumcised ear and every spiritual mind the same deep and precious truth—it "shows the Lord's death till He come." The body has been broken, the blood has been shed ONCE, no more to be repeated; and the breaking of bread is but the memorial of this emancipating truth.

With what profound interest and thankfulness, therefore, should the believer contemplate "the bread and the cup"! Without a word spoken, there is the setting forth of truths at once the most precious and glorious: grace reigning—redemption finished—sin put away—everlasting righteousness brought in—the sting of death gone—eternal glory secured—"grace and glory" revealed as the free gift of God and the Lamb—the unity of the "one body," as baptized by "one Spirit." What a feast! It carries the soul back, in the twinkling of an eye, over a lapse of eighteen hundred years, and shows us the Master Himself, "in the same night in which He was betrayed," sitting at the supper table, and there instituting a feast which, from that solemn moment, that memorable night, until the dawn of the morning, should lead every believing heart at once backward to the cross and forward to the glory.

This feast has ever since, by the very simplicity of its character, and yet the deep significance of its elements, rebuked the superstition that would deify and worship it, the profanity that would desecrate it, and the infidelity that would set it aside altogether: and furthermore, while it has rebuked all these, it has strengthened, comforted and refreshed the hearts of millions of God's beloved saints. It is sweet to think of this—sweet to bear in mind, as we assemble on the first day of the week round the supper of the Lord, that apostles, martyrs and saints have gathered round that feast, and found therein, according to their measure, refreshment and blessing. Schools of theology have arisen, flourished, and disappeared; doctors and fathers have accumulated ponderous tomes of divinity; deadly heresies have darkened the atmosphere, and rent the professing Church from one end to the other; superstition and fanaticism have put forth their baseless theories and extravagant notions; professing Christians have split into sects innumerable—all these things have taken place; but the Lord's Supper has continued, amid the darkness and confusion, to tell out its simple yet comprehensive tale. "As oft as ye eat this bread, and drink this cup, ye do show[10] the Lord's death till He come" (I Cor. xi. 26). Precious feast! Thank God for the great privilege of celebrating it! And yet is it but a sign, the elements of which must, in nature's view, be mean and contemptible. Bread broken, wine poured out—how simple! Faith alone can read, in the sign, the thing signified; and therefore it needs not the adventitious circumstances which false religion has introduced in order to add dignity, solemnity and awe to that which derives all its value, its power and its impressiveness from its being a memorial of an eternal fact which false religion denies.

May you and I, beloved reader, enter with more freshness and intelligence into the meaning of the Lord's Supper, and with deeper experience into the blessedness of breaking that bread which is "the communion of the body of Christ," and drinking of that cup which is "the communion of the blood of Christ."

In closing these few prefatory lines, I commend this treatise to the Lord's gracious care, praying Him to make it useful to the souls of His people.

C. H. M.

THOUGHTS ON
THE LORD'S SUPPER

"For I have received of the Lord that which also I delivered unto you, That the Lord Jesus, the same night in which He was betrayed, took bread: and when He had given thanks, He brake it, and said, Take, eat; this is My body, which is broken for you: this do in remembrance of Me. After the same manner also He took the cup, when He had supped, saying, This cup is the new testament in My blood: this do ye, as oft as ye drink it, in remembrance of Me. For as often as ye eat this bread, and drink this cup, ye do show the Lord's death till He come."—I Cor. xi. 23-26.

I desire to offer a few brief remarks on the subject of the Lord's Supper, for the purpose of stirring up the minds of all who love the name and institutions of Christ to a more fervent and affectionate interest in this most important and refreshing ordinance.

We should bless the Lord for His gracious consideration of our need in having established such a memorial of His dying love, and also in having spread a table at which *all* His members might present themselves without any other condition than the indispensable one of personal connection with and obedience to Him. The blessed Master knew well the tendency of our hearts to slip away from Him, and from each other, and to meet this tendency was *one*, at least, of His objects in the institution of the Supper. He would gather His people around His own blessed person; He would spread a table for them where, in view of His broken body and shed blood, they might remember Him, and the intensity of His love for them, and from whence, also, they might look forward into the future, and contemplate the glory of which the Cross is the everlasting foundation. There, if anywhere, they would learn to forget their differences, and to love one another; there they might see around them those whom THE LOVE OF GOD had invited to the feast, and whom THE BLOOD OF CHRIST had made fit to be there.

However, in order that I may the more easily and briefly convey to the mind of my reader what I have to say on this subject, I shall confine myself to the four following points, viz.:

1st. The nature of the ordinance of the Lord's Supper.

2d. The circumstances under which it was instituted.

3d. The persons for whom it was designed.

4th. The time and manner of its observance.

I. And first, as to the nature of the ordinance of the Lord's Supper. This is a cardinal point. If we understand not the nature of the ordinance, we shall be astray in all our thoughts about it. The Supper, then, is purely and distinctly a feast of thanksgiving—thanksgiving for grace already received.

The Lord Himself, at the institution of it, marks its character by giving thanks. "He took bread: ... when He had given thanks," etc. Praise, and not prayer, is the suited utterance of those who sit at the table of the Lord.

True, we have much to pray for, much to confess, much to mourn over; but the table is not the place for mourners: its language is, "Give strong drink unto him that is ready to perish, and wine unto those that be of heavy hearts. Let him drink and forget his poverty, and remember his misery no more." Ours is "a cup of blessing," a cup of thanksgiving, the divinely appointed symbol of that precious blood which has procured our ransom. "The bread which we break, is it not the communion of the body of Christ?" How, then, could we break it with sad hearts or sorrowful countenances? Could a family circle, after the toils of the day, sit down to supper with sighs and gloomy looks? Surely not. The supper was the great family meal, the only one that was sure to bring *all the family together*. Faces that might not have been seen during the day were sure to be seen at the supper table, and no doubt they would be happy there. Just so it should be at the Lord's Supper: the family should assemble there; and when assembled, they should be happy, unfeignedly happy, in the love that brings them together. True, each heart may have its own peculiar history—its secret sorrows, trials, failures, and temptations, unknown to all around; but these are not the objects to be contemplated at the supper: to bring them into view is to dishonor the Lord of the feast, and make the cup of blessing a cup of sorrow. The Lord has invited us to the feast, and commanded us, notwithstanding all our shortcomings, to place the fulness of His love and the cleansing efficacy of His blood between our souls and everything; and when the eye of faith is filled with Christ, there is no room for aught beside. If my sin be the object which fills my eye and engages my thoughts, of course I must be miserable, because I am looking right away from what God commands me to contemplate; I am remembering my misery and poverty, the very things which God commands me to forget. Hence the true character of the ordinance is lost, and, instead of being a feast of joy and gladness, it becomes a season of gloom and spiritual depression; and the preparation for it, and the thoughts which are entertained about it are more what might be expected in reference to mount Sinai than to a happy family feast.

If ever a feeling of sadness could have prevailed at the celebration of this ordinance, surely it would have been on the occasion of its first institution, when, as we shall see when we come to consider the second point in our subject, there was everything that could possibly produce deep sadness and desolation of spirit; yet the Lord Jesus could "give thanks;" the tide of joy that flowed through His soul was far too deep to be ruffled by surrounding circumstances; He had a joy even in the breaking and bruising of His body and in the pouring forth of His blood which lay far beyond the reach of human thought and feeling. And if He could rejoice in spirit, and give thanks in breaking that bread which was to be to all future generations of the faithful the memorial of His broken body, should not we rejoice therein, we who stand in the blessed results of all His toil and passion? Yes; it becomes us to rejoice.

But it may be asked, Is there no preparation necessary? are we to sit down at the table of the Lord with as much indifference as if we were sitting down to an ordinary supper table? Surely not—we need to be right in our souls, and the first step toward this is peace with God—that sweet assurance of our eternal salvation which most certainly is not the result of human sighs or penitential tears, but the simple result of the finished work of the Lamb of God, attested by the Spirit of God. Apprehending this by faith, we apprehend that which makes us perfectly fit for God. Many imagine that they are putting honor upon the Lord's table when they approach it with their souls bowed down into the very dust, under a sense of the intolerable burden of their sins. This thought can only flow from the legalism of the human heart, that ever-fruitful source of thoughts at once dishonoring to God, dishonoring to the Cross of Christ, grievous to the Holy Ghost, and completely subversive of our own peace. We may feel quite satisfied that the honor and purity of the Lord's table are more fully maintained when THE BLOOD OF CHRIST is made the only title than if human sorrow and human penitence were superadded.[11]

However, the question of preparedness will come more fully before us as we proceed with our subject; I shall therefore state another principle connected with the nature of the Lord's Supper, viz., that there is involved in it an intelligent recognition of the oneness of the body of Christ. "The bread which we break, is it not the communion of the body of Christ? For we, being many, are one bread, and one body; for we are all partakers of that one bread." Now there was sad failure and sad confusion in reference to this point at Corinth: indeed, the great principle of the Church's oneness would seem to have been totally lost sight of there. Hence the apostle observes that "when ye come together into one place, this is not to eat the Lord's Supper, for every one taketh before other *his own* supper" (I Cor. xi. 20, 21). Here, it was isolation, and not unity; an individual, and not a corporate question: "*his own supper*" is strikingly contrasted with "*the Lord's Supper.*" The *Lord's* Supper demands that the body be fully recognized: if the one body be not recognized, it is but sectarianism: the Lord Himself has lost His place. If the table be spread upon any narrower principle than that which would embrace the whole body of Christ, it is become a sectarian table, and has lost its claim upon the hearts of the faithful. On the contrary, where a table is spread upon this divine principle, which embraces *all* the members of the body *simply as such*, every one who refuses to present himself at it is chargeable with schism, and that, too, upon the plain principles of I Cor. xi. "There must," says the apostle, "be heresies among you, that they which are approved may be made manifest among you."

When the great Church principle is lost sight of by any portion of the body, there must be heresies, in order that the approved ones may be made manifest! and under such circumstances it becomes the business of each one to approve himself, and so to eat. The "approved" ones stand in contrast with the heretics, or those who were doing their own will.[12]

But it may be asked, Do not the numerous denominations at present existing in the professing Church altogether preclude the idea of ever being able to gather the whole body together? and, under such circumstances, is it not better for each denomination to have their own table? If there be any force in this question, it merely goes to prove that the people of God are no longer able to act upon God's principles, but that they are left to the miserable alternative of acting on human expediency. Thank God, such is not the case. The truth of the Lord endureth forever, and what the Holy Ghost teaches in I Cor. xi. is binding upon every member of the Church of God. There were divisions, and heresies, and unholiness, existing in the assembly at Corinth, just as there are divisions, and heresies, and unholiness, existing in the professing Church now; but the apostle did not tell them to set up separate tables on the one hand, nor yet to cease from breaking bread on the other. No; he presses upon them the principles and the holiness connected with "the Church of God," and tells those who could approve themselves accordingly to eat. The expression is, "*So let him eat.*" We are to eat, therefore: our care must be to eat "*so,*" as the Holy Ghost teaches us; and that is in the true recognition of the holiness and oneness of the Church of God.[13] When the Church is despised, the Spirit be grieved and dishonored, and the certain end will be spiritual barrenness and freezing formalism: and although men may substitute intellectual for spiritual power, and human talents and attainments for the gifts of the Holy Ghost, yet will the end be "like the heath in the desert." The true way to make progress in the divine life is to live for the Church, and not for ourselves. The man who lives for the Church is in full harmony with the mind of the Spirit, and must necessarily grow. On the contrary, the man who is living for himself, having his thoughts revolving round, and his energies concentrated upon, himself, must soon become cramped and formal, and, in all probability, openly worldly. Yes; he will become worldly, in some sense of that extensive term; for the world and the Church stand in direct opposition, the one to the other; nor is there any aspect of the world in which this opposition is more fully seen than in its religious aspect. What is commonly called the *religious world* will be found, when examined in the light of the presence of God, to be more thoroughly hostile to the true interests of the Church of God than almost anything.

But I must hasten on to other branches of our subject, only stating another simple principle connected with the Lord's Supper, to which I desire to call the special attention of the Christian reader; it is this: the celebration of the ordinance of the Lord's Supper should be the distinct expression of the unity of ALL believers, and not merely of the unity of a certain number gathered on certain principles, which distinguish them from others. If there be any term of communion proposed, save the all-important one of faith in the atonement of Christ, and a walk consistent with that faith, the table becomes the table of a sect, and possesses no claims upon the hearts of the faithful.

Furthermore, if by sitting at the table I must identify myself with any one thing, whether it be principle or practice, not enjoined in Scripture, as a term of communion, there also the table becomes the table of a sect. It is not a question of whether there may be Christians there or not; it would be hard indeed to find a table amongst the reformed communities of which some Christians are not partakers. The apostle did not say, "there must be heresies among you, that they which are *Christians* may be made manifest among you." No; but "that they which are *approved*." Nor did he say, "Let a man prove himself a Christian, and so let him eat." No; but "let a man approve himself," i. e., let him shew himself to be one of those who are not only upright in their consciences as to their individual act in the matter, but who are also confessing the oneness of the body of Christ. When men set up terms of communion of their own, there you find the principle of heresy; there, too, there must be schism. On the contrary, where a table is spread in such a manner and upon such principles as that a Christian, subject to God, can take his place at it, then it becomes schism not to be there; for, by being there, and by walking consistently with our position and profession there, we, so far as in us lies, confess the oneness of the Church of God—that grand object for which the Holy Ghost was sent from heaven to earth. The Lord Jesus, having been raised from the dead, and having taken His seat at the right hand of God, sent down the Holy Ghost to earth for the purpose of forming one body. Mark, to form *one body*—not many bodies. He has no sympathy with the many bodies, as such; though

He has blessed sympathy with many members in those bodies, because they, though being members of sects or schisms, are nevertheless, members of the one body; but He does not form the many bodies, but the one body, for "by one Spirit are we all baptized into one body, whether we be Jews or Gentiles, whether we be bond or free; and have all been made to drink into one Spirit" (I Cor. xii. 13).

I desire that there may be no misunderstanding on this point. I say the Holy Ghost cannot approve the schisms in the professing Church, for He Himself has said of such, "I praise you not." He is grieved by them—He would counteract them; He baptizes all believers into the unity of the one body, so that it cannot be thought, by any intelligent mind, that the Holy Ghost could sustain schisms, which are a grief and a dishonor to Him.

We must however, distinguish between the Spirit's dwelling in the Church, and His dwelling in individuals. He dwells in the body of Christ, which is the Church (see I Cor. iii. 17; Eph. ii. 22); He dwells also in the body of the believer, as we read, "your body is the temple of the Holy Ghost, which is in you, which ye have of God" (I Cor. vi. 19). The only body or community, therefore, in which the Spirit can dwell, is *the whole Church of God*; and the only person in which He can dwell is the believer. But, as has already been observed, the table of the Lord, in any given locality, should be the exhibition of the unity of the whole Church. This leads us to another principle connected with the nature of the Lord's Supper, viz., this, It is an act whereby we not only shew the death of the Lord until He come, but whereby we also give expression to a fundamental truth, which cannot be too strongly or too frequently pressed upon the minds of Christians, at the present day, viz., that *all believers are "one loaf—one body."* It is a very common error to view this ordinance merely as a channel through which grace flows to the soul of the individual, and not as an act bearing upon the whole body, and bearing also upon the glory of the Head of the Church. That it is a channel through which grace flows to the soul of the individual communicant there can be no doubt, for there is blessing in every act of obedience. But that individual blessing is but a very small part of it, can be seen by the attentive reader of I Cor. xi. It is the Lord's death and the Lord's coming, that are brought prominently before our souls in the Lord's Supper; and where any one of these elements is excluded there must be something wrong. If there be anything to hinder the complete showing forth of the Lord's death, or the exhibition of the unity of the body, or the clear perception of the Lord's coming, then there must be something radically wrong in the principle on which the table is spread, and we only need a single eye, and a mind entirely subject to the Word and Spirit of Christ, in order to detect the wrong.

Let the Christian reader, now, prayerfully examine the table at which he periodically takes his place and see if it will bear the threefold test of I Cor. xi., and if not, let him, in the name of the Lord, and for the sake of the Church, abandon it. There are heresies, and schisms flowing from heresies, in the professing Church, but "let a man approve himself, and so let him eat" the Lord's Supper; and if, once for all, it be asked, What means the term "approved?" it may be answered, It is in the first place, to be personally true to the Lord in the act of breaking bread; and in the next place, to shake off all schism, and take our stand, firmly and decidedly, upon the broad principle which will embrace all the members of the flock of Christ. We are not only to be careful that we ourselves are walking in purity of heart and life before the Lord; but also, that the table of which we partake has nothing connected with it that could at all act as a barrier to the unity of the Church. It is not merely a personal question. Nothing more fully proves the low ebb of Christianity at the present day, or the fearful extent to which the Holy Ghost is grieved, than the miserable selfishness which tinges, yea, pollutes, the thoughts of professing Christians. Everything is made to hinge upon the mere question of self. It is *my* forgiveness—*my* safety—*my* peace—*my* happy frames and feelings, and not the glory of Christ, or the welfare of His beloved Church. Well, therefore, may the words of the prophet be applied to us, "Thus saith the Lord, Consider your ways. Go up to the mountain and bring wood, and BUILD THE23" HOUSE; and I will take pleasure in *it* and I WILL BE GLORIFIED. Ye looked for much, and lo, it came to little; and when ye brought it home, I did blow upon it. Why? saith the Lord of hosts. Because of *My house* that is waste, and ye run every man to *his own* house" (Hag. i. 7-9). Here is the root of the matter. Self stands in contrast with the house of God; and, if self be made the object, no marvel that there should be a sad lack of spiritual joy, energy, and power. To have these, we must be in fellowship with the Spirit's thoughts. He thinks of the body of Christ; and, if we are thinking of self, we must be at issue with Him; and the consequences are but too apparent.

II. Having now treated of what I conceive to be by far the most important point in our subject, I shall proceed to consider, in the second place, the circumstances under which the Lord's Supper was instituted. These were particularly solemn and touching. The Lord was about to enter into dreadful conflict with all the powers of darkness—to meet all the deadly enmity of man; and to drain to the dregs the cup of Jehovah's righteous wrath against sin. He had a terrible morrow before Him—the most terrible that had ever been encountered by man or angel; yet, notwithstanding all this, we read that "on *the same night* in which He was betrayed, He took bread." What unselfish love is here! "The same night"— the night of profound sorrow—the night of His agony and bloody sweat

—the night of His betrayal by one, and His denial by another, and His desertion by all of His disciples—on that very night, the loving heart of Jesus was full of thoughts about His Church—on that very night He instituted the ordinance of the Lord's Supper. He appointed the bread to be the emblem of His body broken, and the wine to be the emblem of His blood shed; and such they are to us now, as often as we partake of them, for the Word assures us that "as often as ye eat *this bread* and drink *this cup*, ye do show *the Lord's death*, till He come."

Now, all this, we may say, attaches peculiar importance and sacred solemnity to the Supper of the Lord; and, moreover, gives us some idea of the consequences of eating and drinking unworthily.[14]

The voice which the ordinance utters in the circumcised ear is ever the same. The bread and the wine are deeply significant symbols; the bruised corn and the pressed grape being both combined to minister strength and gladness to the heart: and not only are they significant in themselves, but they are also to be used in the Lord's Supper, as being the very emblems which the blessed Master Himself ordained on the night previous to His crucifixion; so that faith can behold the Lord Jesus presiding at *His own table*—can see Him take the bread and the wine, and hear Him say, "Take, eat; this is My body;" and again, of the cup, "Drink ye *all* of it. For this is My blood of the New Testament which is shed for many for the remission of sins." In a word, the ordinance leads the soul back to the eventful night already referred to—brings before us all the reality of the cross and passion of the Lamb of God, in which our whole souls can rest and rejoice; it reminds us, in the most impressive manner, of the unselfish love and pure devotedness of Him, who, when Calvary was casting its dark shadow across His path, and the cup of Jehovah's righteous wrath against sin, of which He was about to be the bearer, was being filled for Him, could, nevertheless, busy Himself about us, and institute a feast which was to be both the expression of our connection with Him, and with all the members of His body.

And may we not infer, that the Holy Ghost made use of the expression "*the same night*," for the purpose of remedying the disorders that had arisen in the church at Corinth? Was there not a severe rebuke administered to the selfishness of those who were taking "*their own supper*," in the Spirit's reference to the same night in which the Lord of the feast was betrayed? Doubtless there was. Can selfishness live in the view of the cross? Can thoughts about our own interests, or our own gratification, be indulged in the presence of Him who sacrificed Himself for us? Surely not. Could we heartlessly and wilfully despise the Church of God—could we offend or exclude beloved members of the flock of Christ, while gazing on that cross on which the Shepherd of the flock, and the Head of the body, was crucified?[15] Ah, no; let believers only keep near the cross—let them remember "the same night"—let them keep in mind the broken body and shed blood of the Lord Jesus Christ, and there will soon be an end to heresy, schism, and selfishness. If we could only bear in mind that the Lord Himself presides at the table, to dispense the bread and wine; if we could hear Him say, "Take this, and divide it among yourselves," we should be better able to meet *all* our brethren on the *only* Christian ground of fellowship which God can own. In a word, the person of Christ is God's centre of union. "I," said Christ, "if I be lifted up from the earth, will draw all men unto *Me*." Each believer can hear his blessed Master speaking from the cross, and saying of his fellow believers, "*Behold thy brethren;*" and, truly, if we could distinctly hear this, we should act, in a measure, as the beloved disciple acted towards the mother of Jesus; our hearts and our homes would be open to all who have been thus commended to our care. The word is, "*Receive ye one another, as Christ also received us to the glory of God.*"

There is another point worthy of notice, in connection with the circumstances under which the Lord's Supper was instituted, namely, its connection with the Jewish Passover. "Then came the day of unleavened bread, when the Passover must be killed. And He sent Peter and John, saying, Go and prepare us the Passover, that we may eat.... And *when the hour was come*, He sat down, and the twelve apostles with Him. And He said unto them, With desire I have desired to eat this Passover with you before I suffer; for I say unto you, I will not any more eat thereof, until it be fulfilled in the Kingdom of God. And He took the cup [i. e., the cup of the Passover], and gave thanks, and said, Take this and divide it among yourselves; for I say unto you, I will not drink of the fruit of the vine until the Kingdom of God shall come" (Luke xxii. 7-18). The Passover was, as we know, the great feast of Israel, first observed on the memorable night of their happy deliverance from the thralldom of Egypt. As to its connection with the Lord's Supper, it consists in its being the marked *type* of that of which the Supper is the *memorial*. The Passover pointed *forward* to the cross; the Supper points *back* to it. But Israel was no longer in a fit moral condition to keep the Passover, according to the divine thoughts about it; and the Lord Jesus, on the occasion above referred to, was leading His apostles away altogether from the Jewish element to a new order of things. It was no longer to be a lamb sacrificed, but bread broken and wine drunk in commemoration of a sacrifice ONCE offered, the efficacy of which was to be eternal. Those whose minds are bowed down to Jewish ordinances, may still look, in some way or another, for the periodical repetition, either of a sacrifice, or of something which is to bring them into a place of greater nearness to God.[16]

Some there are who think that in the Lord's Supper the soul makes, or renews, a covenant with God, not knowing that if we were to enter into covenant with God, we should inevitably be ruined; as the only possible issue of a covenant between God and man is the failure of one of the parties (i. e., man), and consequent judgment. Thank God, there is no such thing as a covenant with us. The bread and wine, in the Supper, speak a deep and wondrous truth; they tell of the broken body and shed blood of the Lamb of God—the Lamb of God's own providing. Here the soul can rest with perfect complacency; it is THE NEW TESTAMENT IN THE BLOOD OF CHRIST, and not a covenant between God and man. Man's covenant had signally failed, and the Lord Jesus had to allow the cup of the fruit of the vine (the emblem of joy in the earth) to pass Him by. Earth had no joy for Him—Israel had become "the degenerate plant of a strange vine;" wherefore, He had only to say, "I will not drink of the fruit of the vine, until the Kingdom of God shall come." A long and dreary season was to pass over Israel, ere her King could take any joy in her moral condition: but, during that time, "the Church of God" was to "keep the feast" of unleavened bread, in all its moral power and significance, by putting away the "old leaven of malice and wickedness," as the fruit of fellowship with Him whose blood cleanseth from all sin.

However, the fact of the Lord's Supper having been instituted immediately after the Passover, teaches us a very valuable principle of truth, viz., this: the destinies of the Church and of Israel are inseparably linked with the cross of the Lord Jesus Christ. True, the Church has a higher place, even identification with her risen and glorified Head; yet all rests upon the Cross. Yes; it was on the cross that the pure sheaf of corn was bruised and the juices of the living vine pressed forth by the hand of Jehovah Himself, to yield strength and gladness to the hearts of His heavenly and earthly people forever. The Prince of Life took from Jehovah's righteous hand the cup of wrath, the cup of trembling, and drained it to the dregs in order that He might put into the hands of His people the cup of salvation, the cup of God's ineffable love, that they might drink and forget their poverty, and remember their misery no more. The Lord's Supper expresses all this. There the Lord presides; there the redeemed should meet in holy fellowship and brotherly love, to eat and drink before the Lord; and while they do so, they can look back at their Master's *night* of deep sorrow, and forward to His day of glory—that "morning without clouds," when "He shall come to be glorified in His saints, and to be admired in all them that believe."

III. We shall now consider, in the third place, the persons for whom, and for whom *alone*, the Lord's Supper was instituted.

The Lord's Supper, then, was instituted for the Church of God—the family of the redeemed. All the members of that family should be there; for none can be absent without incurring the guilt of disobedience to the plain command of Christ and His inspired apostle; and the consequence of this disobedience will be positive spiritual decline and a complete failure in testimony for Christ. Such consequences, however, are the result only of wilful absence from the Lord's table. There are circumstances which, in certain cases, may present an insurmountable barrier, though there might be the most earnest desire to be present at the celebration of the ordinance, as there ever will be where the mind is spiritual; but we may lay it down as a fixed principle of truth that no one can make progress in the divine life who wilfully absents himself from the Lord's table. "ALL the congregation of Israel" were commanded to keep the passover (Ex. xii.).

No member of the congregation could with impunity be absent. "The man that is clean, and is not in a journey, and forbeareth to keep the passover, even the same soul shall be cut off from among his people: because he brought not the offering of the Lord in his appointed season, that man shall bear his sin" (Num. ix. 13).

I feel that it would be rendering really valuable service to the cause of truth, and a furtherance of the interests of the Church of God, if an interest could be awakened on this important subject. There is too much lightness and indifference in the minds of Christians as to the matter of their attendance at the table of the Lord; and where there is not this indifference, there is an unwillingness arising from imperfect views of justification. Now both these hindrances, though so different in their character, spring from one and the same source, viz., selfishness. He who is indifferent about the matter will selfishly allow trifling circumstances to interfere with his attendance: he will be hindered by family arrangements, love of personal ease, unfavorable weather, trifling or, as it frequently happens, imaginary bodily ailments—things which are lost sight of or counted as nothing when some worldly object is to be gained. How often does it happen that men who have not spiritual energy to leave their houses on the Lord's day have abundant natural energy to carry them some miles to gain some worldly object on Monday. Alas that it should be so! How sad to think that worldly gain could exert a more powerful influence on the heart of the Christian than the glory of Christ and the furtherance of the Church's benefit! for this is the way in which we must view the question of the Lord's Supper. What would be our feelings, amid the glory of the coming kingdom, if we could remember that, while on earth, a fair or a market, or some such worldly object, had commanded our time and energies, while the assembly of the Lord's people around His table was neglected?

Beloved Christian reader, if you are in the habit of absenting yourself from the assembly of Christians, I pray you to ponder the matter before the Lord ere you absent yourself again. Reflect upon the pernicious effect of your absence in every way. You are failing in your testimony for Christ; you are injuring the souls of your brethren, and you are hindering the progress of your own soul in grace and knowledge. Do not suppose that your actings are without their influence on the whole Church of God: you are at this moment either helping or hindering every member of that body on earth. "If *one* member suffer, all the members suffer with it." This principle has not ceased to be true, though professing Christians have split into so many different divisions. Nay, it is so divinely true, that there is not a single believer on earth who is not acting either as a helper to, or a drain upon, the whole body of Christ; and if there be any truth in the principle already laid down (viz., that the assembly of Christians and the breaking of bread in any given locality is, or ought to be, the expression of the unity of the whole body), you cannot fail to see that if you absent yourself from that assembly, or refuse to join in giving expression to that unity, you are doing serious damage to all your brethren as well as to your own soul. I would lay these considerations on your heart and conscience, in the name of the Lord, looking to Him to make them influential.[17]

But not only does this culpable and pernicious indifference of spirit act as a hindrance to many, in presenting themselves at the Lord's table; imperfect views of justification produce the same unhappy result. If the conscience be not perfectly purged, if there be not perfect rest in God's testimony about the finished work of Christ, there will either be a shrinking from the Supper of the Lord, or an unintelligent celebration of it. Those only can show the Lord's death who know, through the teaching of the Holy Spirit, the value of the Lord's death. If I regard the ordinance as a means whereby I am to be brought into a place of greater nearness to God, or whereby I am to obtain a clearer sense of my acceptance, it is impossible that I can rightly observe it. I must believe, as the gospel commands me to believe, that ALL my sins are FOREVER put away ere I can take my place with any measure of spiritual intelligence at the Lord's table. If the matter be not viewed in this light, the Lord's Supper can only be regarded as a kind of step to the altar of God, and we are told in the law that we are not to go up by steps to God's altar, lest our nakedness be discovered (Ex. xx. 26). The meaning of which is, that all human efforts to approach God must issue in the discovery of human nakedness.

Thus we see that if it be indifference that prevents the Christian from being at the breaking of bread, it is most culpable in the sight of God, and most injurious to his brethren and himself; and if it be an imperfect sense of justification that prevents, it is not only unwarrantable, but most dishonoring to the love of the Father, the work of the Son, and the clear and unequivocal testimony of the Holy Ghost.

But it is not unfrequently said, and that, too, by those who profess spirituality and intelligence, "I derive no spiritual benefit by going to the assembly: I am as happy in my own room, reading my Bible." I would affectionately ask such, Are we to have no higher object before us in our actings than our own happiness? Is not obedience to the command of our blessed Master—a command delivered on "the same night in which He was betrayed"—a far higher and nobler object to set before us than anything connected with self? If He desires that His people should assemble in His name, for the express object of showing forth His death till He come, shall we refuse because we feel happier in our own rooms? He tells us to be there: we reply, "We feel happier at home." Our happiness, therefore, must be based on disobedience; and, as such, it is an unholy happiness. It is much better, if it should be so, to be unhappy in the path of obedience than happy in the path of disobedience. But I verily believe, the thought of being happier at home is a mere delusion, and the end of those deluded by it will prove it such. Thomas might have deemed it indifferent whether he was present with the other disciples, but he had to do without the Lord's presence, and to wait for eight days, until the disciples came together on the first day of the week; for there and then the Lord was pleased to reveal Himself to his soul. And just so will it be with those who say, "We feel happier at home than in the assembly of believers." They will surely be behindhand in knowledge and experience; yea, it will be well if they come not under the terrible woe denounced by the prophet: "Woe to the idol shepherd that *leaveth the flock*! the sword shall be upon his arm, and upon his right eye; his arm shall be clean dried up, and his right eye shall be utterly darkened" (Zech. xi. 17). And again, "Not forsaking the assembling of ourselves together, *as the manner of some is*; but exhorting one another, and so much the more as ye see the day approaching. For if we sin wilfully, after that we have received the knowledge of the truth, there remaineth no more sacrifice for sins, but a certain fearful looking for of judgment and fiery indignation, which shall devour the adversaries" (Heb. x. 25-27).

As to the objection upon the grounds of the barrenness and unprofitableness of Christian assemblies, it will generally be remarked that the greatest spiritual barrenness will always be found in connection with a captious and complaining spirit; and I doubt not that if those who complain of the unprofitableness of meetings, and draw from thence an argument in favor of their remaining at home, were to spend more time in secret waiting on the Lord for His blessing on the meetings, they would have a very different experience.

And now, having shown from Scripture who ought to be at the breaking of bread, we shall proceed to consider who ought *not*. On this point Scripture is equally explicit: in a word, then, none should be there who are not members of the true Church of God. The same law which commanded *all* the congregation of Israel to eat the passover, commanded all uncircumcised strangers *not* to eat; and now that Christ our Passover has been sacrificed for us, none can keep the feast, (which is to extend throughout this entire dispensation,) nor break the bread nor drink the wine in true remembrance of Him, save those who know the cleansing and healing virtues of His precious blood. To eat and drink without this knowledge, is to eat and drink unworthily—to eat and drink judgment; like the woman in Num. v. who drank the water of jealousy, to make the condemnation more manifest and awfully solemn.

Now it is in this that Christendom's guilt is specially manifest. In taking the Lord's Supper, the professing Church has, like Judas, put her hand on the table with Christ and betrayed Him; she has eaten with Him, and at the same time lifted up her heel against Him. What will be her end? Just like the end of Judas. "He, then, having received the sop, *went immediately out*: and"—the Holy Ghost adds, in awful solemnity—"IT WAS NIGHT." Terrible night! The strongest expression of divine love only elicited the strongest expression of human hatred. So will it be with the false professing Church collectively, and each false professor individually; and all those who, though baptized in the name of Christ, and sitting down at the table of Christ, have nevertheless been His betrayers, will find themselves at last thrust out into outer darkness—involved in a night which shall never see the beams of the morning—plunged in a gulf of endless and ineffable woe; and though they may be able to say to the Lord, "We have eaten and drunk in Thy presence, and Thou hast taught in our streets," yet His solemn, heartrending reply will be, while He shuts the door against them, "Depart from Me! I never knew you." O reader, think of this, I pray you; and if you be yet in your sins, defile not the Lord's table by your presence; but instead of going thither as a hypocrite, repair to Calvary as a poor ruined and guilty sinner, and there receive pardon and cleansing from Him who died to save just such as you are.

IV. Having now considered, through the Lord's mercy, the nature of the Lord's Supper; the circumstances under which it was instituted; and the persons for whom it was designed; I would only add a word as to what Scripture teaches us about the time and manner of its celebration.

Although the Lord's Supper was not *first* instituted on the first day of the week, yet the twenty-fourth of Luke and the twentieth of Acts are quite sufficient to prove, to a mind subject to the Word, that that is the day on which the ordinance should specially be observed. The Lord broke bread with His disciples on "the first day of the week" (Luke xxiv. 30); and "on the first day of the week the disciples came together to break bread" (Acts xx. 7). These scriptures are quite sufficient to prove that it is not once a month, nor once in three months, nor once in six months, that disciples should come together to break bread, but once a week at least, and that upon the first day of the week. Nor can we have any difficulty in seeing that there is a moral fitness in the first day of the week for the celebration of the Lord's Supper: it is the resurrection day—the Church's day, in contrast with the seventh, which was Israel's day; and as, in the institution of the ordinance, the Lord led His disciples away from Jewish things altogether, (by refusing to drink of the fruit of the vine—the passover cup,—and then instituting another ordinance) so, in the day on which that ordinance was to be celebrated, we observe the same contrast between heavenly and earthly things. It is in the power of resurrection that we can rightly show the Lord's death. When the conflict was over, Melchizedek brought forth bread and wine, and blessed Abram, in the name of the Lord. Thus, too, our Melchizedek, when all the conflict was over and the victory gained, came forth in resurrection with bread and wine, to strengthen and cheer the hearts of His people, and to breathe upon them that peace which He had so dearly purchased.

If, then, the first day of the week be the day on which Scripture teaches the disciples to break bread, it is clear that man has no authority to alter the period to once a month, or once in six months. And I doubt not, when the affections are lively and fervent toward the person of the Lord Himself, the Christian will desire to show the Lord's death as frequently as possible: indeed, it would seem, from the opening of Acts, that the disciples broke bread daily. This we may infer from the expression "breaking bread from house to house" (or "at home"). However, we are not left to depend upon mere inference as to the question of the first day of the week being the day on which the disciples came together to break bread: we are distinctly taught this, and we see its moral fitness and beauty.

Thus much as to the *time*. And now one word about the *manner*. It should be the special aim of Christians to show that the breaking of bread is their grand and primary object in coming together on the first day of the week. They should show that it is not for preaching or teaching that they assemble, though teaching may be a happy adjunct, but that the breaking of bread is the leading object before their minds. It is the work of Christ which we show forth in the Supper, wherefore it should have the first place; and when it has been duly set forth, there should be a full and unqualified opening left for the work of the Holy Ghost in ministry. The office of the Spirit is to set forth and exalt the name, the person and the work of Christ; and if He be allowed to order and govern the assembly of

Christians, as He undoubtedly should, He will ever give the work of Christ the primary place.

I cannot close this paper without expressing my deep sense of the feebleness and shallowness of all that I have advanced, on a subject of really commanding interest. I do feel before the Lord, in whose presence I desire to write and speak, that I have so failed to bring out the full truth about this matter, that I almost shrink from letting these pages see the light. It is not that I have a shadow of doubt as to the truth of what I have endeavored to state; no: but I feel that, in writing upon such a subject as the breaking of bread, at the time when there is such sad confusion among professing Christians, there is a demand for pointed, clear, and lucid statements, to which I am little able to respond.

We have but little conception of how entirely the question of the breaking of bread is connected with the Church's position and testimony on earth; and we have as little conception of how thoroughly the question has been misunderstood by the professing Church. The breaking of bread ought to be the distinct enunciation of the fact that all believers are *one body*; but the professing Church, by splitting into sects, and by setting up a table for each sect, has practically denied that fact.

In truth, the breaking of bread has been cast into the background. The table, at which the Lord should preside, is almost lost sight of, by being placed in the shade of the pulpit, in which man presides: the pulpit, which, alas! is too often the instrument of creating and perpetuating disunion, is, to many minds, the commanding object; while the table, which if properly understood would perpetuate love and unity, is made quite a secondary thing. And even in the most laudable effort to recover from such a lamentable condition of things, what complete failure have we seen. What has the Evangelical Alliance effected? It has effected this, at least, it has developed a need existing among professing Christians, which they are confessedly unable to meet. They want union, and are unable to attain it. Why? Because they will not give up everything which has been *added* to the truth to meet together according to the truth, to break bread as disciples. I say, *as disciples*, and not as Church-men, Independents, Baptists, etc. It is not that all such may not have much valuable truth, I mean those of them who love our Lord Jesus Christ: they certainly may; but they have no *truth* that should prevent them from meeting *together* to break bread. How could truth ever hinder Christians from giving expression to the unity of the Church? Impossible! A sectarian spirit in those who hold truth may do this, but truth never can. But how is it now in the professing Church? Christians, of various communities, can meet for the purpose of reading, praying, and singing together during the week, but when the first day of the week arrives, they have not the least idea of giving the only real and effectual expression of their unity, which the Holy Ghost can recognize, which is the breaking of bread. "We being many are one bread and one body; for we are *all* partakers of that *one* bread."

The sin at Corinth was their not tarrying one for another. This appears from the exhortation with which the apostle sums up the whole question (I Cor. xi.), "Wherefore, my brethren, when ye come together to eat, tarry one for another." Why were they to tarry one for another? Surely, in order that they might the more clearly express their unity. But what would the apostle have said, if, instead of coming together, into one place, they had gone to different places, according to their different views of truth? He might then say with, if possible, greater force, "Ye cannot eat the Lord's Supper." (See *margin.*)

It may, however, be asked, "How could all the believers in London meet in one place?" I reply, if they could not meet in one place, they could, at least, meet on one principle. But how did the believers at Jerusalem meet together? The answer is, they were "*of one accord.*" This being so, they had little difficulty about the question of a meeting-room. "Solomon's porch," or anywhere else, would suit their purpose. They gave expression to their unity, and that, too, in a way not to be mistaken. Neither various localities, nor various measures of knowledge and attainment, could, in the least, interfere with their unity. There was "one body and one Spirit."

Finally, I would say, the Lord will assuredly honor those who have faith to believe and confess the unity of the Church on earth; and the greater the difficulty in the way of doing so, the greater will be the honor. The Lord grant to all His people a single eye, and a humble and honest spirit.

Thy broken body, gracious Lord,Is shadowed by this broken bread;The wine which in this cup is pouredPoints to the blood which Thou hast shed.

And while we meet together thus,We show that we are one in Thee;Thy precious blood was shed for us--Thy death, O Lord, has set us free.

Brethren in Thee, in union sweet--Forever be Thy grace adored--'Tis in Thy name, that now we meet,And know Thou'rt with us, gracious Lord.

We have one hope--that Thou wilt come;Thee in the air we wait to see,When Thou wilt take Thy people home,And we shall ever reign with Thee.

THE ASSEMBLY OF GOD OR, THE ALL-SUFFICIENCY OF THE NAME OF JESUS

In a day like the present, when almost every new idea becomes the centre or gathering-point of some new association, we cannot but feel the value of having divinely formed convictions as to what the assembly of God really is. We live in a time of unusual mental activity, and hence there is the more urgent need of calm and prayerful study of the word of God. That Word, blessed be its Author, is like a rock amid the ocean of human thought. There it stands unmoved, notwithstanding the raging of the storm and the ceaseless lashing of the waves. And not only does it thus stand unmoved itself, but it imparts its own stability to all who simply take their stand upon it. What a mercy to make one's escape from the heavings and tossings of the stormy ocean, and find a calm resting place on that everlasting Rock.

This, truly, is a mercy. Were it not that we have "the law and the testimony," where should we be? Whither should we go? What should we do? What darkness! What confusion! What perplexity!

A thousand jarring voices fall, at times, upon the ear, and each voice seems to speak with such authority, that if one is not well taught and grounded in the Word, there is great danger of being drawn away, or, at least, sadly unhinged. One man will tell you that *this* is right; another will tell you *that* is right; a third will tell you that *everything* is right; and a fourth will tell you that *nothing* is right. With reference to the question of church position, you will meet with some who go *here*; some who go *there*; some who go *everywhere*; and some who go *nowhere*.

Now, under such circumstances, what is one to do? All cannot possibly be right. And yet, surely, there is something right. It cannot be that we are *compelled* to live in error, in darkness, or uncertainty. "*There is a path*," blessed be God, though "no fowl knoweth it, and the vulture's eye hath not seen it. The lion's whelps have not trodden it, nor the fierce lion passed by it." Where is this safe and blessed path? Hear the divine reply: "Behold, *the fear of the Lord*, that is wisdom: and *to depart from evil* is understanding" (Job xxviii.).

Let us, therefore, in the fear of the Lord, in the light of His infallible truth, and in humble dependence upon the teaching of the Holy Spirit, proceed to the examination of the subject which stands at the head of this paper; and may we have grace to abandon all confidence in our own thoughts, and the thoughts of others, so that we may heartily and honestly yield ourselves up to be taught only of God.

Now, in order to get fairly into the grand and all-important subject of the assembly of God, we have first to state *a fact*; and, secondly, to ask *a question*. The fact is this, *There is an assembly of God on the earth.* The question is, *What is that assembly?*

I. And, first then, as to our *fact*. There is such a thing as the assembly of God on the earth. This is a most important fact, surely. God has an assembly on the earth. I do not refer to any merely human organization, such as the Greek Church; the Church of Rome; the Church of England; the Church of Scotland; or to any of the various systems which have sprung from these, framed and fashioned by man's hand, and carried on by man's resources. I refer simply to that assembly which is gathered by God the Holy Ghost, round the person of God the Son, to worship and hold fellowship with God the Father.

If we set forth upon our search for the assembly of God, or for any expression thereof, with our minds full of prejudice, preconceived thoughts, and personal predilections; or if, in our searchings, we seek the aid of the flickering light of the dogmas, opinions, and traditions of men, nothing is more certain than that we shall fail to reach the truth. To recognize God's assembly, we must be exclusively taught by God's Word, and led by God's Spirit; for, of God's assembly, as well as of the sons of God, it may be said, "the world knoweth it not."

Hence, then, if we are, in any wise, governed by the spirit of the world; if we desire to exalt man; if we seek to commend ourselves to the thoughts of men; if our object be to gain the attractive ends of a plausible and soul-ensnaring expediency, we may as well, forthwith, abandon our search for any true expression of the assembly of God, and take refuge in that form of human organization which most fully commends itself to our thinkings or our conscientious convictions.

Further, if our object be to find a religious community in which the word of God is read, or in which the people of God are found, we may speedily satisfy ourselves, for it would be hard indeed to find a section of the professing Christian body in which one or both of these objects might not be realized.

Finally, if we merely aim at doing all the good we can, without any question as to how we do it; if *Per fas aut nefas*, "right or wrong," be our motto in whatever we undertake; if we are prepared to reverse those weighty words of Samuel, and say that, "To sacrifice is better than to obey, and the fat of rams better than to harken," then is it worse than vain for us to pursue our search for the assembly of God, inasmuch as that assembly can only be discovered and approved by one who has been taught to flee from the thousand flowery pathways of human expediency, and to submit his conscience, his heart, his understanding, his whole moral being to the supreme authority of "Thus saith the Lord."

In one word, then, the obedient disciple knows that there is such a thing as God's assembly: and he it is, too, that will be enabled, through grace, to understand what is a true expression of it. The sincere student of Scripture knows, full well, the difference between that which is founded, formed, and governed by the wisdom and the will of man, and that which is gathered round, and governed by Christ the Lord. How vast is the difference! It is just the difference between God and man.

But we may here be asked for the Scripture proofs of our fact that there is such a thing on the earth as *the* assembly of God, and we shall, at once, proceed to furnish these; for we may be permitted to say that, without the authority of the Word, all statements are utterly valueless. What, therefore, saith the Scripture?

Our first proof shall be that famous passage, in Matthew xvi., "When Jesus came into the coast of Cæsarea Philippi, He asked His disciples, saying Whom do men say that I, the Son of man, am? And they said, Some say that Thou art John the Baptist; some, Elias; and others, Jeremias, or one of the prophets. He saith unto them, But whom say ye that I am? And Simon Peter answered and said, Thou art the Christ, the Son of the living God. And Jesus answered and said unto him, Blessed art thou, Simon Bar-jona: for flesh and blood hath not revealed it unto thee, but My Father which is in heaven. And I say also unto thee, that thou art Peter; and upon this rock I will build My assembly[18] ([Greek: ekklêsian]); and the gates of hell shall not prevail against it" (vers. 13-18).

Here our blessed Lord intimates His purpose to build an assembly, and sets forth the true foundation of that assembly, namely, "Christ, the Son of the living God." This is an all-important point in our subject. The building is founded on the Rock, and that Rock is not the poor failing, stumbling, erring Peter, but CHRIST, the eternal Son of the living God; and every stone in that building partakes of the Rock-life which, as being victorious over all the power of the enemy, is indestructible.[19]

Again, passing over a section of Matthew's Gospel, we come to an equally familiar passage: "Moreover, if thy brother shall trespass against thee, go and tell him his fault between thee and him alone: if he shall hear thee, thou hast gained thy brother. But if he will not hear thee, then take with thee one or two more, that in the mouth of two or three witnesses every word may be established. And if he shall neglect to hear them, tell it unto the assembly, but if he neglect to hear the assembly, let him be unto thee as a heathen man and a publican. Verily I say unto you, Whatsoever ye shall bind on earth shall be bound in heaven; and whatsoever ye shall loose on earth, shall be loosed in heaven. Again, I say unto you, that if two of you shall agree on earth as touching anything that they shall ask, it shall be done for them of My Father which is in heaven. For where two or three are *gathered* together *in My name*, there am I in the midst of them" (chap. xviii. 15-20).

We shall have occasion to refer to this passage again, under the second division of our subject. It is here introduced merely as a link in the chain of Scripture evidence of the fact that there is such a thing as the assembly of God on the earth. This assembly is not a name, a form, a pretence, an assumption. It is a divine reality—an institution of God, possessing His seal and sanction. It is a something to be appealed to in all cases of personal trespass and dispute which cannot be settled by the parties involved. This assembly may consist of only "two or three" in any particular place—the smallest plurality, if you please; but there it is, owned of God, and its decisions ratified in heaven.

Now, we are not to be scared away from the truth on this subject, by the fact that the church of Rome has attempted to base her monstrous pretensions on the two passages which we have just quoted. That church is not God's assembly, built8 on the Rock Christ, and gathered in the name of Jesus; but a human apostasy, founded on a failing mortal, and governed by the traditions and doctrines of men. We must not, therefore, suffer ourselves to be deprived of God's reality by reason of Satan's counterfeit. God has His assembly on the earth, and we are responsible to confess the truth of it, and to be a practical expression of it. This may be difficult, in a day of confusion like the present. It will demand a single eye—a subject will—a mortified mind. But let the reader be assured of this, that it is his privilege to possess as divine certainty as to what is a true expression of the assembly of God, as surely as the truth concerning his own salvation through the blood of the Lamb; nor should he be satisfied without this. I should not be content to go on for an hour without the assurance that I am, in spirit and principle, associated with those whose ground of gathering is purely their common membership in the assembly of God—that assembly which includes all saints. I say, in spirit and principle, because I may happen to be in a place where there is no such local expression of the assembly; in which case I must be satisfied to hold fellowship, in spirit, with all those who are thus gathered.

This simplifies the matter amazingly. If I cannot have a true expression of God's assembly, I shall have nothing. It will not do to point me to a religious community, with some Christians therein, the gospel preached, and the ordinances administered.

I must be convinced that in very truth, they are gathered on that ground which, in my heart and conscience, frees them from the charge of sectarianism. I can own the children of God individually anywhere; but sectarianism I cannot own or sanction.

No doubt this will give offence. It will be called bigotry, narrow-mindedness, intolerance, and the like. But this need not discourage us. All we have to do is to ascertain the truth as to God's assembly, and cleave to it, heartily and energetically, at all cost. If God has an assembly—and Scripture says He has—then let me be with those who maintain its principles, and nowhere else. It must be in this as in all other matters, truth or nothing. If there be a local expression of that assembly, well; be there in person. If not, be content to hold spiritual communion with all who humbly and faithfully own and occupy that holy ground. It may sound and seem like liberality to be ready to sanction and go with everything and everybody. It may appear very easy and very pleasant to be in a place "where everybody's will is indulged, and nobody's conscience is exercised"—where we may hold what we like, and say what we like, and do what we like, and go where we like. All this may seem very delightful—very plausible—very popular—very attractive; but oh! it will be barrenness and bitterness in the end; and, in the day of the Lord, it will assuredly be burnt up as so much wood, hay, and stubble, that cannot stand the action of His judgment.

But let us proceed with our Scripture proofs. In the Acts of the Apostles, or rather, the Acts of the Holy Ghost, we find the assembly formally set up. A passage or two will suffice: "And they, continuing daily with one accord in the temple, and breaking bread from house to house, did eat their meat with gladness and singleness of heart, praising God, and having favor with all the people. And the Lord added to the assembly, daily, such as should be saved" (Acts ii. 46, 47). Such was the original, simple apostolic order. When a person was converted, he thereby belonged to the assembly and took his place in it: there was no difficulty in the matter, there were no sects or parties, each claiming to be considered *a* church, a cause, or an interest. There was just the one thing, and that was the assembly of God, where He dwelt, acted, and ruled. It was not a system formed according to the will, the judgment, or even the conscience of man. Man had not, as yet, entered upon the business of church-making. This was God's work. It was just as exclusively God's province and prerogative to baptize the saved into one body by one Spirit, as to save the scattered.[20]

Why, we may justly inquire, should it be different now? Why should the regenerated seek to belong to something else than that to which they already belong—the assembly of God? Is not that sufficient? Assuredly. Should they seek aught else? Assuredly not. We repeat, with emphasis, "*Either that or nothing.*"

True it is, alas! that failure, and ruin, and apostasy have come in. Man's wisdom, and his will; or, if you please, his reason, his judgment, and his misguided conscience have wrought, in matters ecclesiastical, and the result appears before us in the almost numberless and nameless sects and parties of the present moment. Still, we are bold to say, that the ground of assembling as at the beginning, simply as being members of the assembly of God, remains the same, spite of all the failure, the error, and the confusion, which have come in. The difficulty in reaching it practically may be great, but its reality, when reached, is unaltered, and unalterable. In apostolic times the assembly stood out, in bold relief, from the dark background of Judaism on the one hand, and Paganism on the other. It was impossible to mistake it; there it stood, a grand reality! a company of living men, gathered, indwelt, ruled and regulated by God the Holy Ghost, so that the unlearned or unbelieving coming in, were convinced of all, and constrained to acknowledge that God was there. (See carefully, I Cor. xii., xiv. throughout.)

Thus, in this Gospel, our blessed Lord intimates His purpose of building an assembly. This assembly is historically presented to us in the Acts of the Apostles. Then, when we turn to the Epistles of Paul, we find him addressing the assembly in seven distinct places, namely, Rome, Corinth, Galatia, Ephesus, Philippi, Colosse, and Thessalonica; and finally, in the opening of the book of Revelation, we have addresses to seven distinct assemblies. Now, in all these places, the assembly of God was a plain, palpable, real thing, established and maintained by God Himself. It was not a human organization, but a divine institution—a testimony—a light bearer for God, in each place.

Thus much as to our Scripture proofs of the fact that God has an assembly on the earth, gathered, indwelt, and governed by the Holy Ghost who is the true and only Vicar of Christ upon earth. The Gospel prophetically intimates the assembly; the Acts historically presents the assembly; and the Epistles formally address the assembly. All this is plain. And if it be broken into fragments now, it is for us to be gathered on the ground of the *one* assembly of God, and to be a true expression of it.

And let it be carefully noted that we will listen to nothing on this subject but the voice of Holy Scripture. Let not reason speak, for we own it not. Let not tradition lift her voice, for we wholly disregard her. Let not expediency thrust itself upon us, for we shall give it no place whatever. We believe in the all-sufficiency of Holy Scripture—that it is sufficient to furnish the man of God thoroughly—to equip him perfectly for all good works (2 Tim. iii. 16, 17). The word of God is either sufficient or it is not. We believe it to be amply sufficient for every exigency of God's assembly. It could not be otherwise if God be its author. We must either deny the divinity or admit the sufficiency of the Bible. There is not a single hair's breadth of middle ground. It is impossible that God could have written an imperfect, an insufficient book.

This is a very grave principle in connection with our subject. Many of our protestant writers have, in assailing popery, maintained the sufficiency and authority of the Bible; but it does seem very plain to us that they are always at fault when their opponents turn sharp round upon them and demand proof from Scripture for many things sanctioned and adopted by protestant communities.

There are many things adopted and practised in the National Establishment and other protestant communities, which have no sanction in the Word; and when the shrewd and intelligent defenders of popery have called attention to these things, and demanded authority for them, the weakness of mere protestantism has been strikingly apparent. If we admit, for a moment, that, in some things, we must have recourse to tradition and expediency, then who will undertake to fix the boundary line? If it be allowable to depart from Scripture at all, how far are we to go? If the authority of tradition be admitted at all, who is to fix its domain? If we leave the narrow and well-defined pathway of divine revelation, and enter upon the wide and bewildering field of human tradition, has not one man as much right as another to make a choice? The gates of hell shall assuredly prevail against every human system—against all those corporations and associations which men have set on foot. And in no case has that triumph been, even already, made more awfully manifest than in that of the church of Rome itself, although it has arrogantly laid claim to this very declaration of our Lord as the bulwark of its strength. Nothing can withstand the power of the gates of hell but the assembly of the living God, for that is built upon "the living Stone." Now the local expression of that assembly may be but "two or three gathered in the name of Jesus," a poor, feeble, despised handful.

It is well to be clear and decided as to this.

Christ's promise can never fail. He has, blessed be His name, come down to the lowest possible point by which the assembly can be represented, even "*two*." How gracious! How tender! How considerate! How like Himself! He attaches all the dignity—all the value—all the efficacy of His own divine and deathless name to an obscure handful gathered round Himself. It must be very evident to the spiritual mind that the Lord Jesus, in speaking of the "two or three" thought not of those vast systems which have sprung up in ancient, mediæval, and modern times, throughout the eastern and western world, numbering their adherents and votaries, not by "twos or threes," but by kingdoms, provinces, and parishes. It is very plain that a baptized kingdom, and "two or three" living souls gathered in the name of Jesus, do not and cannot mean the same thing. Baptized Christendom is one thing, and the assembly of God is another. What this latter is, we have yet to unfold; we are here asserting that they are not, and cannot be, the same thing. They are constantly confounded, though no two things can be more distinct.[21]

If we would know under what figure Christ presents the baptized world, we have only to look at the "leaven" and the "mustard tree" of Matt. xiii.

The former gives us the internal, and the latter the external character of "the kingdom of heaven"—of that which was originally set up in truth and simplicity—a real thing, though small, but which, through Satan's crafty working, has become inwardly a corrupt mass, though outwardly a far-spreading, showy, popular thing in the earth, gathering all sorts beneath the shadow of its patronage. Such is the lesson—the simple but deeply solemn lesson to be learnt by the spiritual mind from the "leaven" and the "mustard-tree" of Matt. xiii. And we may add, one result of learning this lesson would be an ability to distinguish between "the kingdom of heaven" and "the assembly of God." The former may be compared to a wide morass, the latter to a running stream passing through it, and in constant danger of losing its distinctive character, as well as its proper direction, by intermingling with the surrounding waters. To confound the two things is to deal a deathblow to all godly discipline and consequent purity in the assembly of God. If the kingdom and the assembly mean one and the same thing, then how should we act in the case of "that wicked person" in I Cor. v.? The apostle tells us "to put him away." Where are we to put him? Our Lord Himself tells us distinctly that "the field is *the world*;" and again, in John xvii., He says that His people are not of the world. This makes all plain enough. But men tell us, in the very face of our Lord's statement, that the field is the assembly, and the tares and wheat, ungodly and godly, are to grow together, that they are on no account to be separated. Thus the plain and positive teaching of the Holy Ghost in I Cor. v. is set in open opposition to the equally plain and positive teaching of our Lord in Matt. xiii.; and all this flows from the effort to confound two distinct things, namely, "the kingdom of heaven" and "the assembly of God."

It would not by any means comport with the object of this paper to enter further upon the interesting subject of "the kingdom." Enough has been said, if the reader has thereby been convinced of the immense importance of duly distinguishing that kingdom from the assembly. What this latter is we shall now proceed to inquire; and may God the Holy Ghost be our teacher!

II. In handling our question as to the assembly of God, it will give clearness and precision to our thoughts to consider the four following points, namely:—

First, what is the *material* of which the assembly is composed?

Secondly, what is the *centre* round which the assembly is gathered?

Thirdly, what is the *power* by which the assembly is gathered?

Fourthly, what is the *authority* on which the assembly is gathered?

I. And, first, then, as to the material of which God's assembly is composed; it is, in one word, those possessing salvation, or eternal life. We do not enter the assembly in order to be saved, but as those who are saved. The word is, "*On* this rock I will build My Church." He does not say, "On My Church I will build the salvation of souls." One of Rome's boasted dogmas is this—"There is no salvation out of the true Church." Yes, but we can go deeper still, and say, "Off the true Rock there is no Church." Take away the Rock, and you have nothing but a baseless fabric of error and corruption. What a miserable delusion, to think of being saved by that! Thank God, it is not so. We do not get to Christ through the Church, but to the Church through Christ. To reverse this order is to displace Christ altogether, and thus have neither Rock, nor Church, nor salvation. We meet Christ as a life-giving Saviour, before we have anything to say to the assembly at all; and hence we could possess eternal life, and enjoy full salvation, though there were no such thing as the assembly of God on the earth.[22]

We cannot be too simple in grasping this truth, at a time like the present, when ecclesiastical pretention is rising to such a height. The church, falsely so called, is opening her bosom with delusive tenderness, and inviting poor sin-burdened, world-sick, and heavy-laden souls to take refuge therein. She, with crafty liberality, throws open her treasury door, and places her resources at the disposal of needy, craving, yearning souls. And truly those resources have powerful attractions for those who are not on "The Rock." There is an ordained priesthood, professing to stand in an unbroken line with the apostles.—Alas! how different the two ends of the line!—There is a continual sacrifice. Alas! a bloodless one, and therefore a worthless one. (Heb. ix. 22.)—There is a splendid ritual. Alas! it seeks its origin amid the shadows of a by-gone age—shadows which have been for ever displaced by the Person, the work, and the offices of the eternal Son of God. For ever be His peerless name adored!

The believer has a very conclusive answer to all the pretensions and promises of the Romish system. He can say he has found his *all* in a crucified and risen Saviour. What does he want with the sacrifice of the mass? He is washed in the blood of Christ. What does he want with a poor, sinful, dying priest, who cannot save himself? He has the Son of God as his priest. What does he want with a pompous ritual, with all its imposing adjuncts? He worships in spirit and in truth, within the holiest of all, whither he enters with boldness, through the blood of Jesus.

Nor is it merely with Roman Catholicism we have to do in the establishment of our first point. We fear there are thousands besides Roman Catholics who, in heart, look to the church, if not for salvation, at least to be a stepping-stone thereto. Hence the importance of seeing clearly that the materials of which God's assembly is composed are those possessing salvation, in whom is eternal life; so that whatever be the object of that assembly, it most certainly is not to provide salvation for its members, seeing that all its members are saved ere they enter it at all. God's assembly is a houseful of saved ones from one end to the other. Blessed fact! It is not an institution set on foot for the purpose of providing salvation for sinners, nor yet for providing for their religious wants. It is a saved, living body, formed and gathered by the Holy Ghost, to make known to "Principalities and powers in the heavenlies, the manifold wisdom of God," and to declare to the whole universe the all-sufficiency of the name of Jesus.

Now, the great enemy of Christ and the Church is well aware of what a powerful testimony the assembly of God is called and designed to yield on the earth; and therefore he has put forth all his hellish energy to quash that testimony in every possible way. He hates the name of Jesus, and everything tending to glorify that name. Hence his intense opposition to the assembly as a whole, and to each local expression thereof, wherever it may happen to exist. He has no objection to a mere religious establishment set on foot for the purpose of providing for man's religious wants, whether maintained by government or by voluntary effort. You may set up what you please. You may join what you please. You may be what you please; anything and everything for Satan but the assembly of God, and the practical expression of it in any given place. That he hates most cordially, and will seek to blacken and blast by every means in his power. But those consolatory accents of the Lord Christ fall with divine power on the ear of faith: "On this rock I will build My assembly, and the gates of hell shall not prevail against it."

2. This conducts us naturally to our second point, namely, What is the centre round which God's assembly is gathered? The centre is Christ—the living Stone, as we read in the Epistle of Peter, "To whom coming as unto a living stone, disallowed indeed of men, but chosen of God, and precious, ye also, as living stones, are built up a spiritual house, a holy priesthood, to offer up spiritual sacrifices, acceptable to God by Jesus Christ" (chap. ii. 4, 5).

It is around the person of a living Christ then, that God's assembly is gathered. It is not round a doctrine, however true; nor round an ordinance, however important; but round a living, divine Person. This is a great cardinal and vital point which must be distinctly seized, tenaciously held, and faithfully and constantly avowed and carried out. "To whom coming." It is not said "To *which* coming." We do not come to a thing, but to a Person. "Let us go forth therefore unto *Him*" (Heb. xiii.). The Holy Ghost leads us *only* to Jesus. Nothing short of this will avail. We may speak of joining *a* church, becoming a member of a congregation, attaching ourselves to a party, a cause, or an interest. All these expressions tend to darken and confuse the mind, and hide from our view the divine idea of the assembly of God. It is not our business to join anything. When God converted us, He joined us by His Spirit to Christ and to all the members of Christ, and that should be enough for us. Christ is the only centre of God's assembly.

And, we may ask, is not He sufficient? Is it not quite enough for us to be "joined to the Lord?" Why add aught thereto? "Where two or three are gathered together *in My name*, there am I in the midst of them" (Matt. xviii. 20). What more can we need? If Jesus is in our midst, why should we think of setting up a human president? Why not unanimously and heartily allow Him to take the president's seat, and bow to Him in all things? Why set up human authority, in any shape or form, in the house of God? But this is done, and it is well to speak plainly about it. Man is set up in that which professes to be an assembly of God. We see human authority exercised in that sphere in which divine authority alone should be acknowledged. It matters not, so far as the foundation principle is concerned, whether it be pope, parson, priest, or president. It is man set up in Christ's place. It may be the pope appointing a cardinal, a legate, or a bishop to his sphere of work; or it may be a president appointing a man to exhort or to pray for ten minutes. The principle is one and the same. It is human authority acting in that sphere where only God's authority should be owned. If Christ be in our midst, we can count on Him for everything.

Now, in saying this, we anticipate a very probable objection. It may be said by the advocates of human authority, "How could an assembly ever get on without some human presidency? Would it not lead to all sorts of confusion? Would it not open the door for everyone to intrude himself upon the assembly, quite irrespective of gift or qualification?

Our answer is a very simple one. Jesus is all-sufficient. We can trust Him to keep order in His house. We feel ourselves far safer in His gracious and powerful hand than in the hands of the most attractive human president. We have all spiritual gifts treasured up in Jesus. He is the fountain-head of all ministerial authority. "He hath the seven stars." Let us only confide in Him, and the order of our assembly will be as perfectly provided for as the salvation of our souls. This is just the reason of our connecting, in the title of this pamphlet, "The all-sufficiency of the name of Jesus" with the "Assembly of God." We believe that the name of Jesus is, in very truth, all-sufficient, not only for personal salvation, but for all the exigencies of the assembly—for worship, communion, ministry, discipline, government, everything. Having Him, we have all and abound.

This is the real marrow and substance of our subject. Our one aim and object is to exalt the name of Jesus; and we believe He has been dishonored in that which calls itself His house. He has been dethroned, and man's authority has been set up. In vain does He bestow a ministerial gift; the possessor of that gift is not free to exercise it without the seal, the sanction, and the authority of man. And not only is this so, but if man thinks proper to give his seal, his sanction and authority, to one possessing not a particle of spiritual gift—yea, it may be, not a particle of spiritual life—he is nevertheless a recognized minister. In short, man's authority without Christ's gift makes a man a minister; whereas Christ's gift without man's authority does not. If this be not a dishonor done to the Lord Christ, what is?

Christian reader, pause here, and deeply ponder this principle of human authority. We confess we are anxious you should get to the root of it, and judge it thoroughly, in the light of Holy Scripture, and the presence of God. It is, be assured of it, the grand point of distinction between the principles of the assembly of God and every human system of religion under the sun. If you look at all those systems, from Romanism down to the most refined form of religious association, you will find man's authority recognized and demanded. With that you may minister; without it you must not. On the contrary, in the assembly of God, Christ's gift *alone* makes man a minister, apart from all human authority. "Not of men, neither by man, but by Jesus Christ, and God the Father, who raised Him from the dead." (Gal. i. I). This is the grand principle of ministry in the assembly of God.

Now, in classing Romanism with all the other religious systems of the day, let it, once for all, be distinctly understood that it is *only* in reference to the principle of ministerial authority. God forbid that we should think of comparing a system which shuts out the word of God, and teaches idolatry, the worship of saints and angels, and a whole mass of gross, abominable error and superstition, with those systems where the word of God is held up, and more or less of scriptural truth promulgated. Nothing can be further from our thoughts. We believe popery to be Satan's master-piece, in the way of a religious system, although many of the people of God have been, and may yet be, involved therein.

Further, let us at this stage plainly aver that we believe the saints of God are to be found in every Protestant community, both as ministers and members; and that the Lord uses them in many ways—blesses their work, service, and personal testimony.

And, finally, we feel it right to declare that we would not move a finger to touch any one of those systems. It is not with the systems we have to do; the Lord will deal with them. Our business is with the saints in those systems, to seek by every spiritual and scriptural agency to get them to own and act upon the divine principles of the assembly of God.

Having said thus much, in order to prevent misunderstanding, we return with increased power to our point, namely, that the thread of human authority runs through every religious system in Christendom, and that, in good truth, there is not a hair's breadth of consistent standing ground between the church of Rome and a true expression of the assembly of God. We believe that an honest seeker after truth, setting out from amid the dark shadows of popery, cannot possibly halt until he finds himself in the clear and blessed light of that which is a true expression of God's assembly. He may take years to travel over the intervening space. His steps may be slow and measured; but if only he follows the light, in simplicity and godly sincerity, he will find no rest between those two extremes. The ground of the assembly of God is the true position for all the children of God. Alas! they are not all there; but this is only their loss and their Lord's dishonor. They should be there because not only is God there, but He is allowed to act and *rule* there.

This latter is of all-importance, inasmuch as it may be truly said, Is not God everywhere? And does He not act in various places? True, He is everywhere, and He works in the midst of palpable error and evil. But He is not allowed to *rule* in the systems of men, seeing that man's authority is really supreme, as we have already shown. And in addition to this, if the fact of God's converting and blessing souls in a system be a reason why we should be there, then we ought to be in the church of Rome, for how many have been converted and blessed in that awful system? Even in the recent revival we have heard of persons being stricken in Roman Catholic chapels. What proves too much proves nothing at all, and hence no argument can be based on the fact of God's working in a place. He is sovereign, and may work where He pleases. We are to be subject to His authority, and work where we are commanded, My Master may go where He pleases, but I must go where I am told.

But some may ask, "Is there no danger of incompetent men intruding their ministry upon an assembly of God? And in the event of this, where is the difference between that assembly and the systems of men?" We reply, assuredly there is very great danger. But then such a thing would be *despite*, not in virtue of, the principle. This makes all the difference. Yes, indeed, we have seen mistakes and failures which are most humiliating.

Let no one imagine that, while we contend for the truth concerning the assembly of God, we are at all ignorant or forgetful of the dangers and trials to which any carrying out its principles are exposed. Far from it. No one could be for twenty-eight years on that ground without being painfully conscious of the difficulty of maintaining it. But then the very trials, dangers, and difficulties only prove to be so many proofs—painful if you please, but proofs of the truth of the position; and were there no remedy but an appeal to human authority—a setting up of man in Christ's place—a return to worldly systems, we should without hesitation pronounce the remedy to be far worse than the disease. For were we to adopt the remedy, we should have the very worst symptoms of the disease, not to be mourned over as disease, but gloried in as the fruits of so-called order.

But blessed be God, there is a remedy. What is it? "*There am I* in the midst." This is enough. It is not, "There is a pope, a priest, a parson, or a president in their midst, at their head, in the chair, or in the pulpit." No thought of such a thing, from cover to cover of the New Testament. Even in the assembly of God at Corinth, where there was most grievous confusion and disorder, the inspired apostle never hints at such a thing as a human president, under any name whatsoever. "*God is the author* of peace in all the assemblies of the saints" (I Cor. xiv. 33). God was there to keep order. They were to look to Him, not to a man, under any name. To set up man to keep order in God's assembly is sheer unbelief, and an open insult to the Divine Presence.

Now, we have been often asked to adduce Scripture in proof of the idea of divine presidency in an assembly. We at once reply, "There am I;" and "God is the Author." On these two pillars, even had we no more, we can triumphantly build the glorious truth of divine presidency—a truth which *must* deliver all, who receive and hold it from God, from every system of man, call it by what name you please. It is, in our judgment, impossible to recognize Christ as the centre and sovereign ruler in the assembly, and continue to sanction the setting up of man. When once we have tasted the sweetness of being under Christ, we can never again submit to the servile bondage of being under man. This is not insubordination or impatience of control. It is only the utter refusal to bow to a false authority—to sanction a sinful usurpation. The moment we see man usurping authority in that which calls itself the church, we simply ask, "Who are you?" and retire to a sphere where God alone is acknowledged.

"But, then, there are errors, evils, and abuses even in this very sphere." Doubtless; but if there are, we have the word of God to correct them. And hence, if an assembly should be troubled by the intrusion of ignorant and foolish men—men who have never yet measured themselves in the presence of God—men who boldly overleap the wide domain over which common sense, good taste, and moral propriety preside, and then vainly talk of being led by the Holy Spirit—restless men, who *will* be at something, and who keep the assembly in a continual state of nervous apprehension, not knowing what is to come next—should any assembly be thus grievously afflicted, what should they do? Abandon the ground in impatience, chagrin, and disappointment? give all up as a myth, a fable, an idle chimera? go back to that from which they once came out? Alas! this is what some have done, thus proving that they never understood what they had been doing; or if they had understood it, that they had not faith to pursue it. May the Lord have mercy upon such, and open their eyes that they may see from whence they have fallen, and get a true view of the assembly of God, in contrast with the most attractive of the systems of men.

But what is an assembly to do when abuses creep in? Correct them by the word of God. This is God's authoritative voice.

We are fully aware of the difficulties and trials connected with any expression of the assembly of God. We believe its difficulties and trials are perfectly characteristic. There is nothing under the canopy of heaven that the devil hates as he hates that. He will leave no stone unturned to oppose it. We have seen this exemplified again and again. An evangelist may go to a place and preach the all-sufficiency of the name of Jesus for the salvation of the soul, and he will have thousands hanging on his lips. Let the same man return, and, while he preaches the same gospel, take another step and proclaim the all-sufficiency of that same Jesus for all the exigencies of an assembly of believers, and he will find himself opposed on all hands. Why is this? Because the devil hates the very feeblest expression of the assembly of God. You may see a town left for ages and generations to its dark and dull routine of religious formalism—a dead people gathering once a week to hear a dead man go through a dead service, and all the rest of the week living in sin and folly. There is not a breath of life, not a leaf stirring. The devil likes it well. But let some one come and unfurl the standard of the name of Jesus—Jesus for the soul and Jesus for the assembly—and you will soon see a mighty change. The rage of hell is excited, and the dark and dreadful tide of opposition rises.

This, we most fully believe, is the true secret of many of the bitter attacks that have been recently made on those who maintain the principles of the assembly of God. No doubt we have to mourn over many mistakes, errors, and failures. We have given much occasion to the adversary in various ways. We have been a poor blotted epistle, a faint and feeble witness, a flickering light. For all this we have to be deeply humbled before our God. Nothing could be more unbecoming in us than pretention or assumption, or the putting forth of high-sounding ecclesiastical claims. The dust is our place. Yes, beloved brethren, the place of confession and self-judgment becomes us, in the presence of our God.

Still, we are not to let slip the glorious principles of the assembly of God because we have so shamefully failed in carrying them out: we are not to judge the truth by our exhibition of it, but to judge our exhibition by the truth. It is one thing to occupy divine ground, and another thing to carry ourselves properly thereon; and while it is perfectly right to judge our practice by our principles, yet truth is truth for all that, and we may rest assured that the devil hates the truth which characterizes the assembly. A mere handful of poor people, gathered in the name of Jesus, as members of His body, to break bread in remembrance of Him, is a thorn in the side of the devil. True it is that such an assembly evokes the wrath of men, inasmuch as it throws their office and authority overboard, and they cannot bear that. Yet we believe the root of the whole matter will be found in Satan's hatred of the special testimony which such an assembly bears to the all-sufficiency of the name of Jesus for every possible need of the saints of God.

This is a truly noble testimony, and we earnestly long to see it more faithfully carried out. We may fully count upon intense opposition. It will be with us as it was with the returned captives in the days of Ezra and Nehemiah. We may expect to encounter many a Rehum and many a Sanballat. Nehemiah might have gone and built any other wall in the whole world but the wall of Jerusalem, and Sanballat would never have molested him. But to build the wall of Jerusalem was an unpardonable offence. And why? Just because Jerusalem was God's earthly centre, round which He will yet gather the restored tribes of Israel. This was the secret of the enemy's opposition. And mark the affected contempt. "If a fox go up, he shall even break down their stone wall." And yet Sanballat and his allies were not able to break it down. They might cause it to cease because of the Jews' lack of faith and energy; but they could not break it down when God would have it up. How like is this to the present moment! Surely there is nothing new under the sun. There is affected contempt, but real alarm. And, oh! if those who are gathered in the name of Jesus were only more true in heart to their blessed Centre, what testimony there would be! What power! What victory! How it would tell on all around. "Where two or three are gathered together in My name, there am I." There is nothing like this under the sun, be it ever so feeble and contemptible. The Lord be praised for raising up such a witness for Himself in these last days. May He greatly increase its effectiveness, by the power of the Holy Ghost!

3. We must now very briefly glance at our third point, namely, what is the power by which the assembly is gathered. Here again man and his doings are set aside. It is not man's will choosing; nor man's reason discovering; nor man's judgment dictating; nor man's conscience demanding; it is the Holy Ghost gathering souls to Jesus. As Jesus is the only centre, so the Holy Ghost is the only gathering power. The one is as independent of man as the other. It is "where two or three are *gathered*." It does not say "where two or three are *met*." Persons may meet together round any centre, on any ground, by any influence, and merely form a society, an association, a community. But the Holy Ghost gathers saved souls only to Christ.

An assembly may not embrace all the saints of God in a locality. In such a case they cannot be called the assembly of God in that place. But if they are assembled as members of the body of Christ, they occupy the ground of the assembly of God.

This is a very simple truth. A soul led by the Holy Ghost will gather only to the name of the Lord; and if we gather to aught else, be it a point of truth, or some ordinance or another, we are not in that matter led by the Holy Ghost. It is not a question of life or salvation. Thousands are saved by Christ that do not own Him as their centre. They are gathered to some form of church government, some favorite doctrine, some special ordinance, some gifted man. The Holy Ghost will never gather to any one of these. He gathers only to a risen Christ. This is true of the whole Church of God upon earth; and each local assembly, wherever convened, is the expression of the whole.

Now, the *power* in an assembly will very much depend upon the measure in which each member thereof is gathered in integrity of heart to the name of Jesus. If I am gathered to a party holding peculiar opinions—if I am attracted by the people, or by the teaching—if, in a word, it be not the power of the Holy Ghost, leading me to the true Centre of God's assembly, I shall only prove a hindrance, a weight, a cause of weakness. I shall be to an assembly what a waster is to a candle; and instead of adding to the general light and usefulness, I shall do the very reverse.

All this is deeply practical. It should lead to much exercise of heart and self-judgment as to what has drawn me to an assembly, and as to my ways therein. We are fully persuaded that the tone and testimony of an assembly have been greatly weakened by the presence of persons not understanding their position. Some present themselves there because they get teaching and blessing there which they cannot get anywhere else. Some come because they like the simplicity of the worship. Others come looking for love. None of these things are up to the mark. We should be in an assembly simply because the name of Jesus is the only standard set up there, and the Holy Spirit has "gathered" us thereto.

No doubt ministry is most precious, and we shall have it, in more or less power, where all is ordered aright. So also as to simplicity of worship: we are sure to be simple, and real, and true, when the divine presence is realized, and the sovereignty of the Holy Ghost fully owned and submitted to. And as to love, if we go *looking for it* we shall surely be thoroughly disappointed: but if we are enabled to *cultivate* and *manifest it*, we shall be sure to get a great deal more than we expect or deserve. It will generally be found that those persons who are perpetually complaining of want of love in others are utterly failing in love themselves; and, on the other hand, those who are really walking in love will tell you that they receive a thousand times more than they deserve. Let us remember that the best way to get water out of a dry pump is to pour a little water in. You may work at the handle until you are tired, and then go away in fretfulness and impatience, complaining of that horrible pump; whereas, if you would just pour in a little water, you would get in return a gushing stream to satisfy your utmost desire.

We have but little conception of what an assembly would be were each one distinctly led by the Holy Ghost, and gathered *only* to Jesus. We should not then have to complain of dull, heavy, unprofitable, trying meetings. We should have no fear of an unhallowed intrusion of mere nature and its restless doings—no *making* of prayer—no talking for talking's sake—no hymn-book seized to fill a gap. Each one would know his place in the Lord's immediate presence—each gifted vessel would be filled, fitted, and used by the Master's hand—each eye would be directed to Jesus—each heart occupied with Him. If a chapter were read, it would be the very voice of God. If a word were spoken, it would tell with power upon the heart. If prayer were offered, it would lead the soul into the very presence of God. If a hymn were sung, it would lift the spirit up to God, and be like sweeping the strings of the heavenly harp. We should have no ready-made sermons—no teaching or preaching prayers, as though we would explain doctrines to God, or tell Him a whole host of things about ourselves—no praying *at* our neighbors, or asking for all manner of graces for them, in which we ourselves are lamentably deficient—no singing for music's sake, or being disturbed if harmony be interfered with. All these evils should be avoided. We should feel ourselves in the very sanctuary of God, and enjoy a foretaste of that time when we shall worship in the courts above, and go no more out.

We may be asked, "Where will you find all this down here?" Ah! this is the question. It is one thing to present a *beau ideal* on paper, and another thing to realize it in the midst of error, failure, and infirmity. Through mercy, some of us have tasted, at times, a little of this blessedness. We have occasionally enjoyed moments of heaven upon earth. Oh, for more of it! May the Lord, in His great mercy, raise the tone of the assemblies everywhere! May He greatly enlarge our capacity for more profound communion and spiritual worship! May He enable us so to walk, in private life, from day to day so as to judge ourselves and our ways in His holy presence, that at least we may not prove a lump of lead or a waster to any of God's assemblies.

And then, even though we may not be able to reach in experience the true expression of the assembly, yet let us never be satisfied with anything less. Let us honestly aim at the loftiest standard, and earnestly pray to be lifted up thereto. As to the *ground* of God's assembly, we should hold it with jealous tenacity, and never consent for an hour to occupy any other. As to the tone and character of an assembly, they may and will vary immensely, and will depend upon the faith and spirituality of those gathered. Where the tone of things is felt to be low,—when meetings are felt to be unprofitable—where things are said and done repeatedly which are felt by the spiritual to be wholly out of place, let all who feel it wait on God—wait continually—wait believingly—and He will assuredly hear and answer. In this way the very trials and exercises which are peculiar to an assembly will have the happy effect of casting us more immediately upon Him, and thus the eater will yield meat, and the strong sweetness. We must count upon trials and difficulties in any expression of the assembly, just because it is *the* right and divine way for God's people on earth. The devil will put forth every effort to drive us from that true and holy ground. He will try the patience, try the temper, hurt the feelings, cause offence in nameless and numberless ways—anything and everything to make us forsake the true ground of the assembly.

It is well to remember this. We can only hold the divine ground by faith. This marks the assembly of God, and distinguishes it from every human system. You cannot get on there save by faith. And, further, if you want to be somebody, if you are seeking a place, if you want to exalt *self*, you need not think of any true expression of the assembly. You will soon find your level there, if it be in any measure what it should be. Fleshly or worldly greatness, in any shape, will be of no account in such an assembly. The Divine Presence withers up everything of that kind, and levels all human pretension. Finally, you cannot get on in the assembly if you are living in secret sin. The Divine Presence will not suit you. Have we not often experienced in the assembly a feeling of uneasiness, caused by the recollection of many things which had escaped our notice during the week? Wrong thoughts—foolish words—unspiritual ways—all these things crowd in upon the mind, and exercise the conscience, in the assembly! How is this? Because the atmosphere of the assembly is more searching than that which we have been breathing during the week. We have not been in the presence of God in our private walk. We have not been judging ourselves; and hence, when we take our place in a spiritual assembly, our hearts are detected—our ways are exposed in the light; and that exercise which ought to have gone on in private—even the needed exercise of self-judgment, must go on at the table of the Lord. This is poor, miserable work for us, but it proves the power of the presence of God in the assembly. Things must be in a miserably low state in any assembly when hearts are not thus detected and exposed. It is a fine evidence of the power of the Holy Spirit in an assembly when careless, carnal, worldly, self-exalting, money-loving, unprincipled persons are compelled to judge themselves in God's presence, or, failing this, are driven away by the spirituality of the atmosphere. Such an assembly is no place for these. They can breathe more freely outside.

Now, we cannot but judge that numbers that have departed from the ground of the assembly have done so because their practical ways did not comport with the purity of the place. No doubt it is easy, in all such cases, to find an excuse in the conduct of those who are left behind. But if the *roots* of things were in every case laid bare, we should find that many leave an assembly because of inability or reluctance to bear its searching light. "Thy testimonies are very sure; holiness becometh Thy house, O Lord, forever." Evil *must* be judged, for God cannot sanction it. If an assembly does not it is not practically God's assembly at all, though composed of Christians, as we say. To pretend to be an assembly of God, and not judge false doctrine and evil ways, would involve the blasphemy of saying that God and wickedness can dwell together. The assembly of God must keep itself pure, because it is His dwelling-place. Men may sanction evil, and call it liberality and large-heartedness so to do; but the house of God must keep itself pure. Let this great practical truth sink down into our hearts, and produce its sanctifying influence upon our course and character.

4. A very few words will suffice to set forth, in the last place, "the *authority*" on which the assembly is gathered. It is the word of God alone. The charter of the assembly is the eternal Word of the living and true God. It is not the traditions, the doctrines, nor the commandments of men. A

passage of Scripture, to which we have more than once referred in the progress of this paper, contains at once the standard round which the assembly is gathered, the power by which it is gathered, and the authority by which it is gathered—"the name of Jesus"—"the Holy Ghost"—"the word of God."

Now these are the same all over the world. Whether I go to New Zealand, to Australia, to Canada, to London, to Paris, to Edinburg, or Dublin, the Centre, the gathering Power, and the authority are one and the same. We can own no other centre but Christ; no gathering energy but the Holy Ghost; no authority but the word of God; no characteristic but holiness of life and soundness in doctrine.

Such is a true expression of the assembly of God, and we cannot acknowledge aught else. Saints of God we can acknowledge, love, and honor as such, wherever we find them; but human systems we look upon as dishonoring to Christ, and hostile to the true interest of the saints of God. We long to see all Christians on the true ground of the assembly. We believe it to be the place of real blessing and effective testimony. We believe there is a character of testimony yielded by carrying out the principles of the assembly which cannot be yielded otherwise, even were each member a Whitefield in evangelistic power. We say this not to lower evangelistic work. God forbid. We would that all were Whitefields. But then we cannot shut our eyes to the fact that many affect to despise the assembly, under the plea of going out as evangelists; and when we trace their path, and examine the results of their work, we find that they have no provision for the souls that have been converted by their means. They seem not to know what to do with them. They quarry the stones, but do not build them together. The consequence is that souls are scattered hither and thither, some persuing a desultory course, others living in isolation, all at fault as to true Church ground.

Now, we believe that all these should be gathered on the ground of the assembly of God, to have "fellowship in the breaking of bread and in prayer." They should "come together on the first day of the week, to break bread," looking to the Lord Christ to edify them by the mouth of whom He will. This is the simple path—the normal, the divine idea, needing, it may be, more faith to realize it, because of the clashing and conflicting elements of the present day, but none the less simple and true on that account.

We are aware, of course, that all this will be pronounced proselytizing, and party spirit, by those who seem to regard it as the very *beau ideal* of Christian liberality and large-heartedness to be able to say, "I belong to nothing." Strange, anomalous position! It just resolves itself in this: it is *somebody* professing *nothingism* in order to get rid of all responsibility, and go with all and everything. This is a very easy path for nature, and amiable nature, but we shall see what will come of it in the day of the Lord. Even now we regard it as positive unfaithfulness to Christ, from which may the good Lord deliver His people.

But let none imagine that we want to place the evangelist and the assembly in opposition. Nothing is further from our thoughts. The evangelist should go forth from the bosom of the assembly, in full fellowship therewith; he should work not only to gather souls to Christ, but also bring them to an assembly, where divinely-gifted pastors might watch over them, and divinely-gifted teachers instruct them. We do not want to clip the evangelist's wings, but only to guide his movements. We are unwilling to see real spiritual energy expended in desultory service. No doubt it is a grand result to bring souls to Christ. Every soul linked to Jesus is a work done forever. But ought not the lambs and sheep to be gathered and cared for? Would anyone be satisfied to purchase sheep, and then leave them to wander whithersoever they list? Surely not. But whither should Christ's sheep be gathered? Is it into the folds of man's erection, or into an assembly gathered on divine ground? Into the latter unquestionably; for that, we may rest assured, however feeble, however despised, however blackened and maligned, is the place for all the lambs and sheep of the flock of Christ.

Here, however, there will be responsibility, care, anxiety, labor, a constant demand for watchfulness and prayer; all of which flesh and blood would like to avoid, if possible. There is much that is agreeable and attractive in the idea of going through the world as an evangelist, having thousands hanging on one's lips, and hundreds of souls as the seals of one's ministry: but what is to be done with these souls? By all means show them their true place with those gathered on the ground of the assembly of God, where, notwithstanding the ruin and apostasy of the professing body, they can enjoy spiritual communion, worship, and ministry. This will involve much trial and painful excise. It was so in apostolic times. Those who really cared for the flock of Christ had to shed many a tear, send up many an agonizing prayer, spend many a sleepless night. But, then, in all these things, they tasted the sweetness of fellowship with the chief Shepherd; and when He appears, their tears, their prayers, their sleepless nights will be remembered and rewarded; while those who are building up human systems will find them all come to an end, to be heard of no more forever; and the false shepherds, who ruthlessly seize the pastoral staff only to use it as an instrument of filthy gain to themselves, shall have their faces covered with everlasting confusion.

But, we may be asked, "Is it not worse than useless to seek to carry out the principles of the assembly of God, seeing that the professing Church is in such complete ruin?" We reply by asking, "Are we to be disobedient because the Church is in ruin? Are we to continue in error because the dispensation has failed?" Surely not. We own the ruin, mourn over it, confess it, take our share in it, and in its sad consequences, seek to walk softly and humbly in the midst of it, confessing ourselves to be most unfaithful and unworthy. But though we have failed, Christ has not failed. He abideth faithful; He cannot deny Himself. He has promised to be with His people to the end of the age. Matt. xviii. 20 holds as good to-day as it did 1800 years ago. "Let God be true and every man a liar." We utterly repudiate the idea of men setting about church-making, or pretending to ordain ministers. We look upon it as a pure assumption, without a single shadow of Scripture authority. It is God's work to gather His Church and raise up ministers. We have no business to form ourselves into a church, or to ordain office-bearers. No doubt the Lord is very gracious, tender, and pitiful. He bears with our weakness, and overrules our mistakes, and where the heart is true to Him, even though in ignorance, He will assuredly lead on into higher light.

But we must not use God's grace as a plea for unscriptural acting, any more than we should use the Church's ruin as a plea for sanctioning error. We have to confess the ruin, count on the grace, and act in simple obedience to the word of the Lord. Such is the path of blessing at all times. The remnant, in the days of Ezra, did not pretend to the power and splendor of Solomon's days, but they obeyed the word of Solomon's Lord, and they were abundantly blessed in their deed. They did not say, "Things are in ruin, and therefore we had better remain in Babylon, and do nothing." No; they simply confessed their own and their people's sin, and counted on God. This is precisely what we are to do. We are to own the ruin, and count on God.

Finally, if we be asked, "Where is the true expression of this assembly of God now?" We reply, "Where Christ is truly the Centre of gathering; the one body the ground; the Holy Spirit the Leader; the Holy Scriptures the sole authority; and holiness the practice."

Reader, are you assembled on this divine ground? If so, cling to it with your whole soul. Are you in this path? If so, press on with all the energies of your moral being. Never be content with anything short of His dwelling in you, and your conscious nearness to Him. Let not Satan rob you of your proper portion by leading you to rest in a mere name. Let him not tempt you to mistake your ostensible *position* for your real *condition*. Cultivate secret communion—secret prayer—constant self-judgment. Be especially on your guard against every form of spiritual pride. Cultivate lowliness, meekness, and brokenness of spirit, tenderness of conscience, in your own private walk. Seek to combine the sweetest grace towards others with the boldness of a lion where truth is concerned. Then will you be a blessing in the assembly of God, and an effective witness of the all-sufficiency of the name of Jesus.

The veil is rent:--our souls draw nearUnto a throne of grace;The merits of the Lord appear,They fill the holy place.

His precious blood has spoken there,Before and on the throne:And His own wounds in heaven declare,Th' atoning work is done.

'Tis finished!--here our souls have rest,His work can never fail:By Him, our Sacrifice and Priest,We pass within the veil.

Within the holiest of all,Cleansed by His precious blood,Before the throne we prostrate fall,And worship Thee, O God!

Boldly the heart and voice we raise,His blood, His name, our plea:Assured our prayers and songs of praiseAscend, by Christ, to Thee.

THE CHRISTIAN
HIS POSITION AND HIS WORK

PART I

What is the true position of a Christian? and what has he got to do? are questions of the very deepest practical importance. It is assumed, of course, that he has eternal life: without this, one cannot be a Christian at all. "He that believeth on the Son of God hath everlasting life." This is the common portion of all believers. It is not a matter of attainment, a matter of progress, a thing which some Christians have and others have not. It belongs to the very feeblest babe in the family of God, as well as to the most matured and experienced servant of Christ. All are possessed of eternal life, and can never by any possibility lose it.

But our present theme is not life, but position and work; and in considering it, we shall ask the reader to turn for a moment to a passage in Heb. xiii. Perhaps we cannot do better than quote it for him. There is nothing like the plain and solid word of Holy Scripture.

"Be not carried about with divers and strange doctrines; for it is a good thing that the heart be established with grace; not with meats, which have not profited them that have been occupied therein. We have an altar, whereof they have no right to eat which serve the tabernacle. For the bodies of those beasts, whose blood is brought into the sanctuary by the high priest for sin are burned without the camp. Wherefore Jesus also, that He might sanctify the people with His own blood, suffered without the gate. Let us go forth therefore unto Him without the camp, bearing His reproach. For here have we no continuing city, but we seek one to come" (vers. 9-14).

Here, then, we have one grand aspect of the Christian's position. It is defined by the position of his Lord. This makes it divinely simple; and, we may add, divinely settled. The Christian is identified with Christ. Amazing fact! "As He is so *are* we in this world." It is not said, "As He is, so *shall* we be in the world to come." No; this would not come up to the divine idea. It is, "so are we *in this world*." The position of Christ defines the position of the Christian.

But this glorious fact tells in a double way; it tells upon the Christian's place before God; and it tells on his place as regards this present world. It is upon the latter that Heb. xiii. instructs us so blessedly, and it is that which is now more especially before us.

Jesus suffered without the gate. This fact is the basis on which the apostle grounds his exhortation to the Hebrew believers to go forth without the camp. The cross of Christ closed his connection with the camp of Judaism; and all who desire to follow Him must go outside to where He is. The final breach with Israel is presented, morally, in the death of Christ; doctrinally, in the Epistle to the Hebrews; historically, in the destruction of Jerusalem. In the judgment of faith, Jerusalem was as thoroughly rejected when the Messiah was nailed to the cross, as it was when the army of Titus left it a smouldering ruin. The instincts of the divine nature, and the inspired teachings of Scripture, go before the actual facts of history.

"Jesus suffered without the gate." For what end? "That He might sanctify (or set apart to God) the people with His own blood." What follows? What is the necessary practical result? "Let us go forth therefore unto Him without the camp, bearing His reproach."

But what is "the camp?" Primarily, Judaism; but, most unquestionably, it has a moral application to every organized system of religion under the sun. If that system of ordinances and ceremonies which God Himself had set up—if Judaism, with its imposing ritual, its splendid temple, its priesthood and its sacrifices, has been found fault with, condemned, and set aside, what shall be said of any or all of those organizations which have rebuilt it? If our Lord Christ is outside of that, how much more out of these!

Yes, Christian reader, we may rest assured that the outside place, the place of rejection and reproach is that to which we are called, if we would know aught of true fellowship with our Lord Jesus Christ. Mark the words! "Let us go forth." Will any Christian say, "No; I cannot go forth. My place is inside the camp. I must work there?" If so, then, there must be moral distance between you and Jesus, for He is as surely outside the camp as He is on the throne of God. If your sphere of work lies inside the camp, when your Master tells you to go forth, what shall we say for your work? Can it be "gold, silver, precious stones?" Can it have your Lord's approving smile? It may exhibit His overruling hand, and illustrate His sovereign goodness; but can it possibly have His unqualified approval while carried on in a sphere from which He commands you to go forth?

The all-important thing for every true servant is to be found exactly where his Master would have him. The question is not, "Am I doing a great deal of work? but am I pleasing my Master? I may seem to be doing wonders in the way of work; my name may be heralded to the ends of the earth as a most laborious, devoted, and successful workman; and, all the while, I may be in an utterly false position, indulging my own unbroken will, pleasing myself, and seeking some personal end or object."

All this is very solemn indeed, and demands the consideration of all who really desire to be found in the current of God's thoughts. We live in a day of much wilfulness. The commandments of Christ do not govern all. We think for ourselves, in place of submitting ourselves absolutely to the authority of the Word. When our Lord tells us to go forth without the camp, we, instead of yielding a ready obedience, begin to reason as to the results which we can reach by remaining within. Scripture seems to have little or no power over our souls. We do not aim at simply pleasing Christ. Provided we can make great show of work, we think all is right. We are more occupied with results which, after all, may only tend to magnify ourselves, than with the earnest purpose to do what is agreeable to the mind of Christ.

But are we to be idle? Is there nothing for us to do in the outside place to which we are called? Is Christian life to be made up of a series of negations? Is there nothing positive? Let Heb. xiii. furnish the clear and forcible answer to all these inquiries. We shall find it quite as distinct in reference to our *work* as it is in reference to our *position*.

What, then, have we got to do? Two things; and these two in their comprehensive range take in the whole of a Christian's life in its two grand aspects. They give us the inner and the outer life of the true believer. In the first place, we read, "By Him therefore let us offer the sacrifice of praise to God continually, that is, the fruit of our lips, giving thanks to His name.

Is not this something? Have we not here a very elevated character of work? Yes, verily, the most elevated that can possibly engage the energies of our renewed being. It is our privilege to be occupied, morning, noon, eventide, and midnight, in presenting the sacrifice of praise to God—a sacrifice which, He assures us, is ever most acceptable to Him. "Whoso offereth praise," He says, "glorifieth Me."

Let us carefully note this. Praise is to be the primary and continual occupation of the believer. We, in our fancied wisdom, would put work in the first place. We are disposed to attach chief importance to bustling activity. We have such an overweening sense of the value of *doing*, that we lose sight of the place which worship occupies in the thoughts of God.

Again, there are some who vainly imagine that they can please God by punishing their bodies. They think that He delights in their vigils, fastings, floggings, and flagellations. Miserable, soul-destroying, God-dishonoring delusion! Will not those who harbor it and act upon it bend their ears and their hearts to those gracious words which we have just penned, "Whoso offereth praise glorifieth Me?" True, it is, that those words are immediately followed by that grand practical statement, "And to him that ordereth his conversation aright, will I show the salvation of God." But still, here, as everywhere, the highest place is assigned to praise, not to work. And, most assuredly, no man can be said to be ordering his conversation aright who abuses his body and renders it unfit to be the vessel or instrument by which he can serve God.

No, reader, if we really desire to please God, to gratify His heart and to glorify His name, we shall give our heart's attention to Heb. xiii. 15, and seek to offer the sacrifice of praise *continually*. Yes, "continually." Not merely now and then, when all goes on smoothly and pleasantly. Come what may, it is our high and holy privilege to offer the sacrifice of praise to God. It does so glorify God when His people live in an atmosphere of praise. It imparts a heavenly tone to their character, and speaks more powerfully to the hearts of those around them than if they were preaching to them from morning till night. A Christian should "rejoice in the Lord alway," always reflecting back upon this dark world the blessed beams of his Father's countenance.

Thus it should ever be. Nothing is so unworthy of a Christian as a fretful spirit, a gloomy temper, a sour, morose-looking face. And not only is it unworthy of a Christian, but it is dishonoring to God, and it causes the enemies of truth to speak reproachfully. No doubt, tempers and dispositions vary; and allowance must be made in cases of weak bodily health, and of circumstances of sorrow. It is not easy to look pleasant when the body is in suffering; and, further, we should be very far indeed from the commending anything like levity or the everlasting smile of mere unsubdued nature.

But Scripture is clear and explicit. It tells us to "offer the sacrifice of praise to God continually, that is, the fruit of our lips giving thanks to His name." How simple! "*The fruit of our lips.*" This is what our God delights in. It is His joy to be surrounded with the praises of hearts filled to overflowing with His abounding goodness. Thus it will be throughout eternity, in that bright home of love and glory to which we are so rapidly hastening.

And let the reader specially note the words, "*By Him.*" We are to offer our sacrifice of praise by the hand of our Great High Priest, who is ever in the presence of God for us. This is most consolatory and assuring to our hearts. Jesus presents our sacrifice of praise to God. It must therefore be ever acceptable, coming thus by the priestly hand of the Great Minister of the sanctuary. It goes up to God, not as it proceeds from us, but as it is presented by Him. Divested of all the imperfection and failure attaching to us, it ascends to God in all the fragrance and acceptancy belonging to Him. The feeblest note of praise, the simple "Thank God!" is perfumed with the incense of Christ's infinite preciousness. This is unspeakably precious: and it should greatly encourage us to cultivate a spirit of praise. We should be "continually" praising and blessing God. A murmuring or fretful word should never cross the lips of one who has Christ for his portion, and who stands identified with that blessed One in His position and His destiny.

But we must draw this paper to a close by a rapid glance at the other side of the Christian's work. If it is our privilege to be continually praising and blessing God, it is also our privilege to be doing good to man. "But to do good and to communicate forget not; for with such sacrifices God is well pleased." We are passing through a world of misery, of sin and death and sorrow. We are surrounded by broken hearts and crushed spirits, if we would only look them out.

Yes; this is the point; *if we would only look them out.* It is easy for us to close our eyes to such things, to turn away from them, to forget that there are such things always within reach of us. We can sit in our easy chair, and speculate about truth, doctrines, and the letter of Scripture; we can discuss the theories of Christianity, and split hairs about prophecy and dispensational truth, and, all the while, be shamefully failing in the discharge of our grand responsibility as Christians. We are in imminent danger of forgetting that Christianity is a living reality. It is not a set of dogmas, a number of principles strung together on a thread of systematized divinity, which unconverted people can have at their fingers' ends. Neither is it a set of ordinances to be gone through, in dreary formality, by lifeless, heartless professors. No; it is life—life eternal—life implanted by the Holy Ghost, and expressing itself in those two lovely forms on which we have been dwelling, namely, praise to God and doing good to man. Such was the life of Jesus when He trod this earth of ours. He lived in the atmosphere of praise; and He went about doing good.

And He is our life, and He is our model on which the life is to be formed. The Christian should be the living expression of Christ, by the power of the Holy Ghost. It is not a mere question of leading what is called a religious life, which very often resolves itself into a tiresome round of duties which neither yield "praise" to God nor one atom of "good" to man. There must be *life*, or it is all perfectly worthless. "The kingdom of God is not meat or drink; but righteousness and peace and joy in the Holy Ghost. For he that in these things serveth Christ is acceptable to God, and approved of men" (Rom. xiv. 17, 18).

Beloved Christian reader, let us earnestly apply our hearts to the consideration of these great practical truths. Let us seek to be Christians not merely in name but in reality. Let us not be distinguished as the mere vendors of peculiar "*views.*" Oh! how worthless are views! How utterly profitless is discussion! How wearisome are theological hair-splittings! Let us have life, light, and love. These are heavenly, eternal, divine. All else is vanity. How we do long for reality in this world of sham—for deep thinkers and earnest workers in this day of shallow talkers!

NOTE.—The reader will find it profitable to compare Heb. xiii. 13-16 with I Peter ii. 4-9. "Let us go forth therefore unto Him," says Paul. "To whom coming," says Peter. Then we have "The holy priesthood" offering up spiritual sacrifices of praise. And "the royal priesthood" doing good and communicating—"showing forth the virtues of Him who hath called us out of darkness into His marvelous light." The two scriptures give us a magnificent view of fundamental, devotional and practical Christianity.

PART II

We must ask the reader to open his Bible and read Heb. x. 7-24. In it he will find a very deep and marvelous view of the Christian's position and his work. The inspired writer gives us, as it were, three solid pillars on which the grand edifice of Christianity rests. These are, first, *the will of God*; secondly, *the work of Christ;* and, thirdly, *the witness of the Holy Ghost*, in Scripture. If these grand realities be laid hold of in simple faith, the soul *must* have settled peace. We may assert, with all possible confidence, that no power of earth or hell, men or devils, can ever disturb the peace which is founded upon Heb. x. 7-17.

Let us then, in the first place, dwell, for a few moments, on the manner in which the apostle unfolds, in this magnificent passage,

THE WILL OF GOD

In the opening of the chapter, we are instructed as to the utter inadequacy of the sacrifices under the law. They could never make the conscience perfect—they could never accomplish the will of God—never fulfil the gracious desire and purpose of His heart. "The law, having a shadow of good things to come, and not the very image of the things, can never with those sacrifices which they offered year by year continually make the comers thereunto perfect. For then would they not have ceased to be offered? because *the worshipers once purged* should have had *no more conscience of sins.*"

Let the reader carefully note this. "The worshipers once purged should have had no more conscience of sins." He does not say—"No more *consciousness of sins.*" There is an immense difference between these two things; and yet, it is to be feared, they are often confounded. The Christian has, alas, the consciousness of *sin in him*, but he ought to have no conscience of *sins on him*, inasmuch as he is purged once and forever, by the precious blood of Christ.

Some of the Lord's people have a habit of speaking of their continual need of applying to the blood of Christ, which, to say the least of it, is by no means intelligent, or in accordance with the accurate teaching of Holy Scripture. It seems like humility; but, we may rest assured, true humility can only be found in connection with the full, clear, settled apprehension of the truth of God, and as to His gracious will concerning us. If it be His will that we should have "no more conscience of sins," it cannot be true humility, on our part, to go on from day to day, and year to year, with the burden of sins upon us. And, further, if it be true that Christ has borne our sins and put them away forever—if He has offered one perfect sacrifice for sins, ought we not assuredly to know that we are perfectly pardoned and perfectly purged? Is it—can it be, true humility to reduce the blood of Christ to the level of the blood of bulls and of goats? But this is what is virtually done, though, no doubt, unwittingly, by all who speak of applying continually to the blood of Christ. One reason why God found fault with the sacrifices under the law was, as the apostle tells us, "In those sacrifices there is a remembrance again made of sins every year." This, blessed be His name, was not according to His mind. He desired that every trace of guilt and every remembrance of it should be blotted out, once and forever; and hence it cannot be His will that His people should be continually bowed down under the terrible burden of unforgiven sin. It is *contrary* to His will; it is subversive of their peace, and derogatory to the glory of Christ and the efficacy of His one sacrifice.

One grand point of the inspired argument, in Hebrews x., is to show that the continual remembrance of sins and the continual repetition of the sacrifice go together; and therefore, if Christians now are to have the burden of sins constantly on the heart and conscience, it follows that Christ should be offered again and again—which were a blasphemy. His work is done, and hence our burden is gone—gone forever. "It is not possible that the blood of bulls and goats should take away sin. Wherefore, when He cometh into the world, He saith, Sacrifice and offering Thou wouldest not, but a body hast Thou prepared Me. In burnt-offerings and sacrifices for sin Thou hast had no pleasure. Then said I, Lo, I come (in the volume of the book it is written of Me) to do Thy will, O

God. Above, when He said, Sacrifice and offering and burnt-offerings and offerings for sin Thou wouldest not, neither hadst pleasure therein (which are offered by the law) then said He, Lo, I come to do Thy will, O God. He taketh away the first that He may establish the second. By the which will we are sanctified (or set apart) by the offering of the body of Jesus Christ *once*."

Here we are conducted, in the most distinct and forcible manner, to the eternal source of the whole matter, namely, the will of God—the purpose and counsel formed in the divine mind, before the foundation of the world, before any creature was formed, before sin or Satan existed. It was the will of God, from all eternity, that the Son should, in due time, come forth and do a work which was to be the foundation of the divine glory and of all the counsels and purposes of the Trinity.

It would be a very grave error indeed to suppose that redemption was an afterthought with God. He had not, blessed be His holy name, to sit down and plan what He would do, when sin entered. It was all settled beforehand. The enemy, no doubt, imagined that he was gaining a wonderful victory when he meddled with man in the garden of Eden. In point of fact, he was only giving occasion for the display of God's eternal counsels in connection with the work of the Son. There was no basis for those counsels, no sphere for their display in the fields of creation. It was the meddling of Satan—the entrance of sin—the ruin of man, that opened a platform on which a Saviour-God might display the riches of His grace, the glories of His salvation, the attributes of His nature, to all created intelligences.

There is great depth and power in those words of the eternal Son, "In the volume of the book it is written of Me." To what "volume" does He here refer? Is it to Old Testament scripture merely? Surely not; the apostle quotes from the Old Testament, but it is nothing less than the roll of God's eternal counsels in which the "vast plan" was laid, according to which, in the appointed time, the eternal Son was to come forth and appear on the scene, in order to accomplish the divine will, vindicate the divine glory, confound the enemy utterly, put away sin, and save ruined man in a manner which yields a richer harvest of glory to God than ever He could have reaped in the fields of an unfallen creation.

All this gives immense stability to the soul of the believer. Indeed it is utterly impossible for human language to set forth the preciousness and blessedness of this line of truth. It is such rich consolation to every pious soul to know that One has appeared in this world to do the will of God— whatever that will might be. "Lo, I come to do Thy will O God." Such was the one undivided purpose and object of that perfect human heart. He never did His own will in anything. He says, "I came down from heaven, not to do Mine own will, but the will of Him that sent Me." It mattered not to Him what that will might involve to Himself personally. The decree was written down in the eternal volume that He should come and do the divine will; and, all homage to His peerless name! He came and did it perfectly. He could say, "A body hast Thou prepared Me." "Mine ears hast Thou opened." "I clothe the heavens with blackness, and I make sackcloth their covering. The Lord God hath given Me the tongue of the learned, that I should know how to speak a word in season to him that is weary: He wakeneth morning by morning, He wakeneth Mine ear to hear as the learned. The Lord God hath opened Mine ear, and I was not rebellious, neither turned away back. I gave My back to the smiters, and My cheeks to them that plucked off the hair: I hid not My face from shame and spitting" (Isa. l. 3-6).

But this leads us, in the second place, to contemplate

THE WORK OF CHRIST

It was ever the delight of the heart of Jesus to do His Father's will and finish His work. From the manger at Bethlehem to the cross of Calvary, the one grand object that swayed His devoted heart was the accomplishment of the will of God. He perfectly glorified God, in all things. This, blessed be God, perfectly secures our full and everlasting salvation, as the apostle in this passage, so distinctly states. "By the which will we are sanctified, through the offering of the body of Jesus Christ once."

Here our souls may rest, beloved reader, in sweetest peace and unclouded certainty. It was the will of God that we should be set apart to Himself, according to all the love of His heart, and all the claims of His throne; and our Lord Christ, in due time, in pursuance of the everlasting purpose as set forth "in the volume of the book," came forth from the glory which He had with the Father, before all worlds, to do the work which forms the imperishable basis of all the divine counsels and of our eternal salvation.

And—forever be His name adored!—He has finished His work. He has perfectly glorified God in the midst of the scene in which He has been so dishonored. At all cost He has vindicated Him and made good His every claim. He magnified the law and made it honorable. He vanquished every foe, removed every obstacle, swept away every barrier, bore the judgment and wrath of a sin-hating God; destroyed death and him that had the power of it, extracted its sting, and spoiled the grave of its victory. In a word, He gloriously accomplished all that was written in the volume of the book concerning Him; and now we see Him crowned with glory and honor, at the right hand of the Majesty in the heavens. He travelled from the throne to the dust of death, in order to accomplish the will of God, and having done so, He has gone back to the throne, in a new character and on a new footing. His pathway from the throne to the cross was marked by the footprints of divine and everlasting love; and His pathway from the cross back to the throne is sprinkled by His atoning blood. He came from heaven to earth to do the will of God, and, having done it, He returned to heaven again, thus opening up for us "a new and living way" by which we draw nigh to God, in holy boldness and liberty, as purged worshipers.

All is done. Every question is settled. Every barrier is removed. The vail is rent. That mysterious curtain which, for ages and generations, had shut God in from man, and shut man out from God, was rent in twain, from top to bottom, by the precious death of Christ; and now we can look right up into the opened heavens and see on the throne the Man who bore our sins in His own body on the tree. A seated Christ tells out, in the ear of faith, the sweet emancipating tale that all that had to be done is done— done forever—done for God—done for us. Yes; all is settled now, and God can, in perfect righteousness, indulge the love of His heart, in blotting out all our sins and bringing us nigh unto Himself in all the acceptance of the One who sits beside Him on the throne.

And let the reader carefully note the striking and beautiful way in which the apostle contrasts *a seated Christ in heaven with the standing priest on earth.* "Every priest standeth daily ministering, and offering oftentimes the same sacrifices, which can never take away sins. But this Man, after He had offered one sacrifice for sins, forever ([Greek: eis to diênekes]—in perpetuity) sat down on the right hand of God; from henceforth expecting till His enemies be made His footstool. For by one offering He hath perfected forever (in perpetuity) them that are sanctified."

This is exceedingly blessed. The priest, under the Levitical economy, could never sit down, for the obvious reason that his work was never done. There was no seat provided in the temple or in the tabernacle. There is remarkable force and significance in the manner in which the inspired writer puts this. "*Every priest*"—"standeth *daily*"—"offering *oftentimes*"—"*the same sacrifices*"—"which can *never take away sins.*" No human language could possibly set forth, more graphically, the utter inefficacy of the Levitical ceremonial. How strange that, in the face of such a passage of Holy Scripture, Christendom should have set up a human priesthood, with its daily sacrifice!—a priesthood moreover, not belonging to the tribe of Levi, not springing from the house of Aaron, and therefore having no sort of divine title or sanction. And, then as to the sacrifice, it is, according to their own admission, a sacrifice without blood, and therefore a sacrifice without remission, for, "Without the shedding of blood there is no remission" (Heb. ix. 22).

Hence, this self-made priesthood is a daring usurpation, and her sacrifices a worthless vanity—a positive lie—a mischievous delusion. The priests of whom the apostle speaks in Heb. x. were priests of the tribe of Levi and of the house of Aaron—the only house, the only tribe ever recognised of God as having any title to assume the office and the work of an earthly priest. And, further, the sacrifices which the Aaronic priests offered were appointed by God, for the time being, to serve as *figures* of Him that was to come; but they never gave Him any pleasure, inasmuch as they could never take away sins; and the true Priest having come, the true sacrifice having been offered, the figures have been forever abolished.

Now, in view of all this, what shall we say of Christendom's priests and Christendom's sacrifices? What will a righteous Judge say to them? We cannot attempt to dwell upon such an awful theme. We can merely say, alas! alas! for the poor souls that are deluded and ruined by such antichristian absurdities. May God in His mercy deliver them and lead them to rest in the one offering of Jesus Christ—that precious blood that cleanses from all sin. May many be led to see that a repeated sacrifice and a seated Christ are in positive antagonism. If the sacrifice must be repeated, Christ has no right to His seat and to His crown—God pardon the very penning of the words! If Christ has a divine right to His seat and to His crown, then to repeat a sacrifice is simply a blasphemy against His cross, His name, His glory. To repeat in any way, or under any form whatsoever, the sacrifice, is to deny the efficacy of Christ's one offering, and to rob the soul of anything like an approach to the knowledge of remission of sins. A repeated sacrifice and perfect remission are an absolute contradiction in terms.

But we must turn, for a moment, to the third grand point in our subject, namely,

THE WITNESS OF THE HOLY GHOST

This is of the deepest possible moment for the reader to understand. It gives great completeness to the subject. How are we to know that Christ has, by His work on the cross, absolutely and divinely accomplished the will of God? Simply by the witness of the Holy Ghost in Scripture. This is the third pillar on which the Christian's position rests, and it is as thoroughly divine and, therefore, as thoroughly independent of man as the other two. It is very evident that man had nothing to do with the eternal counsels of the Trinity—nothing to do with the glorious work accomplished on the cross. All this is clear; and it is equally clear that man has nothing to do with the authority on which our souls receive the joyful news as to the *will of God*, and *the work of Christ*, inasmuch as it is nothing less than *the witness of the Holy Ghost.*

We cannot be too simple as to this. It is not, by any means, a question of our feelings, our frames, our evidences, or our experiences—things interesting in their right place. We must receive the truth solely and simply on the authority of that august Witness who speaks to us in Holy Scripture. Thus we read, "Whereof the Holy Ghost also is a witness to us; for after that He had said before, This is the covenant that I will make with them after those days, saith the Lord; I will put My laws into their hearts, and in their minds will I write them; and their sins and iniquities will I remember no more."

Here, then, we have fully before us the solid foundation of the Christian's position and the Christian's peace. It is all of God, from first to last. The *will*, the *work*, and the *witness* are all divine. The Lord be praised for this glorious fact! What should we do, what would become of us, were it otherwise? In this day of confusion, when souls are tossed about by every wind of doctrine—when the beloved sheep of Christ are driven hither and thither, in bewilderment and perplexity—when ritualism with its ignorant absurdities, and rationalism with its impudent blasphemies, and spiritualism with its horrible traffic with demons, are threatening the very foundations of our faith, how important it is for Christians to know what those foundations really are, and that they should be consciously resting thereon!

PART III

We would recall for a moment to the reader's attention the third point in our subject, namely, "The witness of the Holy Ghost in Scripture." We feel it to be of too much importance to be dismissed with such a cursory glance as we were able to give it at the close of our last paper.

It is absolutely essential to the enjoyment of settled peace that the heart should rest *solely* on the authority of Holy Scripture. Nothing else will stand. Inward evidences, spiritual experiences, comfortable frames, happy feelings, are all very good, very valuable, and very desirable; indeed we cannot prize them too highly in their right place. But, most assuredly, their right place is not at the foundation of the Christian position. If we look to such things as the ground of our peace, we shall very soon become clouded, uncertain, and miserable.

The reader cannot be too simple in his apprehension of this point. He must rest like a little child upon the testimony of the Holy Ghost in the Word. It is blessedly true that "He that believeth hath the witness in himself." And again, "The Spirit itself beareth witness with our spirit that we are the children of God." All this is essential to Christianity; but it must, in no wise, be confounded with the witness of the Holy Ghost, as given to us in Holy Scripture. The Spirit of God never leads any one to build upon His work as the ground of peace, but only upon the finished work of Christ, and the unchangeable word of God; and we may rest assured that the more simply we rest on these the more settled our peace will be, and the clearer our evidences, the brighter our frames, the happier our feelings, the richer our experiences. In short, the more we look away from self and all its belongings, and rest in Christ, on the clear authority of Scripture, the more spiritually minded we shall be; and the inspired apostle tells us that "to be spiritually minded (or, the minding of the Spirit) is life and peace." The best evidence of a spiritual mind is childlike repose in Christ and His Word. The clearest proof of an unspiritual mind is self-occupation. It is a poor affair to be trafficking in *our* evidences, or *our* anything. It looks like piety, but it leads away from Christ—away from Scripture—away from God; and this is not piety, or faith, or Christianity.

We are intensely anxious that the reader should seize, with great distinctness, the importance of committing his whole moral being to the divine authority of the word of God. It will never fail him. All else may go, but "the word of our God shall stand forever." Heart and flesh may fail. Internal evidences may become clouded; frames, feelings, and experiences may all prove unsatisfactory; but the word of the Lord, the testimony of the Holy Ghost, the clear voice of Holy Scripture, must ever remain unshaken. "And this is the Word which by the gospel is preached unto us."

Thus much, then, as to the divine and everlasting basis of the Christian's position, as set forth in the tenth chapter of the Epistle to the Hebrews. Let us, now, see what this same scripture tells us of the Christian's work, and of the sphere in which that work is to be carried on.

The Christian is brought into the immediate presence of God, inside the veil, into the holiest of all. This is his proper place, if indeed we are to listen to the voice of Scripture. "Having therefore, brethren, boldness to enter into the holiest by the blood of Jesus, by a *new* and *living* way which He hath consecrated for us, through the veil, that is to say, His flesh; and having a high-priest over the house of God; *let us draw near* with a true heart, in full assurance of faith, having our hearts sprinkled from an evil conscience, and our bodies washed with pure water."

Our God, blessed be His holy name, would have us near unto Himself. He has made out for us a title clear and indisputable in "*the blood of Jesus.*" Nothing more is needed. That precious blood stands out before the eye of faith in all its infinite value. In it alone we read our title. It is not the blood *and* something else—be that something what it may. The blood constitutes our exclusive title. We come before God in all the perfect efficacy of that blood which rent the veil, glorified God as to the question of sin, canceled our guilt according to all the demands of infinite holiness, silenced, forever, every accuser, every foe. We enter by a new and living way—a way which can never become old or dead. We enter by the direct invitation, yea, by the distinct command of God. It is positive disobedience not to come. We enter to receive the loving welcome of our Father's heart, it is an insult to that love not to come. He tells us to "come boldly"—to "draw near" with full, unclouded confidence—a boldness and confidence commensurate with the love that invites us; the word that commands us, and the blood that fits and entitles us. It is offering dishonor to the eternal Trinity not to draw near.

Reader, is all this, think you, understood and taught in Christendom? Say, do Christendom's creeds, confessions, and liturgical services harmonize with apostolic teaching in Heb. x.? Alas! alas! they do not. Nay, they are in direct antagonism; and the state of souls, accordingly, is the very reverse of what it ought to be. In place of "draw near" it is keep off. In place of liberty and boldness, it is legality and bondage. In place of a heart sprinkled from an evil conscience, it is a heart bowed down beneath the intolerable burden of unforgiven sin. In place of a great High Priest seated on the throne of God, in virtue of accomplished redemption, we have poor mortal—not to say sinful—priests standing from week to week, all the year round in wearisome routine, actually contradicting, in their barren formularies, the very foundation truths of Christianity.

How truly deplorable is all this! And then the sad condition of the Lord's dear people, the lambs and sheep of that precious flock for which He died! It is this that so deeply affects us. It is of little use attacking Christendom. We quite admit this; but we yearn over the souls of God's people. We long to see them fully delivered from false teaching, from Judaism, legalism, and every other *ism* that robs them of a full salvation and a precious Saviour. We long to reach them with the clear and soul-satisfying teachings of Holy Scripture, so that they may know and enjoy the things that are freely given to them of God. We can truly say there is nothing which gives us such painful concern as the state of the Lord's dear people, scattered upon the dark mountains and desolate moors: and one special object for which we desire to live is to be the instrument of leading them into those green pastures and beside those still waters where the true Shepherd and Bishop of their souls longs to feed them, according to all the deep and tender love of His heart. He would have them near Himself, reposing in the light of His blessed countenance. It is not according to His mind or His loving heart that His people should be kept at a dim cold distance from His presence, in doubt and darkness. Ah, no; reader, His word tells us to draw near—to come boldly—to appropriate freely—to make our very own all the precious privileges to which a Father's love invites us, and a Saviour's blood entitles us.

"*Let us draw near.*" This is the voice of God to us. Christ has opened up the way. The veil is rent, our place is in the holiest of all, the conscience sprinkled, the body washed, the soul entering intelligently into the atoning value of the blood, and the cleansing, sanctifying power of the Word—its action upon our habits, our ways, our associations, our entire course and character.

All this is of the very utmost practical value to every true lover of holiness—and every true Christian is a lover of holiness. "The body washed with pure water" is a perfectly delightful thought. It sets forth the purifying action of the word of God on the Christian's entire course and character. We must not be content with having the heart sprinkled by the blood; we must also have the body washed with pure water.

And what then? "*Let us hold fast* the profession of our hope ([Greek: elpidos]) without wavering (for He is faithful that promised)." Blessed parenthesis! We may well hold fast, seeing He is faithful. Our hope can never make ashamed. It rests, in holy calmness, upon the infallible faithfulness of Him who cannot lie, whose word is settled for ever in heaven, far above all the changes and chances of this mortal life, above the din of controversy, the strife of tongues, the impudent assaults of infidelity, the ignorant ravings of superstition—far away above all these things, eternally settled in heaven is that Word which forms the ground of our "hope."

It well becomes us, therefore, to hold fast. We should not have a single wavering thought—a single question—a single misgiving. For a Christian to doubt is to cast dishonor upon the word of a faithful God. Let sceptics, and rationalists, and infidels doubt, for they have nothing to believe, nothing to rest upon, no certainty. But for a child of God to doubt, is to call in question the faithfulness of the divine Promiser. We owe it to His glory, to say nothing of our own peace, to "hold fast the confession of our hope without wavering." Thus may it be with every beloved member of the household of faith, until that longed-for moment "when faith and hope shall cease, and love abide alone."

But there is one more interesting branch of Christian work at which we must glance ere closing this paper. "*Let us consider one another*, to provoke unto love and to good works."

This is in lovely moral keeping with all that has gone before. The grace of God has so richly met all our personal need—setting before us such an array of precious privileges—an opened heaven—a rent veil—a crowned and seated Saviour—a great High Priest—a perfectly purged conscience—boldness to enter—a hearty welcome—a faithful Promiser—a sure and certain hope: having all these marvelous blessings in full possession, what have we got to do? To consider ourselves? Nay verily; this were superfluous and sinfully selfish. We could not possibly do so well for ourselves as God has done for us. He has left nothing unsaid, nothing undone, nothing to be desired. Our cup is full and running over. What remains? Simply to "consider one another;" to go out in the activities of holy love, and serve our brethren in every possible way; to be on the lookout for opportunities of doing good; to be ready for every good work; to seek in a thousand little ways to make hearts glad; to seek to shed a ray of light on the moral gloom around us; to be a stream of refreshing in this sterile and thirsty wilderness.

These are some of the things that make up a Christian's work. May we attend to them! May we be found provoking one another, not to envy and jealousy, but to love and good works; exhorting one another daily; diligently availing ourselves of the public assembly, and so much the more, as we see the day approaching.

May the Holy Spirit engrave upon the heart of both writer and reader these most precious exhortations so thoroughly characteristic of our glorious Christianity—"*Let us draw near*"—"*Let us hold fast*"—"*Let us consider one another!*"

The veil is rent:--our souls draw nearUnto a throne of grace;The merits of the Lord appear,They fill the holy place.

His precious blood has spoken there.Before and on the throne:

And His own wounds in heaven declare,The atoning work is done.

'Tis finished!--here our souls have rest,His work can never fail:By Him, our Sacrifice and Priest,We pass within the veil.

Within the holiest of all,Cleansed by His precious blood,Before the throne we prostrate fallAnd worship Thee, O God!

THE CHRISTIAN PRIESTHOOD

We want the reader to open his Bible and read I Pet. ii. I-9. In this lovely scripture he will find three words on which we will ask him to dwell with us for a little. They are words of weight and power—words which indicate three great branches of practical Christian truth—words conveying to our hearts a fact which we cannot too deeply ponder, namely, that Christianity is a living and divine reality. It is not a set of doctrines, however true; a system of ordinances, however imposing; a number of rules and regulations, however important. Christianity is far more than any or all of these things. It is a living, breathing, speaking, active, powerful reality—something to be seen in the every day life—something to be felt in the scenes of personal, domestic history, from hour to hour—something formative and influential—a divine and heavenly power introduced into the scenes and circumstances through which we have to move, as men, women, and children, from Sunday morning to Saturday night. It does not consist in holding certain views, opinions, and principles, or in going to this place of worship or that.

Christianity is the life of Christ communicated to the believer—dwelling *in* him—and flowing out2 *from* him, in the ten thousand little details which go to make up our daily practical life. It has nothing ascetic, or sanctimonious about it. It is genial, pure, elevated, holy, divine. Such is Christianity. It is Christ dwelling in the believer, and reproduced, by the power of the Holy Ghost, in the believer's daily practical career.

But let us turn to our three words; and may the Eternal Spirit expound their deep and holy meaning to our souls!

And first, then, we have the word "living." "To whom coming, as unto a living Stone, disallowed indeed of men, but chosen of God, and precious, ye also, as living stones, are built up."

Here we have what we may call the foundation of Christian priesthood. There is evidently an allusion here to that profoundly interesting scene in Matt. xvi. to which we must ask the reader to turn for a moment.

"When Jesus was come into the coasts of Cæsarea Philippi, He asked His disciples, saying, Whom do men say that I, the Son of Man, am?[23] And they said, Some say Thou art John the Baptist; some, Elias; and others, Jeremias, or one of the prophets."

There was endless speculation, simply because there was no real heart-work respecting the blessed One. Some said this, some said that; and, in result, no one cared who or what He was; and hence He turns away from all this heartless speculation, and puts the pointed question to His own, "But whom say ye that I am?" He desired to know what they thought about Him—what estimate their hearts had formed of Him. "And Simon Peter answered and said, Thou art the Christ, the Son of the *living* God."

Here we have the true confession. Here lies the solid foundation of the whole edifice of the Church of God and all true practical Christianity— "Christ the Son of the *living* God." No more dim shadows—no more powerless forms—no more lifeless ordinances—all must be permeated by this new, this divine, this heavenly life which has come into this world, and is communicated to all who believe in the name of the Son of God.

"And Jesus answered and said unto him, Blessed art thou, Simon Bar-jona; for flesh and blood hath not revealed it unto thee, but My Father which is in heaven. And I say also unto thee, That thou art Peter; and upon this rock I *will build* My Church; and the gates of hell shall not prevail against it."

Now, it is evidently to this magnificent passage that the apostle Peter refers in the second chapter of his first epistle, when he says, "To whom coming, as unto a *living* stone, disallowed indeed of men, but chosen of God, and precious, ye also, as *living* stones (the same words), are built up," etc. All who believe in Jesus are partakers of His risen, victorious, *rock* life. The life of Christ, the Son of the living God, flows through all His members, and through each in particular. Thus we have the *living* God, the *living* Stone, the *living* stones. It is all life together—life flowing down from a living source, through a living channel, and imparting itself to all believers, thus making them living stones.

Now, this life having been tried and tested, in every possible way, and having come forth victorious, can never again be called to pass through any process of trial, testing, or judgment whatsoever. It has passed through death and judgment. It has gone down under all the waves and billows of divine wrath, and come forth at the other side in resurrection, in divine glory and power—a life victorious, heavenly, and divine, beyond the reach of all the powers of darkness. There is no power of earth or hell, men or devils, that can possibly touch the life which is possessed by the very smallest and most insignificant stone in Christ's assembly. All believers are built upon the living Stone, Christ; and are thus constituted living stones. He makes them like Himself in every respect, save of course, in His incommunicable deity. Is He a living Stone? They are living stones. Is He a precious Stone? They are precious stones. Is He a rejected Stone? They are rejected stones—rejected, disallowed of men. They are, in every respect, identified with Him. Ineffable privilege!

Here, then, we repeat, is the solid foundation of the Christian priesthood—the priesthood of all believers. Before any one can offer up a spiritual sacrifice, he must come to Christ, in simple faith, and be built on Him as the foundation of the whole spiritual building. "Wherefore also it is contained in the Scripture (Isa. xxviii. 16), Behold, I lay in Sion a chief corner-stone, elect, precious; and he that believeth in Him shall not be confounded."

How precious are these words! God Himself has laid the foundation, and that foundation is Christ; and all who simply believe in Christ—all who give Him the confidence of their hearts—all who rest satisfied with Him, are made partakers of His resurrection-life, and thus made living stones.

How blessedly simple is this! We are not asked to assist in laying the foundation. We are not called upon to add the weight of a feather to it. God has laid the foundation, and all we have to do is to believe and rest thereon; and He pledges His faithful word that we shall never be confounded. The very feeblest believer in Jesus has God's own gracious assurance that he shall never be confounded —never be ashamed—never come into judgment. He is as free from all charge of guilt and every breath of condemnation as that living Rock on whom he is built.

Beloved reader, are you on this foundation? Are you built on Christ? Have you come to Him as God's living Stone, and given Him the full confidence of your heart? Are you thoroughly satisfied with God's foundation? or are you seeking to add something of your own—your own works, your prayers, your ordinances, your vows and resolutions, your religious duties? If so, if you are seeking to add the smallest jot to God's foundation, you may rest assured, you will be confounded. God will not suffer such dishonor to be offered to His tried, elect, precious, chief corner Stone. Think you that He could allow aught, no matter what, to be placed beside His beloved Son, in order to form, with Him, the foundation of His spiritual edifice? The bare thought were an impious blasphemy. No; it must be Christ alone. He is enough for God, and He may well be enough for us; and nothing is more certain than that all who reject, or neglect, turn away from, or add to, God's foundation, shall be covered with everlasting confusion.

But, having glanced at the foundation, let us look at the superstructure. This will lead us to the second of our three weighty words. "To whom coming as unto a *living* Stone ... ye also, as living stones, are built up a spiritual house, a *holy* priesthood, to offer up spiritual sacrifices, acceptable to God by Jesus Christ."

All true believers are holy priests. They are made this by spiritual birth, just as Aaron's sons were priests in virtue of their natural birth. The apostle does not say, Ye *ought to be* living stones, and, Ye ought to be holy priests. He says ye *are* such. No doubt, being such, we are called upon to act accordingly; but we must be in a position before we can discharge the duties belonging to it. We must be in a relationship before we can know the affections which flow out of it. We do not become priests by offering priestly sacrifices. But being, through grace, made priests, we are called upon to present the sacrifice. If we were to live a thousand years twice told, and spend all that time working, we could not work ourselves into the position of holy priests; but the moment we believe in Jesus—the moment we come to Him in simple faith—the moment we give Him the full confidence of our hearts, we are born anew into the position of holy priests, and are then privileged to draw nigh and offer the priestly sacrifice. How could any one, of old, have constituted himself a son of Aaron? Impossible. But being born of Aaron, he was thereby made a member of the priestly house. We speak not now of capacity, but simply of the position. This latter was reached not by effort, but by birth.

And now, let us enquire as to the nature of the sacrifice which, as holy priests, we are privileged to offer. We are "to offer up spiritual sacrifices, acceptable to God by Jesus Christ." So also in Heb. xiii. 15, we read, "By Him therefore let us offer the sacrifice of praise to God continually, that is, the fruit of our lips giving thanks to His name."

Here, then, we have the true nature and character of that sacrifice which, as holy priests, we are to offer. It is praise—"praise to God continually." Blessed occupation! Hallowed exercise! Heavenly employment! And this is not to be an occasional thing. It is not merely at some peculiarly favored moment, when all looks bright and smiling around us. It is not to be merely amid the glow and fervor of some specially powerful public meeting, when the current of worship flows deep, wide, and rapid. No; the word is, "praise *continually.*" There is no room, no time for complaining or murmuring, fretfulness and discontent, impatience and irritability, lamenting about our surroundings, whatever these may be, complaining about the weather, finding fault with those who are associated with us, whether in public or in private, whether in the congregation, in the business, or in the family circle.

Holy priests should have no time for any of these things. They are brought nigh to God, in holy liberty, peace, and blessing. They breathe the atmosphere and walk in the sunlight of the divine presence, in the new creation, where there are no materials for a sour and discontented mind to feed upon. We may set it down as a fixed principle—an axiom—that whenever we hear anyone pouring out a string of complaints about circumstances, his neighbors etc., such an one is not realizing the place of holy priesthood, and, as a consequence, not exhibiting its practical fruits. A holy priest should "rejoice in the Lord always"—ever ready to praise God.

True, he may be tried in a thousand ways; but he brings his trials to God in communion, not to his fellow-man in complaining. "Hallelujah" is the proper utterance of the very feeblest member of the Christian priesthood.

But we must now look, for a moment, at the third and last branch of our present theme. This is presented in that highly expressive word "royal." The apostle goes on to say, "But ye are a chosen generation, a *royal* priesthood ... that ye should show forth the virtues (see margin) of Him who hath called you out of darkness into His marvelous light."

This completes the lovely picture of the Christian priesthood.[24] As *holy* priests, we draw nigh to God, and present the sacrifice of praise. As royal priests we go forth among our fellow-men, in all the details of practical daily life, to show forth the virtues—the graces—the lovely moral features of Christ. Every movement of a royal priest should emit the fragrance of the grace of Christ.

Mark again, the apostle does not say, *Ye ought to be* royal priests. He says ye *are*; and as such we are to show forth the virtues of Christ. Nothing else becomes a member of the royal priesthood. To be occupied with myself, to be taking counsel for my own ease, my own interest, my own enjoyment, to be seeking my own ends, and caring about my own things, is not the act of a royal priest at all. Christ never did so; and I am told to show forth His virtues. He, blessed be His name, grants to His people, in this the time of His absence, to anticipate the day when He shall come forth as a Royal Priest, and sit upon His throne, and send forth the benign influence of His dominion to the ends of the earth. We are called to be the present expression of the kingdom of Christ—the expression of Himself.

And let none suppose that the actings of a royal priest are to be confined to the matter of *giving*. This would be a grave mistake. No doubt, a royal priest will give, and give liberally if he has it; but to limit him to the mere matter of communicating would be to rob him of some of the most precious functions of his position. The very man who penned the words on which we are dwelling said on one occasion—and said it without shame, "Silver and gold have I none;" and yet at that very moment, he was acting as a royal priest, by bringing the precious virtue of the name of Jesus to bear on the impotent man (Acts. iii.). The blessed Master Himself, we know, possessed no money; but He went about doing good; and so should we: nor do we need money to do it. Indeed it very often happens that we do mischief instead of good with our silver and gold. We may take people off the ground on which God has placed them, namely, the ground of honest industry, and make them dependent upon human alms. Moreover, we may often make hypocrites and sycophants of people by our injudicious use of money.

Hence, therefore, let no one imagine that he cannot act as a royal priest without earthly riches. What riches are required to speak a kindly word—to drop the tear of sympathy—to give the soothing, genial look? None whatever save the riches of God's grace—the unsearchable riches of Christ, all of which are laid open to the most obscure member of the Christian priesthood. I may be poorly clad, without a penny in the world, and yet carry myself truly as a royal priest, by diffusing around me the fragrance of the grace of Christ.

But, perhaps, we cannot more suitably close these few remarks on the Christian priesthood, than by giving a very vivid illustration drawn from the inspired page—the narrative of two beloved servants of Christ who were enabled, under the most distressing circumstances, to acquit themselves as holy and royal priests.

Turn to Acts xvi. 19-34. Here we have Paul and Silas thrust into the innermost part of the prison at Philippi, their backs covered with stripes, and their feet fast in the stocks, in the darkness of the midnight hour. What were they doing? murmuring and complaining? Ah, no! They had something better and brighter to do. Here were two really "living stones," and nothing that earth or hell could do could hinder the life that was in them expressing itself in its proper accents.

But what, we repeat, were these living stones doing? these partakers of the rock-life—the victorious, resurrection-life of Christ—how did they employ themselves? Well, then, in the first place, as *holy* priests they offered the sacrifice of praise to God. Yes, "at midnight, Paul and Silas prayed and sang praises to God." How precious is this! How morally glorious! How truly refreshing! What are stripes, or stocks, or prison walls, or gloomy nights, to living stones and holy priests? Nothing more than a dark background to throw out into bright and beauteous relief the living grace that is in them. Talk of circumstances! Ah, it is little any of us know of trying circumstances. Poor things that we are, the petty annoyances of daily life are often more than enough to cause us to lose our mental balance. Paul and Silas were really in trying circumstances; but they were there as living stones and holy priests.

Yes, reader, and they were there as royal priests, likewise. How does this appear? Certainly not by scattering silver and gold. It is not likely the dear men had much of these to scatter. But oh, they had what was better, even "the virtues of Him who had called them out of darkness into His marvelous light." And where do these virtues shine out? In those touching words addressed to the jailer, "*Do thyself no harm.*" These were the accents of a *royal* priest, just as the song of praise was the voice of a *holy* priest. Thank God for both! The voices of the holy priests went directly up to the throne of God and did their work there; and the words of the royal priests went directly to the jailer's hard heart and did their work there. God was glorified and the jailer saved by two men rightly discharging the functions of "*the Christian priesthood.*"

FATHER! Thy sovereign love has soughtCaptives to sin, gone far from Thee:The work that Thine own Son hath wrought,Has brought us back, in peace, and free!

And now, as sons before Thy Face,With joyful steps the path we tread,Which leads us on to that blest placePrepared for us, by Christ our Head.

Thou gav'st us, in eternal love,To Him, to bring us home to Thee;Suited to Thine own thoughts aboveAs sons, like Him, with Him to be.

Oh, boundless grace! What fills with joyUnmingled all that enter there;God's Nature, Love without alloy,Our hearts are given e'en now to share!

Oh, keep us, Love Divine, near Thee!That we our nothingness may know;And ever to Thy glory be,Walking in faith while here below.

J. N. D.

PAPERS ON EVANGELIZATION

CHAPTER I
A WORD TO THE EVANGELIST

We trust it may not be deemed out of place if we venture to offer a word of counsel and encouragement to all who have been and are engaged in the blessed work of preaching *the gospel of the grace of God.* We are, in some measure, aware of the difficulties and discouragements which attend upon the path of every evangelist,. whatever may be his sphere of labor or measure of gift; and it is our heart's desire to hold up the hands and cheer the hearts of all who may be in danger of falling under the depressing power of these things. We increasingly feel the immense importance of an earnest, fervent gospel testimony everywhere; and we dread exceedingly any falling off therein. We are imperatively called to "do the work of an evangelist," and not to be moved from that work by any arguments or considerations whatsoever.

Let none imagine that, in writing thus, we mean to detract, in the smallest degree, from the value of teaching, lecturing, or exhortation. Nothing is further from our thoughts. "These things ought ye to have done, and not to leave the other undone." We mean not to compare the work of the evangelist with that of the teacher, or to exalt the former at the expense of the latter. Each has its own proper place, its own distinctive interest and importance.

But is there not a danger, on the other hand, of the evangelist abandoning his own precious work in order to give himself to the work of teaching and lecturing? Is there not a danger of the evangelist becoming merged in the teacher? We fear there is; and it is under the influence of this very fear that we pen these few lines. We observe, with deep concern, some who were once known amongst us as earnest and eminently successful evangelists, now almost wholly abandoning their work and becoming teachers and lecturers.

This is most deplorable. *We really want evangelists.* A true evangelist is almost as great a rarity as a true pastor. Alas! alas! how rare are both! The two are closely connected. The evangelist gathers the sheep; the pastor feeds and cares for them. The work of each lies very near the heart of Christ—the Divine Evangelist and Pastor; but it is with the former we have now more immediately to do—to encourage him in his work, and to warn him against the temptation to turn aside from it. We cannot afford to lose a single ambassador just now, or to have a single preacher silent. We are perfectly aware of the fact that there is in some quarters a strong tendency to throw cold water upon the work of evangelization. There is a sad lack of sympathy with the preacher of the gospel; and, as a necessary consequence, of active co-operation with him in his work. Further, there is a mode of speaking of gospel preaching which argues but little sympathy with the heart of Him who wept over impenitent sinners, and who could say, at the very opening of His blessed ministry, "The Spirit of the Lord is upon Me, because He hath anointed Me *to preach the gospel to the poor*" (Isa. lxi.; Luke iv.). And again, "Let us go into the next towns, that I may preach there also: for therefore came I forth" (Mark i. 38).

Our blessed Lord was an indefatigable preacher of the gospel, and all who are filled with His mind and spirit will take a lively interest in the work of all those who are seeking in their feeble measure to do the same. This interest will be evinced, not only by earnest prayer for the divine blessing upon the work, but also by diligent and persevering efforts to get immortal souls under the sound of the gospel.

This is the way to help the evangelist, and this way lies open to every member of the Church of God—man, woman, or child. All can thus help forward the glorious work of evangelization. If each member of the assembly were to work diligently and prayerfully in this way, how different would it be with the Lord's dear servants who are seeking to make known the unsearchable riches of Christ.

But, alas! how often is it otherwise. How often do we hear even those who are of some repute for intelligence and spirituality, when referring to meetings for gospel testimony, say, "Oh, I am not going there; it is *only* the gospel." Think of that! "*Only the gospel.*" If they would put the idea into other words, they might say, "It is *only* the heart of God—*only* the precious blood of Christ—*only* the glorious record of the Holy Ghost."

This would be putting the thing plainly. Nothing is more sad than to hear professing Christians speak in this way. It proves too clearly that their souls are very far away from the heart of Jesus. We have invariably found that those who think and speak slightingly of the work of the evangelist are persons of very little spirituality; and on the other hand, the most devoted, the most true hearted, the best taught saints of God, are always sure to take a profound interest in that work. How could it be otherwise? Does not the voice of Holy Scripture bear the clearest testimony to the fact of the interest of the Trinity in the work of the gospel? Most assuredly it does. Who first preached the gospel? Who was the first herald of salvation? Who first announced the good news of the bruised Seed of the woman? The Lord God Himself, in the garden of Eden. This is a telling fact in connection with our theme. And further, let us ask, who was the most earnest, laborious, and faithful preacher that ever trod this earth? The Son of God. And who has been preaching the gospel for the last eighteen centuries? The Holy Ghost sent down from heaven.

Thus then we have the Father, the Son, and the Holy Ghost all actually engaged in the work of evangelization; and if this be so, who are we to dare to speak slightingly of such a work? Nay, rather may our whole moral being be stirred by the power of the Spirit of God so that we may be able to add our fervent and deep Amen to those precious words of inspiration, "How beautiful are the feet of them that preach the gospel of peace, and bring glad tidings of good things!" (Isa. lii. 7; Rom. x. 15.)

But it may be that these lines shall be scanned by some one who has been engaged in the work of preaching the gospel, and is beginning to feel rather discouraged. It may be that he has been called to preach in the same place for years, and he feels burdened by the thought of having to address the same audience, on the same subject, week after week, month after month, year after year. He may feel at a loss for something new, something fresh, some variety. He may sigh for some new sphere, where the subjects which are familiar to him will be new to the people. Or, if this cannot be, he may feel led to substitute lectures and expositions for the fervid, pointed, earnest preaching of the gospel.

If we have in any measure set forth the reader's feelings on this subject, we think it will greatly help him in his work to bear in mind that the one grand theme of the true evangelist is Christ. The power to handle that theme is the Holy Ghost. The one to whom that theme is to be unfolded is the poor lost sinner. Now, Christ is ever new; the power of the Holy Ghost is ever fresh; the soul's condition and destiny ever intensely interesting. Furthermore, it is well for the evangelist to bear in mind, on every fresh occasion of rising to preach, that his unconverted hearers are totally ignorant of the gospel, and hence he should preach as though it were the first time they had ever heard the message, and the first time he had ever delivered it. For, be it remembered, the preaching of the gospel, in the divine acceptation of the phrase, is not a mere barren statement of evangelical doctrine—a certain form of words enunciated over and over again in wearisome routine. Far, very far from it. The gospel is really the large loving heart of God welling up and flowing forth toward the poor lost sinner in streams of life and salvation. It is the presentation of the atoning death and glorious resurrection of the Son of God; and all this in the present energy, glow, and freshness of the Holy Ghost, from the exhaustless mine of Holy Scripture. Moreover, *the* one absorbing object of the preacher is to win souls for Christ, to the glory of God. For this he labors and pleads; for this he prays, weeps, and agonizes; for this he thunders, appeals, and grapples with the heart and conscience of his hearer. His object is not to teach doctrines, though doctrines may be taught; his object is not to expound Scripture, though Scripture may be expounded. These things lie within the range of the teacher or lecturer; but let it never be forgotten, the preacher's object is to bring the Saviour and the sinner together—to win souls to Christ. May God by His Spirit keep these things ever before our hearts, so that we may have a deeper interest in the glorious work of evangelization!

We would, in conclusion, merely add a word of exhortation in reference to the Lord's Day evening. We would, in all affection, say to our beloved and honored fellow-laborers, Seek to give that one hour to the great business of the soul's salvation. There are 168 hours in the week, and, surely, it is the least we may devote *one* of these to this momentous work. It so happens that during that interesting hour we can get the ear of our fellow-sinner. Oh, let us use it to pour in the sweet story of God's free love and of Christ's full salvation.

CHAPTER II
A MOTTO FOR THE EVANGELIST

(2 Cor. x. 16.)

"To *preach the gospel in the regions beyond you.*" These words, while they set forth the large-heartedness of the self-denying and devoted apostle, do also furnish a fine model for the evangelist, in every age. The gospel is a traveler; and the preacher of the gospel must be a traveler likewise. The divinely-qualified and divinely-sent evangelist will fix his eye upon "*the world.*" He will embrace, in his benevolent design, the human family. From house to house; from street to street; from city to city; from province to province; from kingdom to kingdom; from continent to continent; from pole to pole. Such is the range of the "good news" and the publisher thereof. "The regions beyond" must ever be the grand gospel motto. No sooner has the gospel lamp cast its cheering beams over a district, than the bearer of that lamp must think of the regions beyond. Thus the work goes on. Thus the mighty tide of grace rolls, in enlightening and saving power, over a dark world which lies in "the region of the shadow of death."

"Waft, waft, ye winds, the story,And you, ye waters, roll,Till, like the sea of glory,It spreads from pole to pole."

Christian reader, are you thinking of "the regions beyond you?" This expression may, in your case, mean the next house, the next street, the next village, the next city, the next kingdom, or the next continent. The application is for your own heart to ponder: but say, are you thinking of "the regions beyond you?" I do not want you to abandon your present post at all; or, at least, not until you are fully persuaded that your work, at the post, is done. But, remember, the gospel plough should never stand still. "*Onward*" is the motto of every true evangelist. Let the shepherds abide by the flocks; but let the evangelists betake themselves hither and thither, to gather the sheep. Let them sound the gospel trump, far and wide, o'er the dark mountains of this world, to gather together the elect of God. This is the design of the gospel. This should be the object of the evangelist, as he sighs after "the regions beyond." When Cæsar beheld, from the coast of Gaul, the white cliffs of Britain, he earnestly longed to carry his arms thither. The evangelist, on the other hand, whose heart beats in unison with the heart of Jesus, as he casts his eye over the map of the world, longs to carry the gospel of peace into regions which have heretofore been wrapped in midnight gloom, covered with the dark mantle of superstition, or blasted beneath the withering influences of "a form of godliness without the power."

It would, I believe, be a profitable question for many of us to put to ourselves, how far are we discharging our holy responsibilities to "the regions beyond." I believe the Christian who is not cultivating and manifesting an evangelistic spirit, is in a truly deplorable condition. I believe, too, that the assembly which is not cultivating and manifesting an evangelistic spirit is in a dead state. One of the truest marks of spiritual growth and prosperity, whether in an individual or in an assembly, is earnest anxiety after the conversion of souls. This anxiety will swell the bosom with most generous emotions; yea, it will break forth in copious streams of benevolent exertion, ever flowing toward "the regions beyond." It is hard to believe that "the word of Christ" is "dwelling richly" in any one who is not making some effort to impart that word to his fellow-sinners. It matters not what may be the amount of the effort; it may be to drop a few words in the ear of a friend, to give a tract, to pen a note, to breathe a prayer. But one thing is certain, namely, that a healthy, vigorous Christian will be an evangelistic Christian—a teller of good news—one whose sympathies, desires, and energies, are ever going forth toward "the regions beyond." "I must preach the gospel to other cities also, for therefore am I sent." Such was the language of the true Evangelist.

It is very doubtful whether many of the servants of Christ have not erred in allowing themselves, through one influence or another, to become too much localized—too much tied in one place. They have dropped into routine work—into a round of stated preaching in the same place, and, in many cases, have paralyzed themselves and paralyzed their hearers also. I speak not, now, of the labors of the pastor, the elder, or the teacher, which must, of course, be carried on in the midst of those who are the proper subjects of such labors. I refer more particularly to the evangelist. Such an one should never suffer himself to be localized. The world is his sphere—"the regions beyond," his motto—to gather out God's elect, his object—the current of the Spirit, his line of direction. If the reader should be one whom God has called and fitted to be an evangelist, let him remember these four things—the sphere, the motto, the object, and the line of direction, which all must adopt if they would prove fruitful laborers in the gospel field.

Finally, whether the reader be an evangelist or not, I would earnestly intreat him to examine how far he is seeking to further the gospel of Christ. We must not stand idle. Time is short! Eternity is rapidly posting on! The Master is most worthy! Souls are most precious! The season for work will soon close! Let us, then, in the name of the Lord, be up and doing. And when we have done what we can, in the regions around, let us carry the precious seed into "THE REGIONS BEYOND."

CHAPTER III
THE WORK OF AN EVANGELIST

(Acts xvi. 8-31.)

We ventured to offer a word to the evangelist, which we now follow up with a paper on the evangelist's work; and we cannot do better than select, as the basis of our remarks, a page from the missionary record of one of the greatest evangelists that ever lived. The passage of Scripture that stands at the head of this article furnishes specimens of three distinct classes of hearers, and also the method in which they were met by the great apostle of the Gentiles, guided, most surely, by the Holy Ghost. We have, first, *the earnest seeker*; secondly, *the false professor*; and thirdly, *the hardened sinner*. These three classes are to be met everywhere, and at all times, by the Lord's workman; and hence we may be thankful for an inspired account of the right mode of dealing with such. It is most desirable that those who go forth with the gospel should have skill in dealing with the various conditions of soul that come before them, from day to day; and there can be no more effectual way of attaining this skill than the careful study of the models given us by God the Holy Ghost.

Let us then, in the first place, look at the narrative of

THE EARNEST SEEKER

The laborious apostle, in the course of his missionary journeyings, came to Troas, and there a vision appeared to him in the night, "There stood a man of Macedonia, and prayed him, saying, Come over into Macedonia and help us. And after he had seen the vision, immediately we endeavored to go into Macedonia, assuredly gathering that the Lord had called us for to preach the gospel unto them. Therefore loosing from Troas, we came with a straight course to Samothracia, and the next day to Neapolis; and from thence to Philippi, which is the chief city of that part of Macedonia, and a colony: and we were in that city abiding certain days. And on the Sabbath we went out of the city by a river side, where prayer was wont to be made; and we sat down, and spake unto the women which resorted thither. And a certain woman named Lydia, a seller of purple, of the city of Thyatira, which worshiped God, heard us; whose heart the Lord opened, that she attended unto the things that were spoken of Paul. And when she was baptized, and her household, she besought us, saying, If ye have judged me to be faithful to the Lord, come into my house and abide there. And she constrained us" (Acts xvi. 8-15).

Here, then, we have a touching picture—something well worth gazing at and pondering. It is a picture of one who, having through grace gotten a measure of light, was living up to it, and was earnestly seeking for more. Lydia, the seller of purple, belonged to the same interesting generation as the eunuch of Ethiopia, and the centurion of

Cæsarea. All three appear on the page of inspiration as quickened souls not emancipated—not at rest—not satisfied. The eunuch had gone from Ethiopia to Jerusalem in search of something on which to rest his anxious soul. He had left that city still unsatisfied, and was devoutly and earnestly hanging over the precious page of inspiration. The eye of God was upon him, and He sent His servant Philip with the very message that was needed to solve his difficulties, answer his questions, and set his soul at rest. God knows how to bring the Philips and the eunuchs together. He knows how to prepare the heart for the message and the message for the heart. The eunuch was a worshiper of God; but Philip is sent to teach him how to see God in the face of Jesus Christ. This was precisely what he wanted. It was a flood of fresh light breaking in upon his earnest spirit, setting his heart and conscience at rest, and sending him on his way rejoicing. He had honestly followed the light as it broke in upon his soul, and God sent him more.

Thus it is ever. "To him that hath shall more be given." There never was a soul who sincerely acted up to his light that did not get more light. This is most consolatory and encouraging to all anxious enquirers. If the reader belongs to this class, let him take courage. If he is one of those with whom God has begun to work, then let him rest assured of this, that He who hath begun a good work will perform the same until the day of Jesus Christ. He will, most surely, perfect that which concerneth His people.

But let no one fold his arms, settle upon his oars, and coolly say, "I must wait God's time for more light. I can do nothing—my efforts are useless. When God's time comes I shall be all right; till then, I must remain as I am." These were not the thoughts or feelings of the Ethiopian eunuch. He was one of the earnest seekers; and all earnest seekers are sure to be happy finders. It must be so, for "God is a rewarder of them that diligently seek Him" (Heb. xi. 6).

So also with the centurion of Cæsarea. He was a man of the same stamp. He lived up to his light. He fasted, he prayed, and gave alms. We are not told whether he had read the sermon on the mount: but it is remarkable that he exercised himself in the three grand branches of practical righteousness set forth by our Lord in the sixth chapter of Matthew.[25] He was moulding his conduct and shaping his way according to the standard which God had set before him. His righteousness exceeded the righteousness of the scribes and Pharisees, and therefore he entered the kingdom. He was, through grace, a real man, earnestly following the light as it streamed in upon his soul, and he was led into the full blaze of the gospel of the grace of God. God sent a Peter to Cornelius, as he had sent a Philip to the eunuch. The prayers and alms had gone up as a memorial before God, and Peter was sent with a message of full salvation through a crucified and risen Saviour.

Now it is quite possible that there are persons who, having been rocked in the cradle of easy-going evangelical profession, and trained up in the flippant formalism of a self-indulgent, heaven-made-easy religion, are ready to condemn the pious conduct of Cornelius, and pronounce it the fruit of ignorance and legality. Such persons have never known what it was to deny themselves a single meal, or to spend an hour in real, earnest prayer, or to open their hand, in true benevolence, to meet the wants of the poor. They have heard and learnt, perchance, that salvation is not to be gained by such means—that we are justified by faith without works—that it is to him that worketh not, but believeth on Him that justifieth the ungodly.

All this is most true; but what right have we to imagine that Cornelius was praying, fasting, and giving alms in order to earn salvation? None whatever—at least if we are to be governed by the inspired narrative, and we have no other means of knowing aught about this truly excellent and interesting character. He was informed by the angel that his prayers and his alms had gone up as a memorial before God. Is not this a clear proof that these prayers and alms were not the trappings of self-righteousness, but the fruits of a righteousness based on the knowledge which he had of God? Surely the fruits of self-righteousness and legality could never have ascended as a memorial to the throne of God; nor could Peter ever have said concerning a mere legalist that he was one who feared God and worked righteousness.

Ah, no, reader; Cornelius was a man thoroughly in earnest. He lived up to what he knew, and he would have been quite wrong to go further. To him the salvation of his immortal soul, the service of God, and eternity, were grand and all-absorbing realities. He was none of your easy-going professors, full of flippant, vapid, worthless talk, but *doing* nothing. He belonged to another generation altogether. He belonged to the *working*, not the *talking* class. He was one on whom the eye of God rested with complacency, and in whom the mind of heaven was profoundly interested.

And so was our friend of Thyatira, Lydia, the seller of purple. She belonged to the same school—she occupied the same platform as the centurion and the eunuch. It is truly delightful to contemplate these three precious souls—to think of one in Ethiopia; another at Cæsarea; and a third at Thyatira or Philippi. It is particularly refreshing to contrast such downright thorough-going, earnest souls, with many in this our day of boasted light and knowledge, who have got the plan of salvation, as it is termed, in their heads, the doctrines of grace on the tongue, but the world in the heart; whose absorbing object is self, self, self,—miserable object!

We shall have occasion to refer more fully to these latter under our second head; but, for the present, we shall think of the earnest Lydia; and we must confess it is a far more grateful exercise. It is very plain that Lydia, like Cornelius and the eunuch, was a quickened soul; she was a worshiper of God; she was one who was right glad to lay aside her purple-selling, and betake herself to a prayer-meeting, or to any such like place where spiritual profit was to be had, and where there were good things going. "Birds of a feather flock together," and so Lydia soon found out where a few pious souls, a few kindred spirits, were in the habit of meeting to wait on God in prayer.

All this is lovely. It does the heart good to be brought in contact with this deep-toned earnestness. Surely the Holy Ghost has penned this narrative, like all Holy Scripture, for our learning. It is a specimen case, and we do well to ponder it. Lydia was found diligently availing herself of any and every opportunity; indeed she exhibited the real fruits of divine life, the genuine instincts of the new nature. She found out where saints met for prayer, and took her place among them. She did not fold her arms and settle down on her lees, to wait, in antinomian indolence and culpable idleness, for some extraordinary undefinable thing to come upon her, or some mysterious change to come over her. No; she went to a prayer-meeting—the place of expressed need—the place of expected blessing: and there God met her, as He is sure to meet all who frequent such scenes in Lydia's spirit. God never fails an expectant heart. He has said, "They shall not be ashamed that wait for Me;" and, like a bright and blessed sunbeam on the page of inspiration, shines that pregnant, weighty, soul-stirring sentence, "God is a rewarder of them that DILIGENTLY seek Him." He sent a Philip to the eunuch in the desert of Gaza. He sent a Peter to the centurion, in the town of Cæsarea. He sent a Paul to a seller of purple, in the suburbs of Philippi; and He will send a message to the reader of these lines, if he be a really earnest seeker after God's salvation.

It is ever a moment of deepest interest when a prepared soul is brought in contact with the full gospel of the grace of God. It may be that that soul has been under deep and painful exercise for many a long day, seeking rest but finding none. The Lord has been working by His Spirit, and preparing the ground for the good seed. He has been making deep the furrows so that the precious seed of His Word may take permanent root, and bring forth fruit to His praise. The Holy Ghost is never in haste. His work is deep, sure and solid. His plants are not like Jonah's gourd, springing up in a night and perishing in a night. All that He does will stand, blessed be His name. "I know that whatsoever God doeth, it shall be forever." When He convicts, converts, and liberates a soul, the stamp of His own eternal hand is upon the work, in all its stages.

Now, it must have been a moment of intense interest when one in Lydia's state of soul was brought in contact with that most glorious gospel which Paul carried (Acts xvi. 14). She was thoroughly prepared for his message; and surely his message was thoroughly prepared for her. He carried with him truth which she had never heard and never thought of. As we have already remarked, she had been living up to her light; she was a worshiper of God; but we are bold to assert that she had no idea of the glorious truth which was lodged in the heart of that stranger who sat beside her at the prayer-meeting. She had come thither—devout and earnest woman that she was—to pray and to worship, to get some little refreshment for her spirit, after the toils of the week. How little did she imagine that at that meeting she should hear the greatest preacher that ever lived, save One, and that she should hear the very highest order of truth that had ever fallen upon mortal ears.

Yet thus it was. And, oh, how important it was for Lydia to have been at that memorable prayer meeting! How well it was she had not acted as so many, now-a-days, act, who after a week of toil in the shop, the warehouse, the factory, or the field, take the opportunity of lying in bed on Sunday!

How many there are whom you will see at their post from Monday morning till Saturday night, working away with all diligence at their calling, but for whom you will look in vain at the meeting on the Lord's day. How is this? They will tell you, perhaps, that they are so worn out on Saturday night that they have no energy to rise on Sunday, and therefore they spend this day in sloth, lounging, and self-indulgence. They have no care for their souls, no care for eternity, no care for Christ. They care for themselves, for their families, for the world, for money-making; and hence you will find them up with the dawn of Monday and off to their work.

Lydia did not belong to this class at all. No doubt she attended to her business, as every right-minded person will. We dare say—indeed, we are sure—she kept very excellent purple, and was a fair, honest trader, in every sense of the word. But she did not spend her Sabbath in bed, or lounging about her house, or nursing herself up, and making a great fuss about all she had to do during the week. Neither do we believe that Lydia was one of those self-occupied folk whom a shower of rain is sufficient to keep away from a meeting. No; Lydia was of a different stamp altogether. She was an earnest woman, who felt she had a soul to save, and an eternity before her, and a living God to serve and worship.

Would to God we had more Lydias in this our day! It would give a charm, and an interest, and a freshness to the work of an evangelist, for which many of the Lord's workmen have to sigh in vain. We seem to live in a day of terrible unreality as to divine and eternal things. Men, women, and children are real enough at their money-making, their pursuits, and their pleasures; but oh, when the things of God, the things of the soul, the things of eternity, are in question, the aspect of people is that of a yawning indifference. But the moment is rapidly approaching—every beat of the pulse, every tick of the watch, brings us nearer to it—when the yawning indifference shall be exchanged for "weeping, wailing, and gnashing of teeth." If this were more deeply felt, we should have many more Lydias, prepared to lend an attentive ear to Paul's gospel.

What force and beauty in those words, "Whose heart the Lord opened, that *she attended* unto the things that were spoken of Paul." Lydia was not one of those who go to meetings to think of anything and everything but the things that are spoken by the Lord's messengers. She was not thinking of her purple, or of the prices, or the probable gains or losses. How many of those who fill our preaching rooms and lecture halls follow the example of Lydia? Alas! we fear but very few indeed. The business, the state of the markets, the state of the funds, money, pleasure, dress, folly—a thousand and one things are thought of, and dwelt upon, and attended to, so that the poor vagrant, volatile heart is at the ends of the earth instead of "*attending*" to the things that are spoken.

All this is very solemn, and very awful. It really ought to be looked into and thought of. People seem to forget the responsibility involved in hearing the gospel preached. They do not seem to be in the smallest degree impressed with the weighty fact that the gospel never leaves any unconverted person where it finds him. He is either saved by receiving, or rendered more guilty by rejecting it. Hence it becomes a serious matter to hear the gospel. People may attend gospel meetings as a matter of custom, as a religious service, or because they have nothing else to do, and the time would hang heavy upon their hands; or they may go because they think that the mere act of going has a sort of merit attached to it. Thus thousands attend preachings at which Christ's servants, though not Pauls in gift, power, or intelligence, unfold the precious grace of God in sending His only begotten Son into the world to save us from everlasting torment and misery. The virtue and efficacy of the atoning death of the divine Saviour— the Lamb of God—the dread realities of eternity—the awful horrors of hell, and the unspeakable joys of heaven—all these weighty matters are handled, according to the measure of grace bestowed upon the Lord's messengers, and yet how little impression is produced! They "reason of righteousness, temperance, and judgment to come," and yet how few are made even to "tremble!"

And why? Will anyone presume to excuse himself for rejecting the gospel message on the ground of his inability to believe it? Will he appeal to the very case before us, and say, "The Lord opened her heart; and if He would only do the same for me, I, too, should attend; but until He does, I can do nothing"? We reply, and with deep seriousness, Such an argument will not avail thee in the day of judgment. Indeed we are most thoroughly convinced that thou wilt not dare to use it then. Thou art making a false use of Lydia's charming history. True it is, blessedly true, the Lord opened her heart; and He is ready to open thine also, if there were in thee but the hundredth part of Lydia's earnestness.

And dost thou not know full well, reader, that there are two sides to this great question, as there are to every question? It is all very well, and sounds very forcibly, for thee to say, "I can do nothing." But who told thee this? Where hast thou learnt it? We solemnly challenge thee, in the presence of God, Canst thou look up to Him and say, "I can do nothing—I am not responsible?" Say, is the salvation of thy never-dying soul just *the* one thing in which thou canst do nothing? Thou canst do a lot of things in the service of the world, of self, and of Satan; but when it becomes a question of God, the soul, and eternity, you coolly say, "I can do nothing—I am not responsible."

Ah! it will never do. All this style of argument is the fruit of a one-sided theology. It is the result of the most pernicious reasoning of the human mind upon certain truths in Scripture which are turned the wrong way and sadly misapplied. But it will not stand. This is what we urge upon the reader. It is of no possible use arguing in this way. The sinner is responsible; and all the theology, and all the reasoning, and all the fallacious though plausible objections that can be scraped together, can never do away with this weighty and most serious fact.

Hence, therefore, we call upon the reader to be, like Lydia, in earnest about his soul's salvation—to let every other question, every other point, every other subject, sink into utter insignificance in comparison with this one momentous question—the salvation of his precious soul. Then, he may depend upon it, the One who sent Philip to the eunuch, and sent Peter to the centurion, and sent Paul to Lydia, will send some messenger and some message to him, and will also open his heart to attend. Of this there cannot possibly be a doubt, inasmuch as Scripture declares that "God is not willing that any should perish, but that all should come to repentance." All who perish, after having heard the message of salvation—the sweet story of God's free love, of a Saviour's death and resurrection—shall perish without a shadow of an excuse, shall descend into hell with their blood upon their guilty heads. Their eyes shall then be open to see through all the flimsy arguments by which they have sought to prop themselves up in a false position, and lull themselves to sleep in sin and worldliness.

But let us dwell for a moment on "the things that were spoken of Paul." The Spirit of God hath not thought proper to give us even a brief outline of Paul's address at the prayer-meeting. We are therefore left to other passages of Holy Scripture to form an idea of what Lydia heard from his lips on that interesting occasion. Let us take, for example, that famous passage in which he reminds the Corinthians of the gospel which he had preached to them. "Moreover, brethren, I declare unto you the gospel which I preached unto you, which also ye have received, and wherein ye stand; by which also ye are saved if ye keep in memory what I preached unto you, unless ye have believed in vain. For I delivered unto you first of all that which I also received, how that Christ died for our sins according to the Scriptures; and that He was buried, and that He rose again the third day according to the Scriptures" (I Cor. xv. I-4).

Now we may safely conclude that the foregoing passage of Scripture contains a compendium of the things that were spoken of Paul at the prayer-meeting at Philippi. The grand theme of Paul's preaching was Christ—Christ for the sinner—Christ for the saint—Christ for the conscience—Christ for the heart. He never allowed himself to wander from this great centre, but made all his preachings and all his teachings circulate round it with admirable consistency. If he called on men, both Jews and Gentiles, to repent, the lever with which he worked was Christ. If he urged them to believe, the object which he held up for faith was Christ, on the authority of Holy Scripture. If he reasoned of righteousness, temperance, and judgment to come, the One that gave cogency and moral power to his reasoning was Christ. In short, Christ was the very gist and marrow, the sum and substance, the foundation and top stone of Paul's preaching and teaching.

But, for our present purpose, there are three grand subjects, found in Paul's preaching, to which we desire to call the reader's attention. These are, first, the grace of God; secondly, the Person and work of Christ; and thirdly, the testimony of the Holy Ghost as given in the Holy Scriptures.

We do not attempt to go into these vast subjects here; we merely name them, and entreat the reader to ponder them, to muse over them, and seek to make them his own.

(I) The grace of God—His free, sovereign favor—is the source from whence salvation flows—salvation in all the length, breadth, height, and depth of that most precious word—salvation which stretches, like a golden chain, from the bosom of God, down to the very deepest depths of the sinner's guilty and ruined condition, and back again to the throne of God— meets all the sinner's necessities, overlaps the whole of the saint's history, and glorifies God in the highest possible manner.

(2) Then, in the second place, the Person of Christ and His finished work are the *only* channel through which salvation can possibly flow to the lost and guilty sinner. It is not the Church and her sacraments, religion and its rites and ceremonies—man or his doings in any shape or form. It is the death and resurrection of Christ. "He died for our sins, was buried, and rose again the third day." This was the gospel which Paul preached, by which the Corinthians were saved, and the apostle declares, with solemn emphasis, "If any man preach any other gospel, let him be accursed." Tremendous words for this our day!

(3) But, thirdly, the authority on which we receive the salvation is the testimony of the Holy Ghost in Scripture. It is "according to the Scriptures." This is a most solid and comforting truth. It is not a question of feelings, or experiences, or evidences; it is a simple question of faith in God's word wrought in the heart by God's Spirit.

It is a serious reflection for the evangelist, that wherever God's Spirit is at work, there Satan is sure to be busy. We must remember and ever be prepared for this. The enemy of Christ and the enemy of souls is always on the watch, always hovering about to see what he can do, either to hinder or corrupt the work of the gospel. This need not terrify or even discourage the workman; but it is well to bear it in mind and be watchful. Satan will leave no stone unturned to mar or hinder the blessed work of God's Spirit. He has proved himself the ceaseless, vigilant enemy of that work, from the days of Eden down to the present moment.

Now, in tracing the history of Satan, we find him acting in two characters, namely, as a serpent, or as a lion—using craft or violence. He will try to deceive; and, if he cannot succeed, then he will use violence. Thus it is in this sixteenth chapter of the Acts. The apostle's heart had been cheered and refreshed by what we moderns should pronounce, "a beautiful case of conversion." Lydia's was a very real and decided case, in every respect. It was direct, positive, and unmistakable. She received Christ into her heart, and forthwith took Christian ground by submitting to the deeply significant ordinance of baptism. Nor was this all. She immediately opened her house to the Lord's messengers. Hers was no mere lip profession. It was not merely *saying* she believed. She proved her faith in Christ, not only by going down under the water of baptism, but also by identifying herself and her household with the name and cause of that blessed One whom she had received into her heart by faith.

All this was clear and satisfactory. But we must now look at something quite different. The serpent appears upon the scene in the person of

THE DECEIVER

"It came to pass, as we went to prayer, a certain damsel possessed with a spirit of divination met us, which brought her masters much gain by soothsaying. The same followed Paul and us, and cried, saying, These men are the servants of the most high God, which show unto us the way of salvation.

And this did she many days. But Paul, being grieved, turned and said to the spirit, I command thee in the name of Jesus Christ to come out of her. And he came out the same hour" (vers. 16-18).

Here, then, was a case eminently calculated to test the spirituality and integrity of the evangelist. Most men would have hailed such words from the lips of this damsel as an encouraging testimony to the work. Why then was Paul grieved? Why did he not allow her to continue to bear witness to the object of his mission? Was she not saying the truth? Were they not the servants of the most high God? And were they not showing the way of salvation? Why be grieved with—why silence such a witness? Because it was of Satan; and, most assuredly, the apostle was not going to receive testimony from him. He could not allow Satan to help him in his work. True, he might have walked about the streets of Philippi owned and honored as a servant of God, if only he had consented to let the devil have a hand in the work. But Paul could never consent to this. He could never suffer the enemy to mix himself up with the work of the Lord. Had he done so, it would have given the deathblow to the testimony at Philippi. To have permitted Satan to put his hand to the work, would have involved the total shipwreck of the mission to Macedonia.

It is deeply important for the Lord's workman to weigh this matter. We may rest assured that this narrative of the damsel has been written for our instruction.

It is not only a statement of what has occurred, but a sample of what may and indeed what does occur every day.[26]

Besides Christendom is full of false profession. There are multitudes of false professors at this moment, throughout the wide domain of Christian profession. It is sad to have to say it, but so it is, and we must press the fact upon the attention of the reader. We are surrounded, on all sides, by those who give a merely nominal assent to the truths of the

Christian religion. They go on, from week to week, and from year to year, professing to believe certain things which they do not in reality believe at all. There are thousands who, every Lord's Day, profess to believe in the forgiveness of sins, and yet, were such persons to be examined, it would be found that they either do not think about the matter at all, or, if they do think, they deem it the very height of presumption for any one to be sure that his sins are forgiven.

This is very serious. Only think of a person standing up in the presence of God and saying, "I believe in the forgiveness of sins," and all the while he does not believe any such thing! Can anything be more hardening to the heart, or more deadening to the conscience than this? It is our firm persuasion that the forms and the formularies of professing Christianity are doing more to ruin precious souls than all the forms of moral pravity put together. It is perfectly appalling to contemplate the countless multitudes that are at this moment rushing along the well-trodden highway of religious profession, down to the eternal flames of hell. We feel bound to raise a warning note. We want the reader most solemnly to take heed as to this matter.

We have only instanced one special formulary, because it refers to a subject of very general interest and importance. How few, comparatively, are clear and settled as to the question of forgiveness of sins! How few are able, calmly, decidedly, and intelligently, to say, "*I know* that my sins are forgiven!" How few are in the real enjoyment of full forgiveness of sins, through faith in that precious blood that cleanseth from all sin! How solemn, therefore, to hear people giving utterance to such words as these, "I believe in the forgiveness of sins," while, in fact, they do not believe their own very utterance! Is the reader in the habit of using such a form of words? Does he believe it? Say, dear friend, are thy sins forgiven? Art thou washed in the precious atoning blood of Christ? If not, why not? The way is open. There is no hindrance. Thou art perfectly welcome, this moment, to the free benefits of the atoning work of Christ. Though thy sins be as scarlet; though they be black as midnight, black as hell; though they rise like a dreadful mountain before the vision of thy troubled soul, and threaten to sink thee into eternal perdition; yet do these words shine with divine and heavenly lustre on the page of inspiration, "*The blood of Jesus Christ, God's Son, cleanseth us from* ALL *sin*" (I John i. 7).

But mark, friend, do not go on, week after week, mocking God, hardening thine own heart, and carrying out the schemes of the great enemy of Christ, by a false profession. This marks the damsel possessed by a spirit of divination, and here her history links itself with the present awful condition of Christendom. What was the burden of her song, during those "many days" in the which the apostle narrowly considered her case? "These men are the servants of the most high God, which *show unto us* the way of salvation." But she was not saved—she was not delivered—she was, all the while, under Satan's power herself.

Thus it is with Christendom—thus it is with each false professor throughout the length and breadth of the professing Church. We know of nothing, even in the deepest depths of moral evil, or in the darkest shades of heathenism, more truly awful than the state of careless, hardened, self-satisfied, fallow-ground professors, who on each successive Lord's Day give utterance, either in their prayers or their singing, to words which, so far as they are concerned, are wholly false.

The thought of this is, at times, almost over-whelming. We cannot dwell upon it. It is really too sorrowful. We shall therefore pass on, having once more solemnly warned the reader against every shade and degree of false profession. Let him not say or sing aught that he does not heartily believe. The devil is at the bottom of all false profession, and by means thereof he seeks to bring discredit on the work of the Lord.

But how truly refreshing to contemplate the actings of the faithful apostle in the case of the damsel. Had he been seeking his own ends, or had he been merely a minister of religion, he might have welcomed her words as a tributary stream to swell the tide of his popularity, or promote the interest of his cause. But Paul was not a mere minister of religion; he was a minister of Christ—a totally different thing. And we may notice that the damsel does not say a word about Christ. She breathes not the precious, peerless name of Jesus. There is total silence as to Him. This stamps the whole thing as of Satan. "No man can call Jesus Lord but by the Holy Ghost." People may speak of God, and of religion; but Christ has no place in their hearts. The Pharisees, in the ninth of John, could say to the poor man, "Give God the praise;" but in speaking of Jesus, they could say, "This man is a sinner."

Thus it is ever in the case of corrupt religion, or false profession. Thus it was with the damsel in Acts xvi. There was not a syllable about Christ.

There was no truth, no life, no reality. It was hollow and false. It was of Satan; and hence Paul would not and could not own it; he was grieved with it and utterly rejected it.

Would that all were like him! Would that there were the singleness of eye to detect, and the integrity of heart to reject the work of Satan in much that is going on around us! Such an eye Paul, through grace, possessed. He was not to be deceived. He saw that the whole affair was an effort of Satan to mix himself up with the work, that thus he might spoil it altogether. "But Paul, being grieved, turned and said to the spirit, I command thee, in the name of Jesus Christ, to come out of her. And he came out the same hour."

This was true spiritual action. Paul was not in any haste to come into collision with the evil one, or even to pronounce upon the case at all; he waited many days; but the very moment that the enemy was detected he is resisted and repulsed with uncompromising decision. A less spiritual workman might have allowed the thing to pass, under the idea that it might turn to account and help forward the work. Paul thought differently; and he was right. He would take no help from Satan. He was not going to work by such an agency; and hence, in the name of Jesus Christ—that name which the enemy so sedulously excluded—he puts Satan to flight.

But no sooner was Satan repulsed as the serpent, than he assumed the character of a lion. Craft having failed, he tried violence. "And when her masters saw that the hope of their gains was gone, they caught Paul and Silas and drew them into the market-place unto the rulers, and brought them to the magistrates, saying, These men, being Jews, do exceedingly trouble our city, and teach customs which are not lawful for us to receive, neither to observe, being Romans. And the multitude rose up together against them; and the magistrates rent off their clothes, and commanded to beat them. And when they had laid many stripes upon them, they cast them into prison, charging the jailor to keep them safely" (vers. 19-23).

Thus the enemy seemed to triumph; but be it remembered that Christ's warriors gain their most splendid victories by apparent defeat. The devil made a great mistake when he cast the apostle into prison. Indeed it is consolatory to reflect that he has never done anything else but make mistakes, from the moment that he left his first estate down to the present moment. His entire history, from beginning to end, is one tissue of errors.

And thus, as has been already remarked, the devil made a great mistake when he cast Paul into prison at Philippi. To nature's view it might have seemed otherwise; but in the judgment of faith, the servant of Christ was much more in his right place in prison for the truth's sake, than outside at his Master's expense. True, Paul might have saved himself. He might have been an honored man, owned and acknowledged as "a servant of the most high God," if he had only accepted the damsel's testimony, and suffered the devil to help him in his work. But he could not do this, and hence he had to suffer. "And the multitude (ever fickle and easily swayed) rose up together against them: and the magistrates rent off their clothes, and commanded to beat them. And when they had laid many stripes upon them, they cast them into prison, charging the jailor to keep them safely. Who, having received such a charge, *thrust* them into the inner prison, and made their feet fast in the stocks" (vers. 22-24).

Here, then, some might have said, was an end to the work of the evangelist in the city of Philippi. Here was an effectual stop to the preaching. Not so; the prison was the very place, at the moment, for the evangelist. His work was there. He was to find a congregation within the prison walls which he could not have found outside. But this leads us, in the third and last place, to the case of

THE HARDENED SINNER

It was very unlikely that the jailor would ever have found his way to the prayer-meeting at the river side. He had little care for such things. He was neither an earnest seeker, nor a deceiver. He was a hardened sinner, pursuing a very hardening occupation. Jailors, from the occupation of their office, are, generally speaking, hard and stern men. No doubt there are exceptions. There are some tender-hearted men to be found in such situations; but, as a rule, jailors are not tender. It would hardly suit them to be so. They have to do with the very worst class of society. Much of the crime of the whole country comes under their notice; and many of the criminals come under their charge. Accustomed to the rough and the coarse, they are apt to become rough and coarse themselves.

Now, judging from the inspired narrative before us, we may well question if the Philippian jailor was an exception to the general rule with respect to men of his class. Certainly he does not seem to have shown much tenderness to Paul and Silas. "He *thrust* them into the *inner* prison, and made their feet *fast* in the stocks." He seems to have gone to the utmost extreme in making them uncomfortable.

But God had rich mercy in store for that poor, hardened, cruel jailor; and, as it was not at all likely that he would go to hear the gospel, the Lord sent the gospel to him; and, moreover, He made the devil the instrument of sending it. Little did the jailor know whom he was thrusting into the inner prison—little did he anticipate what was to happen ere another sun should rise. And we may add, little did the devil think of what he was doing when he sent the preachers of the gospel into jail, there to be the means of the jailor's conversion. But the Lord Jesus Christ knew what He was about to do, in the case of a poor hardened sinner. He can make the wrath of man to praise Him and restrain the remainder.

"He everywhere hath sway,And all things serve His might,His ev'ry act pure blessing is,His path unsullied light.

"When He makes bare His arm,Who shall His work withstand?When He His people's cause defends,Who then shall stay His hand?"

It was His purpose to save the jailor; and so far from Satan's being able to frustrate that purpose, he was actually made the instrument of accomplishing it. "God's purpose shall stand; and He will do all His pleasure." And where He sets His love upon a poor, wretched, guilty sinner, He will have him in heaven, spite of all the malice and rage of hell.

As to Paul and Silas, it is very evident that they were in their right place in the prison. They were there *for the truth's sake*, and therefore *the Lord was with them*. Hence they were perfectly happy. What, though they were confined within the gloomy walls of the prison, with their feet made fast in the stocks, prison walls could not confine their spirits. Nothing can hinder the joy of one who has the Lord with him. Shadrach, Meshach, and Abednego, were happy in the fiery furnace. Daniel was happy in the lions' den; and Paul and Silas were happy in the dungeon of Philippi: "And at midnight Paul and Silas prayed, and sang praises to God: and the prisoners heard them."

What sounds to issue from the inner prison! We may safely say that no such sounds had ever issued thence before. Curses and execrations and blasphemous words might have been heard; sighs, cries, and groans come forth from those walls. But to hear the accents of prayer and praise, ascending at the midnight hour, must have seemed strange indeed. Faith can sing as sweetly in a dungeon as at a prayer-meeting. It matters not where we are, provided always that we have God with us. His presence lights up the darkest cell, and turns a dungeon into the very gate of heaven. He can make His servants happy anywhere, and give them victory over the most adverse circumstances, and cause them to shout for joy in scenes where nature would be overwhelmed with sorrow.

But the Lord had His eye upon the jailor. He had written his name in the Lamb's book of life before the foundation of the world, and He was now about to lead him into the full joy of His salvation. "And suddenly there was a great earthquake, so that the foundations of the prison were shaken: and immediately all the doors were opened, and every one's bands were loosed" (ver. 26).

Now if Paul had not been in full communion with the mind and heart of Christ, he would assuredly have turned to Silas and said, "Now is the moment for us to make our escape. God has most manifestly appeared for us, and set before us an open door. If ever there was an opening of divine Providence surely this is one." But no; Paul knew better. He was in the full current of His blessed Master's thoughts, and in full sympathy with his

Master's heart. Hence he made no attempt to escape. The claims of *truth* had brought him into prison; the activities of *grace* kept him there. Providence opened the door; but faith refused to walk out. People talk of being guided by Providence; but if Paul had been so guided, the jailor would never have been a jewel in his crown.

"And the keeper of the prison awaking out of his sleep and seeing the prison doors open, he drew out his sword, and would have killed himself, supposing that the prisoners had been fled" (ver. 27). This proves, very plainly, that the earthquake, with all its attendant circumstances, had not touched the heart of the jailor. He naturally supposed, when he saw the doors open, that the prisoners were all gone. He could not imagine a number of prisoners sitting quietly in jail when the doors lay open and their chains were loosed. And then what was to become of him if the prisoners were gone? How could he face the authorities? Impossible. Anything but that. Death, even by his own hand, was preferable to that.

Thus the devil had conducted this hardened sinner to the very brink of the precipice, and he was about to give him the final and fatal push over the edge, and down to the eternal flames of hell; when lo, a voice of love sounded in his ear. It was the voice of Jesus through the lips of His servant—a voice of tender and deep compassion—"*Do thyself no harm.*"

This was irresistible. A hardened sinner could meet an earthquake; he could meet death itself; but he could not withstand the mighty melting power of love. The hardest heart must yield to the moral influence of love. "Then he called for a light, and sprang in, and came *trembling*, and fell down before Paul and Silas, and brought them out, and said, Sirs, what must I do to be saved?" Love can break the hardest heart. And surely there was love in those words, "Do thyself no harm," coming from the lips of one to whom he had done so much harm a few hours before.

And, be it noted, there was not a single syllable of reproach, or even of reflection, uttered by Paul to the jailor. This was Christ-like. It was the way of divine grace. If we look through the Gospels, we never find the Lord casting reproach upon the sinner. He has tears of sorrow; He has touching words of grace and tenderness; but no reproaches—no reflections—no reproach to the poor distressed sinner. We cannot attempt to furnish the many illustrations and proofs of this assertion; but the reader has only to turn to the gospel story to see its truth. Look at the prodigal: look at the thief. Not one reproving word to either.

Thus it is in every case; and thus it was with God's Spirit in Paul. Not a word about the harsh treatment—the thrusting into the inner prison—not a word about the stocks. "Do thyself no harm." And then, "Believe on the Lord Jesus Christ, and thou shalt be saved, and thy house."

Such is the rich and precious grace of God. It shines, in this scene, with uncommon lustre. It delights in taking up hardened sinners, melting and subduing their hard hearts, and leading them into the sunlight of a full salvation; and all this in a style peculiar to itself. Yes, God has His style of doing things, blessed be His name; and when He saves a wretched sinner,

He does it after such a fashion as fully proves that His whole heart is in the work. It is His joy to save a sinner—even the very chief—and He does it in a way worthy of Himself.

And now, let us look at the fruit of all this. The jailor's conversion was most unmistakable. Saved from the very brink of hell, he was brought into the very atmosphere of heaven. Preserved from self-destruction, he was brought into the circle of God's salvation; and the evidences of this were as clear as could be desired. "And they spake unto him the word of the Lord, and to all that were in his house. And he took them the same hour of the night, and washed their stripes; and was baptized, he and all his straightway. And when he had brought them into his house, he set meat before them, and rejoiced, *believing in God, with all his house*."

What a marvelous change! The ruthless jailor has become the generous host! "If any man be in Christ, he is a new creature; old things are passed away: behold, all things are become new." How clearly we can now see that Paul was right in not being guided by *providences*! How much better and higher to be led by the "eye" of God! What an eternal loss it would have proved to him had he walked out at the open door! How much better to be conducted out by the very hand that had thrust him in—a hand once the instrument of cruelty and sin, now the instrument of righteousness and love! What a magnificent triumph! What a scene, altogether! How little had the devil anticipated such a result from the imprisonment of the Lord's servants! He was thoroughly outwitted. The tables were completely turned upon him. He thought to hinder the gospel, and, behold! he was made to help it on. He had hoped to get rid of two of Christ's servants, and, lo! he lost one of his own. Christ is stronger than Satan; and all who put their trust in Him and move in the current of His thoughts shall most assuredly share in the triumphs of His grace now, and shine in the brightness of His glory forever.

Thus much, then, as to "the work of an evangelist." Such are the scenes through which he may have to pass—such the cases with which he may have to come in contact. We have seen the earnest seeker satisfied; the deceiver silenced; the hardened sinner saved. May all who go forth with the gospel of the grace of God know how to deal with the various types of character that may cross their path! May many be raised up to do the work of an evangelist!

CHAPTER IV
LETTERS TO AN EVANGELIST

DEAREST A——,

I have been much interested, and I trust profited, of late, by tracing, through the Gospels and the Acts, the various notices of the work of evangelization; and it has occured to me that it may not be amiss to present to you, as one much occupied in the blessed work, a few of the thoughts that have suggested themselves to my mind. I shall feel myself much more free in this way, than if I were writing a formal treatise.

And, first of all, I have been greatly struck with the simplicity with which the work of evangelizing was carried on in primitive times; so very unlike a great deal of what obtains among us. It seems to me that we moderns are quite too much hampered by conventional rules—too much fettered by the habits of Christendom. We are sadly deficient in what I may call spiritual elasticity. We are apt to think that in order to evangelize there must be a special gift; and even where there is this special gift, there must be a great deal of machinery and human arrangement. When we speak of doing the work of an evangelist, we, for the most part, have before our minds great public halls, and crowded audiences, for which there is a demand for considerable gift and power for speaking.

Now you and I thoroughly believe, that in order to preach the gospel publicly, there must be a special gift from the Head of the Church; and, moreover, we believe according to Eph. iv. 11, that Christ has given, and does still give, "evangelists." This is clear, if we are to be guided by Scripture. But I find in the Gospels, and in the Acts of the Apostles, that a quantity of most blessed evangelistic work was done by persons who were not specially gifted at all, but who had an earnest love for souls, and a deep sense of the preciousness of Christ and His salvation. And, what is more, I find in those who were specially gifted, called, and appointed by Christ to preach the gospel, a simplicity, freedom, and naturalness in their mode of working, which I greatly covet for myself and for all my brethren.

Let us look a little into Scripture. Take that lovely scene in John i. 36-45. John pours out his heart in testimony to Jesus: "Behold the Lamb of God!" His soul was absorbed with the glorious Object. What was the result? "Two disciples heard him speak, and they followed Jesus." What then? "One of the two which heard John speak, and followed Him, was Andrew, Simon Peter's brother." And what does he do? "*He first findeth his own brother* Simon, and saith unto him, We have found the Messias, which is, being interpreted, the Christ. And he brought him to Jesus." Again, "The day following, Jesus would go forth into Galilee, and findeth Philip, and saith unto him, Follow Me.... *Philip findeth Nathanael*, and saith unto him, We have found Him, of whom Moses in the law, and the prophets, did write, Jesus of Nazareth, the son of Joseph.... *Come and see.*"

Here then, dearest A., is the style of thing for which I earnestly long: this individual work, this laying hold of the first man that comes in our way, this finding one's own brother, and bringing him to Jesus. I do feel we are deficient in this. It is all right enough to gather congregations, and address them, as God gives ability and opportunity. Neither you nor I would pen a single word to detract from the value of such a line of work. By all means hire rooms, halls, and theatres; put out bills inviting people to come; leave no lawful means untried to spread the gospel. Seek to get at souls as best you can. Far be it from me to cast a damp upon any who are seeking to carry on the work in this public way.

But does it not strike you that we want more of the individual work? more of the private, earnest, personal dealing with souls? Do you not think that if we had more "Philips" we should have more "Nathanaels?" If we had more "Andrews," we should have more "Simons?" I cannot but believe it. There is amazing power in an earnest personal appeal. Do you not often find that it is after the more formal public preaching is finished, and the close personal work begins, that souls are reached? How is it then that there is so little of this latter? Does it not often happen at our public preachings, that when the formal address is delivered, a hymn sung, and a word of prayer offered, all disperse without any attempt at individual work? I speak not now, mark you, of the preacher—who cannot possibly reach every case, but of the scores of Christians who have been listening to him. They have seen strangers enter the room, they have sat beside them; they have, it may be, noticed their interest, seen the tear stealing down the cheek; and yet they have let them pass away without a single loving effort to reach them, or to follow up the good work.

No doubt it may be said, "It is much better to allow the Spirit of God to follow up His own work. We may do more harm than good. And besides, people do not like to be spoken to: they will look upon it as an impertinent intrusion, and they will be driven away from the place altogether." There is considerable weight in all this. I fully appreciate it; and I am sure you do likewise, dearest A. I fear great blunders are committed by injudicious persons intruding upon the sacred privacy of the soul's deep and holy exercises. It needs tact and judgment; in short, it needs direct spiritual guidance to be able to deal with souls; to know whom to speak to, and what to say.

But allowing all this, as we do in the fullest possible manner, I think you will agree with me that there is, as a rule, something lacking in connection with our public preachings. Is there not a want of that deep, personal, loving interest in souls which will express itself in a thousand ways that act powerfully on the heart? I confess that I have often been pained by what has come under my own notice in our preaching-rooms. Strangers come in and are left to find a seat wherever they can. No one seems to think of them. Christians are there, and they will hardly move to make room for them. No one offers them a Bible or hymn-book. And when the preaching is over, they are allowed to go as they came; not a loving word of inquiry as to whether they enjoyed the truth preached; not even a kindly look which might win confidence and invite conversation. On the contrary, there is a chilling reserve, amounting almost to repulsiveness.

All this is very sorrowful; and perhaps you will tell me that I am drawing too highly colored a picture. Alas! the picture is only too true. And what makes it all the more deplorable is, that one knows as a fact that many persons frequent our preaching-rooms and lecture-halls in the deepest exercise, and they are only longing to open their hearts to some one who could offer them a little spiritual counsel; but through timidity, reserve, or nervousness, they shrink from making any advance, and have but to retire to their homes and to their bedchambers, lonely and sad, there to weep in solitude because no man cares for their precious souls. Now I feel persuaded that much of this might be remedied if those Christians who attend the gospel preachings were more *on the look out* for souls: if they would attend, not so much for their own profit, as in order to be co-workers with God, in seeking to bring souls to Jesus. No doubt it is very refreshing to Christians to hear the gospel fully and faithfully preached. But it would not be the less refreshing because they were intensely interested in the conversion of souls, and in earnest prayer to God in the matter. And, besides, it could in no wise interfere with their personal enjoyment and profit to cultivate and manifest a lively and loving interest in those who surround them, and to seek at the close of the meeting to help any who may need and desire to be helped. It has a surprising effect upon the preacher, upon the preaching, upon the whole meeting, when the Christians who attend are really entering into, and discharging, their high and holy responsibilities to Christ and to souls. It imparts a certain tone and creates a certain atmosphere which must be felt in order to be understood; but when once felt it cannot easily be dispensed with.

But, alas, how often is it otherwise! How cold, how dull, how dispiriting is it at times to see the whole congregation clear out the moment the preaching is over! No loving, lingering groups gathering round young converts or anxious inquirers. Old experienced Christians have been present; but, instead of pausing with the fond hope that God would graciously use them to speak a word in season to him that is weary, they hasten away as though it were a matter of life and death that they should be home at a certain hour.

Do not suppose, dearest A., that I wish to lay down rules for my brethren. Far be the thought.

I am merely, in the freest possible manner, pouring out the thoughts of my heart to one with whom I have been linked in the work of the gospel for many years. I feel convinced there is a something lacking. It is my firm persuasion that no Christian is in a right condition, if he is not seeking in some way to bring souls to Christ. And, on the same principle, no assembly of Christians is in a right condition if it be not a thoroughly evangelistic assembly. We should all be on the lookout for souls; and then we may rest assured we should see soul-stirring results. But if we are satisfied to go on from week to week, month to month, and year to year, without a single leaf stirring, without a single conversion, our state must be truly lamentable.

But I think I hear you saying, "Where is all the Scripture we were to have had? where the many quotations from the Gospels and the Acts?" Well, I have gone on jotting down the thoughts which have for some considerable time occupied my mind; and now, space forbids my going further at present. But if you so desire, I shall write you a second letter on the subject. Meanwhile, may the Lord, by His Spirit, make us more earnest in seeking the salvation of immortal souls, by every legitimate agency. May our hearts be filled with genuine love for precious souls, and then we shall be sure to find ways and means of getting at them!

Ever, believe me, dearest A.,
Your deeply affectionate yoke-fellow,

* * *

LETTER II

There is one point in connection with our subject which has much occupied my mind; and that is, the immense importance of cultivating an earnest faith in the presence and action of the Holy Ghost. We want to remember, at all times, that we can do nothing, and that God the Holy Ghost can do all. It holds good in the great work of evangelization, as in all beside, that it is "not by might, nor by power, but by My Spirit, saith the Lord of hosts." The abiding sense of this would keep us humble, and yet full of joyful confidence. Humble, because we can do nothing; full of joyful confidence, because God can do all. Moreover, it would have the effect of keeping us very sober and quiet in our work—not cold and indifferent, but calm and serious, which is a great matter just now. I was much struck with a remark lately made by an aged workman, in a letter to one who had just entered the field. "Excitement," says this writer, "is not power, but weakness. Earnestness and energy are of God."

This is most true and most valuable. But I like the two sentences taken together. If we were to take either apart, I think you and I would prefer the latter; and for this reason: there are many, I fear, who would regard as "excitement" what you and I might really consider to be "earnestness and energy." Now I do confess, I love a deep-toned earnestness in the work. I do not see how a man can be otherwise than deeply and thoroughly in earnest, who realizes in any measure the awfulness of eternity, and the state of all those who die in their sins. How is it possible for any one to think of an immortal soul standing on the very brink of hell, and in danger at any moment of being dashed over, and not be serious and earnest?

But this is not excitement. What I understand by excitement is the working up of mere nature, and the putting forth of such efforts of nature as are designed to work on the natural feelings—all high pressure—all that is merely sensational. This is all worthless. It is evanescent. And not only so, but it superinduces weakness. We never find aught of this in the ministry of our blessed Lord or His apostles: and yet what earnestness! what untiring energy! what tenderness! We see an earnestness which wore the appearance of being beside oneself; an energy which hardly afforded a moment for rest or refreshment; and a tenderness which could weep over impenitent sinners. All this we see; but no excitement. In a word, all was the fruit of the Eternal Spirit; and all was to the glory of God. Moreover, there was ever that calmness and solemnity which becomes the presence of God, and yet that deep earnestness which proved that man's serious condition was fully realized.

Now, dear brother, this is precisely what we want, and what we ought diligently to cultivate. It is a signal mercy to be kept from all merely natural excitement; and, at the same time, to be duly impressed with the magnitude and solemnity of the work. Thus the mind will be kept properly balanced, and we shall be preserved from the tendency to be occupied with *our* work merely because it is ours. We shall rejoice that Christ is magnified, and souls are saved, whoever be the instrument used.

I have been thinking a good deal lately of that memorable time, now exactly ten years ago, when the Spirit of God wrought so marvelously in the province of Ulster. I think I gathered up some valuable instruction from what then came under my notice. That was a time never to be forgotten by those who were privileged to be eyewitnesses of the magnificent wave of blessing which rolled over the land. But I now refer to it in connection with the subject of the Spirit's action. I have no doubt whatever that the Holy Ghost was grieved and hindered in the year 1859, by man's interference. You remember how that work began. You remember the little school-house by the road side, where two or three men met, week after week, to pour out their hearts in prayer to God, that He would be pleased to break in upon the death and darkness which reigned around: and that He would revive His work, and send out His light and His truth in converting power. You know how these prayers were heard and answered. You and I were privileged to move through these soul-stirring scenes in the province of Ulster; and I doubt not the memory of them is fresh with you, as it is with me, this day.

Well, what was the special character of that work in its earlier stages? Was it not most manifestly a work of God's Spirit? Did not He take up and use instruments the most unfit and unfurnished, according to human thinking, for the accomplishment of His gracious purpose? Do we not remember the style and character of the agents who were chiefly used in the conversion of souls? Were they not for the most part "unlearned and ignorant men?" And further, can we not distinctly recall the fact that there was a most decided setting aside of all human arrangement and official routine? Working men came from the field, the factory, and the workshop, to address crowded audiences; and we have seen hundreds hanging in breathless interest upon the lips of men who could not speak five words of good grammar. In short, the mighty tide of spiritual life and power rolled in upon us, and swept away for the time being a quantity of human machinery, and ignored all question of man's authority in the things of God and the service of Christ.

Now we can well remember, that just in so far as the Holy Ghost was owned and honored, did the glorious work progress; and, on the other hand, in proportion as man intruded himself, in bustling self-importance, upon the domain of the Eternal Spirit, was the work hindered and quashed. I saw the truth of this illustrated in numberless cases. There was a vigorous effort made to cause the living water to flow in official and denominational channels, and this the Holy Ghost would not sanction. Moreover, there was a strong desire manifested, in many quarters, to make sectarian capital out of the blessed movement; and this the Holy Ghost resented.

Nor was this all. The work and the workman were *lionized* in all directions. Cases of conversion which were judged to be "striking" were blazed abroad and paraded in the public prints. Travellers and tourists from all parts visited these persons, took notes of their words and ways, and wafted the report of them to the ends of the earth. Many poor creatures, who had up to that time lived in obscurity, unknown and unnoticed, found themselves, all of a sudden, objects of interest to the wealthy, the noble, and the public at large. The pulpit and the press proclaimed their sayings and doings; and, as might be expected, they completely lost their balance. Knaves and hypocrites abounded on all hands. It became a grand point to have some strange and extravagant experience to tell; some remarkable dream or vision to relate. And even where this ill-advised line of action did not issue in producing knavery and hypocrisy, the young converts became heady and high-minded, and looked with a measure of contempt upon old established Christians, or those who did not happen to be converted after their peculiar fashion—"stricken," as it was termed.

In addition to this, some very remarkable characters—men of desperate notoriety, who seemed to be converted, were conveyed from place to place, and placarded about the various streets, and crowds gathered to see them and hear them recount their history; which history was very frequently a disgusting detail of immoralities and excesses which ought never to have been named. Several of these remarkable men afterwards broke down, and returned with increased ardor to their former practices.

These things, dearest A., I witnessed in various places. I believe the Holy Ghost was grieved and hindered, and the work marred thereby. I am thoroughly convinced of this: and hence it is that I think we should earnestly seek to honor the blessed Spirit; to lean upon Him in all our work; to follow where He leads, not run before Him. His work will stand: "Whatsoever God doeth it shall be forever." "The works that are done upon the earth, He is the doer of them." The remembrance of this will ever keep the mind well balanced. There is great danger of young workmen getting so excited about *their* work, *their* preaching, *their* gifts, as to lose sight of the blessed Master Himself. Moreover, they are apt to make preaching the *end* instead of the *means*. This works badly in every way. It injures themselves, and it mars their work. The moment I make preaching my end, I am out of the current of the mind of God, whose end is to glorify Christ;

and I am out of the current of the heart of Christ, whose end is the salvation of souls and the full blessing of His Church. But where the Holy Ghost gets His proper place, where He is duly owned and trusted, there all will be right. There will be no exaltation of man; no bustling self-importance; no parading of the fruits of our work; no excitement. All will be calm, quiet, real, and unpretending. There will be the simple, earnest, believing, patient waiting upon God. Self will be in the shade; Christ will be exalted.

I often recall a sentence of yours. I remember your once saying to me, "Heaven will be the best and safest place to hear the results of our work." This is a wholesome word for all workmen. I shudder when I see the names of Christ's servants paraded in the public journals, with flattering allusion to their work and its fruits. Surely those who pen such articles ought to reflect upon what they are doing: they should consider that they may be ministering to the very thing which they ought to desire to see mortified and subdued. I am most fully persuaded that the quiet, shady, retired path is the best and safest for the Christian workman. It will not make him less earnest but the contrary. It will not cramp his energy, but increase and intensify it. God forbid that you or I should pen a line or utter a sentence which might in the most remote way tend to discourage or hinder a single worker in all the vineyard of Christ. No, no, this is not the moment for aught of this kind. We want to see the Lord's laborers thoroughly in earnest; but we believe, most assuredly, that true earnestness will ever result from the most absolute dependence upon God the Holy Ghost.

But only see how I have run on! And yet I have not referred to those passages of Scripture of which I spoke in my last. Well, dearly beloved in the Lord, I am addressing one who is happily familiar with the Gospels and Acts, and who therefore knows that the great Workman Himself, and all those who sought to tread in His blessed footsteps, owned and honored the Eternal Spirit as the One by whom all their works were to be wrought.

I must now close for the present, my much loved brother and fellow-laborer; and I do so with a full heart, commending you, in spirit and soul and body, to Him who has loved us, and washed us from our sins in His own blood, and called us to the honored post of workers in His gospel field. May He bless you and yours, most abundantly, and increase your usefulness a thousandfold!

As ever, and for ever,
Your deeply affectionate work-fellow,
* * *

LETTER III

There is another point which stands intimately connected with the subject of my last letter, and that is, the place the word of God occupies in the work of evangelization. In my last letter, as you will remember, I referred to the work of the Holy Ghost, and the immense importance of giving Him His proper place. How clearly the precious word of God is connected with the action of the Holy Spirit, I need not say. Both are inseparably linked in those memorable words of our Lord to Nicodemus—words so little understood—so sadly misapplied: "Except a man be born of water and of the Spirit, he cannot enter into the kingdom of God" (John iii).

Now, you and I, dearest A., fully believe that in the above passage the Word is presented under the figure of "water." Thank God, we are not disposed to give any credit to the ritualistic absurdity of baptismal regeneration. We are, I believe, most thoroughly convinced that no one ever did, ever will, or ever could, get life by water baptism. That all who believe in Christ ought to be baptized we fully admit; but this is a totally different thing from the fatal error that substitutes an ordinance for the atoning death of Christ, the regenerating power of the Holy Ghost, and the life-giving virtues of the word of God. I shall not waste your time or my own in combating this error, but at once assume that you agree with me in thinking that when our Lord speaks of being "born of water and of the Spirit," He refers to the Word and the Holy Ghost.

Thus, then, the Word is the grand instrument to be used in the work of evangelization. Many passages of holy Scripture establish this point with such clearness and decision as to leave no room whatever for dispute. In the first chapter of James, ver. 18, we read, "Of His own will begat He us *with the word of truth*." Again, in I Pet. i. 23, we read, "Being born again, not of corruptible seed, but of incorruptible, *by the word of God*, which liveth and abideth forever." I must quote the whole passage because of its immense importance in connection with our subject: "For all flesh is as grass, and all the glory of man as the flower of grass. The grass withereth, and the flower thereof falleth away; but the word of the Lord endureth forever. *And this is the word which by the gospel is preached unto you.*"

This last clause is of unspeakable value to the evangelist. It binds him, in the most distinct manner, to the word of God as the instrument—the only instrument—the all-sufficient instrument, to be used in his glorious work. He is to give the Word to the people; and the more simply he gives it the better. The pure water should be allowed to flow from the heart of God to the heart of the sinner, without receiving a tinge from the channel through which it flows. The evangelist is to preach the Word; and he is to preach it in simple dependence upon the power of the Holy Ghost. This is the true secret of success in preaching.

But while I urge this great cardinal point in the work of preaching—and I believe it cannot be too strongly urged—I am very far indeed from thinking that the evangelist should give his hearers a quantity of truth. So far from this, I consider it a very great mistake. He ought to leave this to the teacher, lecturer, or pastor. I often fear that very much of our preaching shoots over the heads of the people, owing to the fact of our seeking rather to unfold truth than to reach souls. We rest satisfied, it may be, with having delivered a very clear and forcible lecture, a very interesting and instructive exposition of Scripture, something very valuable for the people of God; but the unconverted hearer has sat unmoved, unreached, unimpressed. There has been nothing for him. The lecturer has been more occupied with his lecture than with the sinner—more taken up with his subject than with the soul.

Now I am thoroughly convinced that this is a serious mistake, and one into which we all—at least I am—very apt to fall. I deplore it deeply, and I earnestly desire to correct it. I question if this very mistake may not be viewed as the true secret of our lack of success. But, dearest A., I should not perhaps say "*our* lack" but *my* lack. I do not think—so far as I know aught of your ministry—that you are exactly chargeable with the defect to which I am now just referring. Of this, however, you will be the best judge yourself; but of one thing I am certain, namely, that the most successful evangelist is the one who keeps his eye fixed on the sinner, who has his heart bent on the salvation of souls, yea, the one with whom the love for precious souls amounts almost to a passion. It is not the man who unfolds the most truth, but the man who longs most after souls, that will have the most seals to his ministry.

I assert all this, mark you, in the full and clear recognition of the fact with which I commenced this letter, namely, that the Word is the grand instrument in the work of conversion. This fact must never be lost sight of, never weakened. It matters not what agency may be used to make the furrow, or in what form the Word may clothe itself, or by what vehicle it may be conveyed; it is only by "the Word of truth" that souls are begotten.

All this is divinely true, and we would ever bear it in mind. But do we not often find that persons who undertake to preach the gospel (particularly if they continue long in one place) are very apt to leave the domain of the evangelist—most blessed domain!—and travel into that of the teacher and lecturer? This is what I deprecate and deeply deplore. I know I have erred in this way myself, and I mourn over the error. I write in all loving freedom to you—the Lord has of late deepened immensely in my soul the sense of the vast importance of earnest gospel preaching. I do not—God forbid that I should—think the less of the work of a teacher or pastor. I believe that wherever there is a heart that loves Christ, it will delight to feed and tend the precious lambs and sheep of the flock of Christ, that flock which He purchased with His own blood.

But the sheep must be gathered before they can be fed; and how are they to be gathered but by the earnest preaching of the gospel? It is the grand business of the evangelist to go forth upon the dark mountains of sin and error, to sound the gospel trumpet and gather the sheep; and I feel convinced that he will best accomplish this work, not by elaborate exposition of truth; not by lectures however clear, valuable, and instructive; not by lovely unfoldings of prophetic, dispensational, or doctrinal truth—most precious and important in the right place—but by fervid, pointed, earnest dealing with immortal souls; the warning voice, the solemn appeal, the faithful reasoning of righteousness, temperance, and judgment to come—the awakening presentation of death and judgment, the dread realities of eternity, the lake of fire and the worm that never dies.

In short, beloved, it strikes me we want awakening preachers. I fully admit that there is such a thing as *teaching* the gospel, as well as *preaching* it. For example, I find Paul teaching the gospel in Rom. i.-viii. just as I find him preaching the gospel in Acts xiii. or xvii. This is of the very last importance at all times, inasmuch as there are almost sure to be a number of what we call "exercised souls" at our public preachings, and these need an emancipating gospel—the full, clear, elevated, resurrection gospel.

But admitting all this, I still believe that what is needed for successful evangelization is, not so much a great quantity of truth as an intense love for souls. Look at that eminent evangelist George Whitefield. What think you was the secret of his success? No doubt you have looked into his printed sermons. Have you found any great breadth of truth in them? I question it. Indeed I must say I have been struck with the contrary. But oh! there was that in Whitefield which you and I may well covet and long to cultivate. There was a burning love for souls—a thirst for their salvation—a mighty grappling with the conscience—a bold, earnest, face-to-face dealing with men about their past ways, their present state, their future destiny. These were the things that God owned and blessed; and He will own and bless them still. I am persuaded—I write as under the very eye of God—that if our hearts are bent upon the salvation of souls, God will use us in that divine and glorious work. But on the other hand, if we abandon ourselves to the withering influences of a cold, heartless, godless fatalism; if we content ourselves with a formal and official statement of the gospel—a very cheerless sort of thing; if, to use a vulgar phrase, our preaching is on the principle of "take it or leave it," need we wonder if we do not see conversions? The wonder would be if there were any to see.

No, no; I believe we want to look seriously into this great practical subject. It demands the solemn and dispassionate consideration of all who are engaged in the work. There are dangers on all sides. There are conflicting opinions on all sides. But I cannot conceive how any Christian man can be satisfied to shirk the responsibility of looking after souls. A man may say, "I am not an evangelist; that is not my line; I am more of a teacher, or a pastor." Well, I understand this; but will any one tell me that a teacher or pastor may not go forth in earnest longing after souls? I cannot admit it for a moment. Nay more; it does not matter in the least what a man's gift is, or even though he should not possess any prominent gift at all, he can and ought, nevertheless, to cultivate a longing desire for the salvation of souls. Would it be right to pass a house on fire, without giving warning, even though one were not a member of the Fire Brigade? Should we not seek to save a drowning man, even though we could not command the use of a patent life-boat? Who in his senses would maintain aught so monstrous? So, in reference to souls, it is not so much a gift or knowledge of truth that is needed, as a deep and earnest longing for souls—a keen sense of their danger, and a desire for their rescue.

Ever, dearest A.,
Your deeply affectionate yoke-fellow,
* * *

LETTER IV

When I took up my pen to address you in my first letter, I had no idea that I should have occasion to extend the series to a fourth. However, the subject is one of intense interest to me; and there are just two or three points further on which I desire very briefly to touch.

And in the first place I deeply feel our lack of a prayerful spirit in carrying on the work of evangelization. I have referred to the subject of the Spirit's work; and also to the place which God's word ought ever to get; but it strikes me we are very deficient in reference to the matter of earnest, persevering, believing prayer. This is the true secret of power. "We," say the apostles, "will give ourselves continually to prayer and to the ministry of the Word."

Here is the order: "Prayer, and the ministry of the Word." Prayer brings in the power of God; and this is what we want. It is not the power of eloquence, but the power of God; and this can only be had by waiting upon Him. "He giveth power to the faint; and to them that have no might He increaseth strength. Even the youths shall faint and be weary, and the young men shall utterly fall: but they that wait upon the Lord shall renew their strength; they shall mount up with wings as eagles; they shall run, and not be weary; and they shall walk, and not faint" (Isa. xl. 29-31).

It seems to me, dearest A., that we are far too mechanical, if I may so express myself, in the work. There is too much of what I may call going through a service. I greatly fear that some of us are more on our legs than on our knees; more in the railway carriage than in the closet; more on the road than in the sanctuary; more before men than before God. This will never do. It is impossible that our preaching can be marked by power and crowned with results, if we fail in waiting upon God. Look at the blessed Master Himself—that great Workman. See how often He was found in prayer. At His baptism; at His transfiguration; previous to the appointment and mission of the twelve. In short, again and again we find that blessed One in the attitude of prayer. At one time He rises up a great while before day, in order to give Himself to prayer. At another time He spends the whole night in prayer, because the day was given up to work.

What an example for us! May we follow it! May we know a little better what it is to agonize in prayer. How little we know of this!—I speak for myself. It sometimes appears to me as if we were so much taken up with preaching engagements that we have no time for prayer—no time for closet work—no time to be alone with God. We get into a sort of whirl of public work; we rush from place to place, from meeting to meeting, in a prayerless, barren condition of soul. Need we wonder at the little result? How could it be otherwise when we so fail in waiting upon God? *We* cannot convert souls—God alone can do this; and if we go on without waiting on Him, if we allow public preaching to displace private prayer, we may rest assured our preaching will prove barren and worthless. We really must "give ourselves to prayer" if we would succeed in the "ministry of the Word."

Nor is this all. It is not merely that we are lacking in the holy and blessed practice of private prayer. This is, alas! too true, as I have said. But there is more than this. We fail in our public meetings for prayer. The great work of evangelization is not sufficiently remembered in our prayer-meetings. It is not definitely, earnestly, and constantly kept before God in our public reunions. It may occasionally be introduced in a cursory, formal manner, and then dismissed. Indeed, I feel there is a great lack of earnestness and perseverance in our prayer-meetings generally, not merely as to the work of the gospel, but as to other things as well. There is frequently great formality and feebleness. We do not seem like men in earnest. We lack the spirit of the widow in Luke xviii., who overcame the unjust judge by the bare force of her importunity. We seem to forget that God will be inquired of; and that He is a rewarder of them that diligently seek Him.

It is of no use for any one to say, "God can work without our earnest pleading; He will accomplish His purposes; He will gather out His own." We know all this; but we know also that He who has appointed the end has appointed the means; and if we fail in waiting on Him, He will get others to do His work. The work will be done, no doubt, but we shall lose the dignity, the privilege, and the reward of working. Is this nothing? Is it nothing to be deprived of the sweet privilege of being co-workers with God, of having fellowship with Him in the blessed work which He is carrying on? Alas! alas! that we prize it so little. Still we do prize it; and perhaps there are few things in which we can more fully taste this privilege than in united earnest prayer. Here every saint can join. Here all can add their cordial Amen. All may not be preachers; but all can pray—all join in prayer; all can have fellowship.

And do you not find, beloved brother, that there is always a stream of deep and real blessing where *the assembly* is drawn out in earnest prayer for the gospel, and for the salvation of souls? I have invariably seen it, and hence it is always a source of unspeakable comfort, joy, and encouragement to my heart when I see the assembly stirred up to pray, for then I am sure God is going to give copious showers of blessing.

Moreover, when this is the case, when this most excellent spirit pervades the whole assembly, you may be sure there will be no trouble as to what is called "The responsibility of the preaching." It will be all the same who does the work, provided it is done as well as it can be. If the assembly is waiting upon God, in earnest intercession for the progress of the work, it will not be a question as to the one who is to take the preaching, provided Christ is preached and souls are blessed.

Then there is another thing which has of late occupied my mind a good deal; and that is our method of dealing with young converts. Most surely there is immense need of care and caution, lest we be found accrediting what is not the genuine work of God's Spirit at all. There is very great danger here. The enemy is ever seeking to introduce spurious materials into the assembly, in order that he may mar the testimony and bring discredit upon the truth of God.

All this is most true, and demands our serious consideration. But does it not seem to you, beloved, that we often err on the other side? Do we not often, by a stiff and peculiar style, cast a chill upon young converts? Is there not frequently something repulsive in our spirit and deportment? We expect young Christians to come up to a standard of intelligence which has taken us years to attain. Nor this only. We sometimes put them through a process of examination which only tends to harass and perplex.

Now assuredly this is not right. The Spirit of God would never puzzle, perplex, or repulse a dear anxious inquirer—never, no never. It could never be according to the mind or heart of Christ to chill the spirit of the very feeblest lamb in all His blood-bought flock. He would have us seeking to lead them on gently and tenderly—to soothe, nourish, and cherish them, according to all the deep love of His heart. It is a great thing to lay ourselves out, and hold ourselves open to discern and appreciate the work of God in souls, and not to mar it by placing our own miserable crotchets as stumbling-blocks in their pathway. We need divine guidance and help in this as much as in any other department of our work. But, blessed be God, He is sufficient for this as for all beside. Let us only wait on Him: let us cling to Him, and draw upon His exhaustless treasury for each case as it arises, for exigence of every hour. He will never fail a trusting, expectant, dependent heart.

I must now close this series of letters. I think I have touched most, if not all, of the points which I had in my mind. You will, I trust, bear in mind, beloved in the Lord, that I have, in all these letters, simply jotted down my thoughts in the utmost possible freedom, and in all the intimacy of true brotherly friendship. I have not been writing a formal treatise, but pouring out my heart to a beloved friend and yoke-fellow. This must be borne in mind by all who may read these letters.

May God bless and keep you, dearest A. May He crown your labours with His richest and best blessing! May He keep you from every evil work, and preserve you unto His own everlasting kingdom!

Ever believe me,
My dearest A.,
Your deeply affectionate
* * *

LETTER V

It seems as though I must once more take up my pen to address you on certain matters connected with the work of evangelization, which have forced themselves upon my attention for some time past. There are three distinct branches of the work which I long to see occupying a far more definite and prominent place among us; and these are, the Tract depot, the Gospel preaching, and the Sunday-school.

It strikes me that the Lord is awakening attention to the importance of the Tract depot as a valuable agency in the work of evangelization; but I question if we, on this side of the Atlantic, are thoroughly in earnest on the subject. How is this? Have books and tracts lost their interest and value in our eyes? Or does the fault lie in the mode of conducting our Tract depots? To my mind there seems to be something lacking in reference to this matter.

I would fain see a well-conducted depot in every important town; by "well-conducted" I mean one taken up and carried on as a direct service to the Lord, in true love for souls, deep interest in the spread of the truth, and at the same time in a sound business way. I have known several depots fall to the ground through lack of business habits on the part of the conductors. They seemed very earnest, sincere persons, but quite unfit to conduct a business. In short, they were persons in whose hands any business would have fallen through. Then in many places there is the most deplorable failure as to the valuable and interesting work of conducting a depot.

And how can we best reach the people, for whom the tracts and books are prepared? I believe by having the books and tracts exposed for sale in a shop window, where that is possible, so that people may see them as they pass, and step in and purchase what they want. Many a soul has been laid hold of in this way. Many, I doubt not, have been saved and blessed by means of tracts, seen for the first time in a shop window or arranged on a counter. But where there is no such opportunity, the assembly's meeting-room is the Tract depot's natural home.

There is, manifestly, a real want of a Tract depot in every large town, conducted by some one of intelligence and sound business habits, who would be able to speak to persons about the tracts, and to recommend such as might prove helpful to anxious inquirers after truth. In this way, I feel persuaded, much good might be done. The Christians in the town would know where to go for tracts, not only for their own personal reading, but also for general distribution. Surely if a thing is worth doing at all, it is worth doing well; and if the Tract depot be not worth attending to, we know not what is.

The Tract depot must be taken up in direct service to Christ. And I feel assured that where it is so taken up and so carried on, in energy, zeal, and integrity, the Lord will own it and He will make it a blessing. Is there no one who will take up this valuable work for Christ's sake and not for the sake of remuneration? Is there no one who will enter upon it in simple faith, looking to the living God?

Here lies the root of the matter, dearest A. For this branch of the work, as for every other branch, we need those who trust God and deny themselves. It seems to me that a grand point would be gained if the Tract depot were placed on its proper footing, and viewed as an integral part of the evangelistic work, to be taken up in responsibility to the Lord, and carried on in the energy of faith in the living God. Every branch of gospel work—the Depot, the Preaching, the Sunday-school—must be carried on in this way. It is all well and most valuable to have fellowship—full cordial fellowship, in all our service; but if we wait for fellowship and co-operation in the starting of work which comes within the range of personal, as well as collective, responsibility, we shall find ourselves very much behind—or the work may not be done at all.

I shall have occasion to refer more particularly to this point, when I come to treat of the Preaching and the Sunday-school. All I want now, is to establish the fact that the Tract depot is a branch, and a most important and efficient branch, of evangelistic work. If this be thoroughly grasped by our friends, a great point is gained. I must confess to you, dearest A., that my moral sense has often been grievously offended by the cold, commercial style in which the publishing and sale of books and tracts are spoken of—a style befitting perhaps a mere commercial business, but most offensive when adopted in reference to the precious work of God. I admit in the fullest way—nay, I actually contend for it—that the proper management of the depot demands good sound business habits, and upright business principles. But at the same time I am persuaded that the Tract depot will never occupy its true ground—never realize the true idea, never reach the desired end—until it is firmly fixed on its holy basis, and viewed as an integral part of that most glorious work to which we are called—even the work of active, earnest, persevering evangelization.

And this work must be taken up in the sense of responsibility to Christ, and in the energy of faith in the living God. It will not do for an assembly of Christians, or some wealthy individual, to take up an inefficient protégé, and commit to such an one the management of the affair in order to afford a means of living. It is most blessed for all to have fellowship in the work; but I am thoroughly convinced that the work must be taken up in direct service to Christ, to be carried on in love for souls, and real interest in the spread of the truth.

I hope to address you again on the other two branches of my theme.

Meanwhile, I remain, dearest A.,
Your deeply affectionate yoke-fellow,
* * *

LETTER VI

I have, in some of the earlier letters of this series, dwelt upon the unspeakable importance of keeping up with zeal and constancy, a faithful preaching of the gospel—a distinct work of evangelization, carried on in the energy of love to precious souls, and with direct reference to the glory of Christ—a work bearing entirely upon the unconverted, and therefore quite distinct from the work of teaching, lecturing, or exhorting, in the bosom of the assembly; which latter is, I need not say, of equal importance in the mind of our Lord Christ.

My object in referring again to this subject is to call your attention to a point in connection with it, respecting which, it seems to me, there is a great want of clearness amongst some of our friends. I question if we are, as a rule, thoroughly clear as to the question of individual responsibility in the work of the gospel. I admit, of course, that the teacher or lecturer is called to exercise his gift, to a very great extent, on the same principle as the evangelist; that is, on his own personal responsibility to Christ; and that the assembly is not responsible for his individual services; unless indeed he teach unsound doctrine, in which case the assembly is bound to take it up.

But my business is with the work of the evangelist; and he is to carry on his work outside of the assembly. His sphere of action is the wide, wide world. "Go ye into all the world, and preach the gospel to every creature." Here is the sphere and here the object of the evangelist—"*All* the world"— "*Every* creature." He may go forth from the bosom of the assembly, and return thither again laden with his golden sheaves; nevertheless he goes forth in the energy of personal faith in the living God, and on the ground of personal responsibility to Christ; nor is the assembly responsible for the peculiar *mode* in which he may carry on his work. No doubt the assembly is called into action when the evangelist introduces the *fruit* of his work in the shape of souls professing to be converted, and desiring to be received into fellowship at the Lord's table. But this is another thing altogether, and must be kept distinct. The evangelist must be left free: this is what I contend for. He must not be tied down to certain rules or regulations, nor cramped by special conventionalities. There are many things which a large-hearted evangelist will feel perfectly free to do which might not commend themselves to the spiritual judgment and feelings of some in the assembly; but, provided he does not traverse any vital or fundamental principle, such persons have no right to interfere with him.

And be it remembered, dearest A., that when I use the expression, "spiritual judgment and feelings," I am taking the very highest possible view of the case, and treating the objector with the highest respect. I feel this is but right and proper. Every true man has a right to have his feelings and judgment—not to speak of conscience—treated with all due respect. There are, alas! everywhere, men of narrow mind, who object to everything that does not square with their own notions—men who would fain tie the evangelist down to the exact line of things and mode of acting which according to their thinking would suit the assembly of God's people when gathered for worship at the table of the Lord.

All this is a thorough mistake. The evangelist should pursue the even tenor of his way, regardless of all such narrowness and meddling. Take, for example, the matter of singing hymns. The evangelist may feel perfectly free to use a class of hymns or gospel songs which would be wholly unsuitable for the assembly. The fact is, he *sings* the gospel for the same object that he *preaches* it, namely, to reach the sinner's heart. He is just as ready to sing "Come" as to preach it.

Such, dearest A., is the judgment which I have had on this subject for many years, though I am not quite sure if it will fully commend itself to your spiritual mind. It strikes me we are in danger of slipping into Christendom's false notion of "establishing a cause," and "organizing a body." Hence it is that the four walls in which the assembly meets are regarded by many as a "chapel," and the evangelist who happens to preach there is looked upon as "the minister of the chapel."

All this has to be carefully guarded against: but my object in referring to it now is to clear up the point with respect to the gospel preaching. The true evangelist is not the minister of any chapel; or the organ of any congregation; or the representative of a body; or the paid agent of any society. No; he is the ambassador of Christ—the messenger of a God of love—the herald of glad tidings. His heart is filled with love to souls; his lips anointed by the Holy Ghost; his words clothed with heavenly power. Let him alone! Fetter him not by your rules and regulations! Leave him to his work and to his Master! And further, bear in mind that the Church of God can afford a platform broad enough for all sorts of workmen and every possible style of work, *provided only* that foundation truth be not disturbed. It is a fatal mistake to seek to reduce every one and every thing to a dead level. Christianity is a living, divine reality. Christ's servants are sent by Him, and to Him they are responsible. "Who art thou that judgest another man's servant? To his own master he standeth or falleth" (Rom. xiv.).

We may depend upon it, dearest A., these things demand our serious consideration, if we do not want to have the blessed work of evangelization marred in our hands.

I have just one other point that I would refer to before closing my letter, as it has been rather a vexed question in certain places—I allude to what has been termed "the responsibility of the preaching."

How many of our friends have been and are harassed about this question! And why? I am persuaded that it is from not understanding the true nature, character, and sphere of the work of evangelization. Hence we have had some persons contending for it that the Sunday evening preaching should be left open. "Open to what?" That is the question. In too many cases it has proved to be "open" to a character of speaking altogether unsuited to many who had come there, or who had been brought by friends, expecting to hear a full, clear, earnest gospel. On such occasions our friends have been disappointed, and the unconverted perfectly unable to understand the meaning of the service. Surely such things ought not to be; nor would they be if men would only discern the simplest thing possible, namely, the distinction between all meetings in which Christ's servants exercise their ministry on their own personal responsibility, and all meetings which are purely reunions of the assembly, whether for the Lord's Supper, for prayer, or for any other purpose whatsoever.

Your deeply affectionate,
* * *

LETTER VII

Through want of space I was obliged to close my last letter without even touching upon the subject of the Sunday-school: I must, however, devote a page or two to a branch of work which has occupied a very large place in my heart for thirty years. I should deem my series incomplete were this subject left untouched.

Some may question how far the Sunday-school can be viewed as an integral part of the work of evangelization. I can only say it is mainly in this light I regard it. I look upon it as one great and most interesting branch of gospel work. The superintendent of the Sunday-school and the teacher of the Sunday-school class are workers in the wide gospel field, just as distinctly as the evangelist or preacher of the gospel.

I am fully aware that a Sunday-school differs materially from an ordinary gospel preaching. It is not convened in the same way, or conducted in the same manner. There is, if I may so express myself, a union of the parent, the teacher, and the evangelist, in the person of the Sunday-school worker. For the time being he takes the place of the parent: he seeks to do the duty of a teacher; but he aims at the object of the evangelist—that priceless object, the salvation of the souls of the precious little ones committed to his charge. As to the mode in which he gains his end—as to the details of his work—as to the varied agencies which he may bring to bear, he alone is responsible.

I am aware that exception is taken to the Sunday-school on the ground that its tendency is to interfere with parental or domestic training. Now I must confess, dearest A., that I cannot see any force whatever in this objection. The true object of the Sunday-school is, not to supersede parental training, but to help it where it exists, or to supply its lack where it does not exist. There are, as you and I well know, hundreds of thousands of dear children who have no parental training at all. Thousands have no parents, and thousands more have parents who are far worse than none. Look at the multitudes that throng the lanes, alleys, and courtyards of our large cities and towns, who seem hardly a degree above mere animal existence—yea, many of them like little incarnate demons.

Who can think upon all these precious souls without wishing a hearty God-speed to all *true* Sunday-school workers, and earnestly longing for more thorough earnestness and energy in that most blessed work?

I say "*true*" Sunday-school workers, because I fear that many engage in the work who are not true, not real, not fit. Many, I fear, take it up as a little bit of fashionable religious work, suited to the younger members of religious communities. Many, too, view it as a kind of set-off to a week of self-indulgence, folly, and worldliness. All such persons are an actual hindrance rather than a help to this sacred service.

Then again, there are many who sincerely love Christ, and long to serve Him in the Sunday-school, but who are not really fitted for the work. They are deficient in tact, energy, order, and rule. They lack that power to adapt themselves to the children, and to engage their young hearts, which is so essential to the Sunday-school worker. It is a great mistake to suppose that every one who stands idle in the market-place is fit to turn into this particular branch of Christian labor. On the contrary, it needs a person thoroughly fitted of God for it; and if it be asked, "How are we ever to be supplied with suited agents for this branch of evangelistic service?" I reply, Just in the same way as you are to be supplied in any other department—by earnest, persevering, believing prayer. I am most thoroughly persuaded that if Christians were more stirred up by God's Spirit to feel the importance of the Sunday-school—if they could only seize the idea that it is, like the Tract depot and the preaching, part and parcel of that most glorious work to which we are called in these closing days of Christendom's history—if they were more permeated by the idea of the evangelistic nature and object of Sunday-school work, they would be more instant and earnest in prayer, both in the closet and in the public assembly, that the Lord would raise up in our midst a band of earnest, devoted, whole-hearted Sunday-school workers.

This is the lack, dearest A.; and may God, in His abounding mercy, supply it! He is able, and surely He is willing. But then He will be waited on and inquired of; and "He is the rewarder of them that *diligently* seek Him." I think we have much cause for thankfulness and praise for what has been done in the way of Sunday-schools during the last few years. I well remember the time when many of our friends seemed to overlook this branch of work altogether. Even now many treat it with indifference, thus weakening the hand and discouraging the hearts of those engaged in it.

But I shall not dwell upon this, inasmuch as my theme is the Sunday-school, and not those who neglect or oppose it. I bless God for what I see in the way of encouragement. I have often been exceedingly refreshed and delighted by seeing some of our very oldest friends rising from the table of their Lord, and proceeding to arrange the benches on which the dear little ones were soon to be ranged to hear the sweet story of a Saviour's love. And what could be more lovely, more touching, or more morally suited, than for those who had just been remembering the Saviour's dying love to seek, even by the arrangement of the benches, to carry out His living words, "Suffer the little children to come unto Me?"

There is very much I should like to add as to the mode of working the Sunday-school; but perhaps it is just as well that each worker should be wholly cast upon the living God for counsel and help as to details. We must ever remember that the Sunday-school, like the Tract depot and the preaching, is entirely a work of individual responsibility. This is a grand point; and where it is fully understood, and where there is real earnestness of heart and singleness of eye, I believe there will be no great difficulty as to the particular mode of working. A large heart, and a fixed purpose to carry on the great work and fulfil the glorious mission committed to us, will effectually deliver us from the withering influence of crotchets and prejudices—those miserable obstructions to all that is lovely and of good report.

May God pour out His blessing on all Sunday-schools, upon the pupils, the teachers, and the superintendents! May He also bless all who are engaged, in any way, in the instruction of the young! May He cheer and refresh their spirits by giving them to reap many golden sheaves in their special corner of the one great and glorious gospel field!

Ever believe me, dearest A.,
Your deeply affectionate
* * *

THE LIVING GOD AND A LIVING FAITH

There is one great substantial fact standing prominently forth on every page of the volume of God, and illustrated in every stage of the history of God's people—a fact of immense weight and moral power at all times, but specially in seasons of darkness, difficulty, and discouragement, occasioned by the low condition of things among those who profess to be on the Lord's side. The fact is this, *That faith can always count on God, and God will always answer faith.*

Such is our fact, such our thesis; and if the reader will turn with us, for a few moments, to 2 Chron xx., he will find a very beautiful and very striking illustration.

This chapter shows us the good king Jehoshaphat under very heavy pressure indeed—it records a dark moment in his history. "It came to pass after this also, that the children of Moab, and the children of Ammon, and with them other besides the Ammonites, came against Jehoshaphat to battle. Then" (for people are ever quick to run with evil tidings) "there came some that told Jehoshaphat, saying, There cometh a great multitude against thee from beyond the sea, on this side Syria." Here was a difficulty of no ordinary nature. This invading host was made up of the descendants of Lot and of Esau; and this fact might give rise to a thousand conflicting thoughts and distracting questions in the mind of Jehoshaphat. They were not Egyptians or Assyrians, concerning whom there could be no question whatever; but both Esau and Lot stood in certain relations to Israel, and a question might suggest itself as to how far such relations were to be recognized.

Not this only. The practical state of the entire nation of Israel—the actual condition of God's people, was such as to give rise to the most serious misgivings. Israel no longer presented an unbroken front to the invading foe. Their visible unity was gone. A grievous breach had been made in their battlements. The ten tribes and the two were rent asunder, the one from the other. The condition of the former was terrible, and that of the latter, shaky enough.

Thus the circumstances of king Jehoshaphat were dark and discouraging in the extreme; and, even as regards himself and his practical course, he was but just emerging from the consequences of a very humiliating fall, so that his reminiscences would be quite as cheerless as his surroundings.

But it is just here that our grand substantial fact presents itself to the vision of faith, and flings a mantle of light over the whole scene. Things looked gloomy, no doubt; but God was to be counted upon by faith, and faith could count upon Him. God is a never failing resource—a great reality, at all times, and under all circumstances.

"God is our refuge and strength, a very present help in trouble. Therefore will not we fear, though the earth be removed, and though the mountains be carried into the midst of the sea. Though the waters thereof roar and be troubled, though the mountains shake with the swelling thereof. There is a river, the stream whereof shall make glad the city of God, the holy place of the tabernacles of the Most High. God is in the midst of her, she shall not be moved: God shall help her, and that right early. The heathen raged, the kingdoms were moved: He uttered His voice, the earth melted. The Lord of hosts is with us; the God of Jacob is our refuge" (Psa. xlvi. I-7).

Here, then, was Jehoshaphat's resource in the day of his trouble; and to it he at once betook himself, in that earnest faith which never fails to draw down power and blessing from the living and true God, to meet every exigency of the way. "And Jehoshaphat feared, and set himself to seek the Lord, and proclaimed a fast throughout all Judah. And Judah gathered themselves together, to ask help of the Lord; even out of all the cities of Judah they came to seek the Lord. And Jehoshaphat stood in the congregation of Judah and Jerusalem, in the house of the Lord, before the new court, and said, O Lord God of our fathers, art not Thou God in heaven? and rulest not Thou over all the kingdoms of the heathen? and in Thy hand is there not power and might, so that none is able to withstand Thee? Art not Thou our God, who didst drive out the inhabitants of this land before Thy people Israel, and gavest it to *the seed of Abraham Thy friend for ever?*"

These are the breathings of faith—faith that enables the soul to take the very highest possible ground. It mattered not what unsettled questions there might be between Esau and Jacob; there were none between Abraham and the Almighty God. Now, God had given the land to Abraham, His friend. For how long? *For ever.* This was enough. "The gifts and calling of God are without repentance." God will never cancel His call, or take back a gift. This is a fixed foundation principle; and on this faith always takes its stand with firm decision. The enemy might throw in a thousand suggestions; and the poor heart might throw up a thousand reasonings. It might seem like presumption and empty conceit, on the part of Jehoshaphat, to plant his foot on such lofty ground. It was all well enough in the days of David, or of Solomon, or of Joshua, when the unity of the nation was unbroken, and the banner of Jehovah floated in triumph over the twelve tribes of Israel. But things were sadly changed; and it ill became one in Jehoshaphat's circumstances to use such lofty language or assume to occupy such a high position.

What is faith's reply to all this? A very simple, but a very powerful one— God never changes. He is the same yesterday, to-day, and forever. Had He not made Abraham a present of the land of Canaan? Had He not bestowed it upon his seed forever? Had He not ratified the gift by His word and His oath—these two immutable things in which it was impossible for Him to lie? Unquestionably. But then what of the law? Did not that make some difference? None whatever, as regards God's gift and promise. Four centuries previous to the giving of the law, was the great transaction settled and stablished between the Almighty God and Abraham His friend—and settled and stablished forever. Hence nothing can possibly touch this. There were no legal conditions proposed to Abraham. All was pure and absolute grace. God gave the land to Abraham by promise, and not by law, in any shape or form.

Now, it was on this original ground that Jehoshaphat took his stand; and he was right. It was the only thing for him to do. He had not one hair's breadth of solid standing ground, short of these golden words, "Thou gavest it to the seed of Abraham Thy friend forever." It was either this or nothing. *A living faith always lays hold on the living God.* It cannot stop short of Him. It looks not at men or their circumstances. It takes no account of the changes and chances of this mortal life. It lives and moves and has its being in the presence of the living God; it rejoices in the cloudless sunlight of His blessed countenance. It carries on all its artless reasonings in the sanctuary, and draws all its happy conclusions from the facts discovered there. It does not lower the standard according to the condition of things around, but boldly and decidedly takes up its position on the very highest ground.

Now, these actings of faith are always most grateful to the heart of God. The living God delights in a living faith. We may be quite sure that the bolder the grasp of faith, the more welcome it is to God. We need never suppose that the blessed One is either gratified or glorified by the workings of a legal mind. No, no; He delights to be trusted without a shadow of reserve or misgiving. He delights to be fully counted upon and largely used; and the deeper the need, and the darker the surrounding gloom, the more is He glorified by the faith that draws upon Him.

Hence, we may assert with perfect confidence, that the attitude and the utterances of Jehoshaphat, in the scene before us, were in full accordance with the mind of God. There is something perfectly beautiful to see him, as it were, opening the original lease, and laying his finger on that clause in virtue of which Israel held as tenants forever under God. Nothing could cancel that clause or break that lease. No flaw there. All was ordered and sure. "Thou *gavest* it to the seed of Abraham Thy friend *forever*."

This was solid ground—the ground of God—the ground of faith, which no power of the enemy can ever shake. True, the enemy might remind Jehoshaphat of sin and folly, failure and unfaithfulness. Nay, he might suggest to him that the very fact of the threatened invasion proved that Israel had fallen, for had they not done so, there would be neither enemy nor evil.

But for this, too, grace had provided an answer—an answer which faith knew well how to appropriate. Jehoshaphat reminds Jehovah of the house which Solomon had built to His name. "They have built Thee a sanctuary therein for Thy name, saying, If, when evil cometh upon us, as a sword, judgment, or pestilence, or famine, we stand before this house, and in Thy presence (for Thy name is in this house), and cry unto Thee in our affliction, then Thou will hear and help. And now, behold, the children of Ammon, and Moab, and Mount Seir, whom Thou wouldest not let Israel invade, when they came out of the land of Egypt, but they turned from them, and distroyed them not. Behold, I say, how they reward us, to come to cast us out of *Thy possession, which Thou hast given us to inherit.* O our God, wilt Thou not judge them? for we have no might against this great company that cometh against us; neither know we what to do, but *our eyes are upon Thee*" (vers. 8-12).

Here, truly, is a living faith dealing with the living God. It is no mere empty profession—no lifeless creed—no cold uninfluential theory. It is not a man "saying he has faith." Such things will never stand in the day of battle. They may do well enough when all is calm, smooth, and bright; but when difficulties have to be grappled with—when the enemy has to be met face to face, all merely nominal faith, all mere lip profession, will prove like autumn leaves before the blast. Nothing will stand the test of actual conflict but a living personal faith in a living personal Saviour-God. This is what is needed. It is this which alone can sustain the heart, come what may. Faith brings God into the scene, and all is strength, victory, and perfect peace.

Thus it was with the king of Judah, in the days of 2 Chron. xx. "We have no might; neither know we what to do; but our eyes are upon Thee." This is the way to occupy God's ground, even with the eyes fixed on God Himself. This is the true secret of stability and peace. The devil will leave no stone unturned to drive us off the true ground which, as Christians, we ought to occupy in these last days; and we, in ourselves, have no might whatever against him. Our only resource is in the living God. If our eyes are upon Him, nothing can harm us. "Thou wilt keep him in perfect peace, whose mind is stayed on Thee, because he trusteth in Thee."

Reader, art thou on God's ground? Canst thou give a "Thus saith the Lord" for the position which thou occupiest, at this moment? Art thou consciously standing on the solid ground of holy Scripture? Is there anything questionable in thy surroundings and associations? We beseech thee to weigh these questions solemnly as in the divine presence. Be assured they are of moment just now. We are passing through critical moments.

Men are taking sides; principles are working and coming to a head. Never was it more needful to be thoroughly and unmistakably on the Lord's side. Jehoshaphat never could have met the Ammonites, Moabites, and Edomites, had he not been persuaded that his feet were on the very ground which God had given to Abraham. If the enemy could have shaken his confidence as to this, he would have had an easy victory. But Jehoshaphat knew where he was; he knew his ground. He understood his bearings; and therefore he could fix his eyes with confidence upon the living God. He had no misgivings as to his position. He did not say, as many do, now-a-days, "I am not quite sure. I hope I am; but sometimes clouds come over my soul, and make me hesitate as to whether I am really on divine ground." Ah! no, reader, the king of Judah would not have understood such language at all. All was clear to him. His eye rested on the original grant. He felt sure he was on the true ground of the Israel of God; and albeit all Israel were not there with him, yet God was with him, and that was enough. His was a living faith in the living God—the only thing that will stand in the day of trial.

There is something in the attitude and utterance of the king of Judah, on that memorable occasion, well worthy of the reader's profound attention. His feet were firmly fixed on God's ground, and his eyes as firmly fixed on God Himself; and in addition to this, there was the deep sense of his own thorough nothingness. He had not so much as a shadow of a doubt as to the fact of his being in possession of the very inheritance which God had given him. He knew that he was in his right place. He did not *hope* it; still less did he doubt it; no, he knew it. He could say, "I believe and am sure."

This is all-important. It is impossible to stand against the enemy, if there is anything equivocal in our position. If there be any secret misgiving as to our being in our right place—if we cannot give a "Thus saith the Lord" for the position which we occupy, the path we tread, the associations in which we stand, the work in which we are engaged, there will, most assuredly, be weakness in the hour of conflict. Satan is sure to avail himself of the smallest misgiving in the soul. All must be settled as to our positive standing, if we would make any headway against the enemy. There must be an unclouded confidence as to our real position before God, else the foe will have an easy victory.

Now, it is precisely here that there is so much weakness apparent among the children of God. Very few, comparatively, are clear, sound, and settled as to their foundation—very few are able, without any reserve, to take the blessed ground of being washed in the blood of Jesus, and sealed with the Holy Spirit. At times they hope it. When things go well with them; when they have had a good time in the closet; when they have enjoyed nearness to God in prayer, or over the Word; while they are sitting under a clear, fervent, forcible ministry —at such moments, perhaps, they can venture to speak hopefully about themselves. But, very soon, dark clouds gather; they feel the workings of indwelling sin; they are afflicted with wandering thoughts; or it may be, they have been betrayed into some levity of spirit, or irritability of temper; then they begin to *reason* about themselves, and to question whether they are, in reality, the children of God. And from reasonings and questionings, they very speedily slip into positive unbelief, and then plunge into the thick gloom of a despondency bordering on despair.

All this is most sad. It is, at once, dishonoring to God, and destructive to the soul's peace; and as to progress, in such a condition, it is wholly out of the question. How can any one run a race, if he has not cleared the starting post? How can he erect a building, if he has not laid the foundation? And, on the same principle, how can a soul grow in the divine life, if he is always liable to doubt whether he has that life or not?

But it may be that some of our readers are disposed to put such a question as the following, "How can I be sure that I am on God's ground?—that I am washed in the blood of Jesus and sealed with the Holy Spirit?" We reply, How do you know that you are a lost sinner? Is it because you feel it? Is mere feeling the ground of your faith? If so, it is not a divine faith at all. True faith rests *only* on the testimony of holy Scripture. No doubt, it is by the gracious energy of the Holy

Ghost that any one can exercise this living faith; but we are speaking now of the true ground of faith—the authority—the basis on which it rests, and that is simply the holy Scriptures which, as the inspired apostle tells us, are able to make us wise unto salvation, and which even a child could know, without the church, the clergy, the fathers, the doctors, the councils, the colleges, or any other human intervention whatsoever.

"Abraham believed God." Here was divine faith. It was not a question of feeling. Indeed, if Abraham had been influenced by his feelings, he would have been a doubter instead of a believer. For what had he to build upon in himself? "His own body now dead." A poor ground surely on which to build his faith in the promise of an innumerable seed. But, we are told, "He considered not his own body now dead" (Rom. iv.). What, then, did he consider? He considered the word of the living God, and on that he rested. Now this is faith. And mark what the apostle says: "He staggered not at the promise of God through unbelief" (for unbelief is always a staggerer), "but was strong in faith, giving glory to God: and being fully persuaded that what He had promised, He was able also to perform. And *therefore* it was imputed to him for righteousness."

"Ah! but," the anxious reader may say, "what has all this to say to my case? I am not an Abraham—I cannot expect a special revelation from God. How am I to know that God has spoken to me?

How can I possess this precious faith?" Well, dear friend, mark the apostle's further statement. "Now," he adds, "it was not written for his (Abraham's) sake alone, that it was imputed to him; but for us also, to whom it shall be imputed, if"—if what?—if we feel, realize, or experience aught in ourselves? Nay, but "if we believe on Him that raised up Jesus our Lord from the dead; who was delivered for our offences, and was raised again for our justification."

All this is full of solid comfort and richest consolation. It assures the anxious inquirer that he has the self-same ground and authority to rest upon that Abraham had, with an immensely higher measure of light thrown on that ground, inasmuch as Abraham was called to believe in a promise, whereas we are privileged to believe in an accomplished fact. He was called to look forward to something which was to be done; we look back at something that is done, even an accomplished redemption, attested by the fact of a risen and glorified Saviour, at the right hand of the Majesty in the heavens.

But as to the ground or authority on which we are called to rest our souls, it is the same in our case as in Abraham's and all true believers' in all ages—it is the word of God—the holy Scriptures. There is no other foundation of faith but this; and the faith that rests on any other is not true faith at all. A faith resting on human tradition—on the authority of the Church—on the authority of so-called general councils—on the clergy—or on learned men, is not divine faith, but mere superstition; it is a faith which "stands in the wisdom of men," and "not in the power of God" (I Cor. ii. 5).

Now, it is utterly impossible for any human pen or mortal tongue to overstate the value or importance of this grand principle—this principle of a living faith. Its value at the present moment is positively unspeakable. We believe it to be the divine antidote against most, if not all, the leading errors, evils, and hostile influences of the day in which our lot is cast. There is a tremendous shaking going on around us. Minds are agitated. Disturbing forces are abroad. There is a loosening of the foundations. Old institutions, to which the human mind clings, as the ivy to the oak, are tottering on every side; and many are actually fallen: and thousands of souls that have been finding shelter in them are dislodged and scared, and know not whither to turn. Some are saying, "The bricks are thrown down, but we will build with hewn stone." Many are at their wit's end, and most are ill at ease.

Nor is this all; there is a numerous class, for the most part, of those who are not so much concerned about the condition and destiny of religious institutions and ecclesiastical systems, as about the condition and destiny of their own precious souls—of those who are not so much agitated by questions about "Broad Church," "High Church," "Low Church," "State Church," or "Free Church," as about this one great question, "What must I do to be saved?" What have we to say to these latter? What is the real want of their souls? Simply this, "A living faith in the living God." This is what is needed for all who are disturbed by what they see without, or feel within. Our unfailing resource is in the living God and in His Son Jesus Christ, as revealed by the Holy Spirit in the holy Scriptures.

Here is the true resting-place of faith, and to this we do, most earnestly, most urgently and solemnly, invite the anxious reader. In one word, we entreat him to stay his whole soul on the word of God—the holy Scriptures. Here we have authority for all that we need to know, to believe, or to do.

Is it a question of anxiety about my eternal salvation? Hear the following words, "Therefore, thus saith the Lord God, Behold, I lay in Zion *for a foundation*, a stone, a tried stone, a precious corner stone, *a sure foundation*: he that believeth shall not make haste" (Isa. xxviii. 16). These precious words, so pregnant with tranquilizing power, are quoted by the inspired apostle in the New Testament Scriptures: "Wherefore also it is contained in the scripture, Behold, I lay in Sion a chief corner stone, elect, precious: and *he that believeth on Him shall not be confounded*" (I Peter ii. 6).

What solid comfort—what deep and settled repose for the anxious soul is here! God has laid the foundation, and that foundation is nothing less than His own eternal and co-equal Son, the Son who had dwelt from all eternity in His bosom.

This foundation is, in every respect, adequate to sustain the whole weight of the counsels and purposes of the eternal THREE IN ONE—to meet all the claims of the nature, the character, and the throne of God.

Being all this, it must needs be fully adequate to meet all the need of the anxious soul, of what kind soever that need may be. If Christ is enough for God He must of necessity be enough for man—for any man—for the reader; and that He is enough is proved by the very passage just quoted. He is God's own foundation, laid by His own hand, the foundation and centre of that glorious system of royal and victorious grace set forth in the word "Zion." (See Heb. xii. 22-24.) He is God's own precious, tried, chief corner stone—that blessed One who went down into death's dark waters—bore the heavy judgment and wrath of God against sin—robbed death of its sting, and the grave of its victory—destroyed him that had the power of death—wrested from the enemy's grasp that terrible weapon with which sin had armed him, and made it the very instrument of his eternal defeat and confusion. Having done all this, He was received up into glory, and seated at the right hand of the Majesty in the heavens.

Such is God's foundation, to which He graciously calls the attention of every one who really feels the need of something divinely solid on which to build, in view of the hollow and shadowy scenes of this world, and in prospect of the stern realities of eternity.

Dear reader, you are now invited to build upon this foundation. Be assured it is for you as positively and distinctly as though you heard a voice from heaven speaking to your own very self. The word of the living God is addressed "to every creature under heaven"—"Whosoever will" is invited to come. The inspired volume has been placed in your hand and laid open before your eyes; and for what think you? Is it to mock or to tantalize you by presenting before you what was never intended for you? Ah! no, reader; such is not God's way. Does He send His sunlight and showers to mock and to tantalize, or to gladden and refresh? Do you ever think of calling in question your own very personal welcome to study the book of Creation? Never; and yet there might be some show of foundation of such a question, inasmuch as, since that wondrous volume was thrown open, sin has entered and thrown its dark blots over the pages thereof. But, spite of sin and all its forms and all its consequences, spite of Satan's power and malice, God has spoken. He has caused His voice to be heard in this dark and sinful world. And what has He said? "Behold, I lay in Zion a foundation." This is something entirely new. It is as though our blessed, loving, and ever gracious God had said to us, "Here, I have begun on the new. I have laid a foundation, on the ground of redemption, which nothing can ever touch, neither sin, or Satan, or aught else. I *lay* the foundation, and pledge My word that whosoever believes—whosoever commits himself, in childlike, unquestioning confidence, to My foundation—whosoever rests in My Christ—whosoever is satisfied with My precious, tried, chief corner stone, shall never—no, never—no, never be confounded—never be put to shame—never be disappointed—shall never perish, world without end."

Beloved reader, dost thou still hesitate? We solemnly avow we cannot see even the shadow of a foundation of a reason why thou shouldest. If there were any question raised, or any condition proposed, or any barrier erected, reason would that thou mightest hesitate. If there were so much as a single preliminary to be settled by thee—if it were made a question of feeling or of experience, or of aught else that thou couldst do, or feel, or be, then verily thou mightest justly pause. But there is absolutely nothing of the sort. There is the Christ of God and the word of God, and—what then? "He that believeth shall not be confounded." In short it is simply "A living faith in the living God." It is taking God at His word. It is believing what He says because He says it. It is committing your soul to the word of Him who cannot lie. It is doing what Abraham did when he believed God and was counted righteous. It is doing what Jehoshaphat did when he planted his foot firmly on those immortal words, "Thou gavest it to the seed of Abraham Thy friend, forever." It is doing what the patriarchs, the prophets, the apostles, the saints in all ages have done, when they rested their souls for time and eternity upon that Word which "is settled forever in heaven," and thus lived in peace and died in hope of a glorious resurrection. It is resting calmly and sweetly on the immovable rock of holy Scripture, and thus proving the divine and sustaining virtue of that which has never failed any who who trusted it, and never will, and never can.

Oh! the unspeakable blessedness of having such a foundation in a world like this where death, decay, and change are stamped upon all; where friendship's fondest links are snapped in the twinkling of an eye by death's rude hand; where all that seems, to nature's view, most stable, is liable to be swept away in a moment by the rushing tide of popular revolution; where there is absolutely nothing on which the heart can lean, and say, "I have now found permanent repose." What a mercy, in such a scene, to have "A living faith in the living God."

"They shall not be ashamed that wait for Me." Such is the veritable record of the living God—a record made good in the experience of all those who have been enabled, through grace, to exercise a living faith. But then we must remember how much is involved in those three words, "*wait for Me.*" The waiting must be a real thing. It will not do to *say* we are waiting on God, when, in reality, our eye is askance upon some human prop or creature confidence. We must be absolutely "shut up" to God. We must be brought to the end of self, and to the bottom of circumstances, in order fully to prove what the life of faith is, and what God's resources are. God and the creature can never occupy the same platform. It must be God alone. "My soul, wait thou *only* upon God; for my expectation is from Him. He *only* is my rock and my salvation" (Psa. lxii. 5, 6).

Thus it was with Jehoshaphat, in that scene recorded in 2 Chron. xx. He was wholly cast upon God. It was either God or nothing. "We have no might." But what then? "Our eyes are upon Thee." This was enough. It was well for Jehoshaphat not to have so much as a single atom of might—a single ray of knowledge. He was in the very best possible attitude and condition to prove what God was. It would have been an incalculable loss to him to have been possessed of the very smallest particle of creature strength or creature wisdom, inasmuch as it could only have proved a hindrance to him in leaning exclusively upon the arm and the counsel of the Almighty God. If the eye of faith rests upon the living God—if He fills the entire range of the soul's vision, then what do we want with might or knowledge of our own? Who would think of resting in that which is human when he can have that which is divine? Who would lean on an arm of flesh, when he can lean on the arm of the living God?

Reader, art thou, at this moment in any pressure, in any trial, need, or difficulty? If so, let us entreat thee to look simply and solely to the living God. Turn away thine eyes completely from the creature: "Cease from man, whose breath is in his nostrils."

Let thy faith take hold now on the strength of God Himself. Put thy whole case into His omnipotent hand. Cast thy burden, whatever it is, upon Him. Let there be no reserve. He is as willing as He is able, and as able as He is willing, to bear all. Only trust Him fully. He loves to be trusted—loves to be used. It is His joy, blessed be His name, to yield a ready and a full response to the appeal of faith. It is worth having a burden, to know the blessedness of rolling it over upon Him. So the king of Judah found it in the day of his trial, and so shall the reader find it now. God never fails a trusting heart. "They shall not be ashamed that wait for Me." Precious words! Let us mark how they are illustrated in the narrative before us.

No sooner had Jehoshaphat cast himself completely upon the Lord, than the divine response fell, with clearness and power, upon his ear. "Harken ye, all Judah, and ye inhabitants of Jerusalem, and thou king Jehoshaphat; thus saith the Lord unto you, Be not afraid or dismayed by reason of this great multitude; for the battle is not yours, but God's ... ye shall not need to fight in this battle. Set yourselves, stand ye still, and see the salvation of the Lord with you, O Judah and Jerusalem: fear not, nor be dismayed; to-morrow go out against them; for the Lord will be with you."

What an answer! "The battle is not yours, but God's." Only think of God's having a battle with people! Assuredly there could be little question as to the issue of such a battle. Jehoshaphat had put the whole matter into God's hands, and God took it up and made it entirely His own. It is always thus. Faith puts the difficulty, the trial, and the burden into God's hands, and leaves Him to act. This is enough. God never refuses to respond to the appeal of faith; nay, it is His delight to answer it. Jehoshaphat had made it a question between God and the enemy. He had said, "They have come to cast us out of *Thy* possession, which Thou hast given us to inherit."

Nothing could be simpler. God had given Israel the land, and He could keep them in it, spite of ten thousand foes. Thus faith would reason. The self-same Hand that had placed them in the land could keep them there. It was simply a question of divine power. "O our God, wilt Thou not judge them? for we have no might against this great company that cometh against us; neither know we what to do; but our eyes are upon Thee."

It is a wonderful point in the history of any soul, to be brought to say, "I have no might." It is the sure precursor of divine deliverance. The moment a man is brought to the discovery of his utter powerlessness, the divine word is, "Stand still, and see the salvation of God." One does not want "might" to "stand still." It needs no effort to "see the salvation of God." This holds good in reference to the sinner in coming to Christ, at the first; and it holds equally good in reference to the Christian in his whole career from first to last. The great difficulty is to get to the end of our own strength.

Once there, the whole thing is settled. There may be a vast amount of struggle and exercise ere we are brought to say "without strength!" But, the moment we take that ground, the word is, "Stand still, and see the salvation of God." Human effort, in every shape and form, can but raise a barrier between our souls and God's salvation. If God has undertaken for us, we may well be still. And has He not? Yes, blessed be His holy name, He has charged Himself with all that concerns us, for time and eternity; and hence we have only to let Him act for us, in all things. It is our happy privilege to let Him go before us, while we follow on "in wonder, love, and praise."

Thus it was in that interesting and instructive scene on which we have been dwelling. "Jehoshaphat bowed his head, with his face to the ground: and all Judah and the inhabitants of Jerusalem fell before the Lord, worshiping the Lord. And the Levites, of the children of the Kohathites, and of the children of the Korhites, stood up to praise the Lord God of Israel with a loud voice on high."

Here we have the true attitude and the proper occupation of the believer. Jehoshaphat withdrew his eyes from "that great company that had come against him," and fixed them upon the living God. Jehovah had come right in and placed Himself between His people and the enemy, just as He had done in the day of the exodus, at the Red Sea, so that instead of looking at the difficulties, they might look at Him.

This, beloved reader, is the secret of victory at all times, and under all circumstances. This it is which fills the heart with praise and thanksgiving, and bows the head in wondering worship. There is something perfectly beautiful in the entire bearing of Jehoshaphat and the congregation, on the occasion before us. They were evidently impressed with the thought that they had nothing to do but to praise God. And they were right. Had He not said to them, "Ye shall not need to fight"? What then had they to do? What remained for them? Nothing but praise. Jehovah was going out before them to fight; and they had but to follow after Him in adoring worship.

"And they rose early in the morning, and went forth in the wilderness of Tekoa: and as they went forth, Jehoshaphat stood and said, Hear me, O Judah, and ye inhabitants of Jerusalem; believe in the Lord your God, so shall ye be established; believe His prophets, so shall ye prosper" (2 Chron. xx. 20).

It is of the very last importance that God's word should ever have its own supreme place in the heart of the Christian. God has spoken. He has given us His Word; and it is for us to lean unshaken thereon. We want nothing more. The divine Word is amply sufficient to give confidence, peace, and stability to the soul. We do not need evidences from man to prove the truth of God's word. That Word carries its own powerful evidences with it. To suppose that we require human testimony to prove that God's word is true, is to imply that man's word is more valid, more trustworthy, more authoritative, than the word of God. If we need a human voice to interpret, to ratify, to make God's revelation available, then we are virtually deprived of that revelation altogether.

We call the special attention of the reader to this point. It concerns the integrity of Holy Scripture. The grand question is this, Is God's word sufficient or not? Do we really want man's authority to make us sure that God has spoken? Far be the thought! This would be placing man's word above God's word, and thus depriving us of the *only* solid ground on which our souls can lean. This is precisely what the devil has been aiming at from the very beginning, and it is what he is aiming at now. He wants to remove from beneath our feet the solid rock of divine revelation, and to give us instead the sandy foundation of human authority. Hence it is that we do so earnestly press upon our readers the urgent need of keeping close to God's word, in simple unquestioning faith. It is really the true secret of stability and peace. If God's word be not enough for us, without man's interference, we are positively left without any sure basis of our soul's confidence; yea, we are cast adrift on the wild watery waste of skepticism, we are plunged in doubt and dark uncertainty: we are most miserable.

But, thanks and praise be to God, it is not so. "*Believe in the Lord your God, so shall ye be established: believe His prophets, so shall ye prosper.*"

Here is the resting-place of faith in all ages. God's eternal Word, which is settled forever in heaven, which He has magnified according to all His name, and which stands forth in its own divine dignity and sufficiency before the eye of faith. We must utterly reject the idea that aught in the way of human authority, human evidences, or human feelings, is needful to make the testimony of God full weight in the balances of the soul. Grant us but this, that God has spoken, and we argue with bold decision that nothing more is needed as a foundation for genuine faith. In a word, if we want to be established and to prosper, we have simply to "Believe in the Lord our God." It was this that enabled Jehoshaphat to bow his head in holy worship. It was this that enabled him to praise God for victory ere a single blow was struck. It was this that conducted him into "the valley of Berachah" (*blessing*) and surrounded him with spoil more than he could carry away.

And now we have the soul-stirring record: "And when he had consulted with the people, he appointed *singers unto the Lord*, and that should praise the beauty of holiness, as they went out before the army, and to say, Praise the Lord: for His mercy endureth forever." What a strange advance guard for an army! A company of singers! Such is faith's way of ordering the battle.

"And when they began to sing and to praise, the Lord set ambushments against the children of Ammon, Moab, and Mount Seir, which were come against Judah, and they were smitten." Only think of the Lord setting ambushments! Think of His engaging in the business of military tactics! How wonderful! God will do any thing that His people need, if only His people will confide in Him, and leave themselves and their affairs absolutely in His hand.

"And when Judah came toward the watch-tower in the wilderness, they looked unto the multitude, and, behold, they were dead bodies fallen to the earth, and none escaped." Such was the end of "that great company"—that formidable host—that terrible foe. All vanished away before the presence of the God of Israel. Yes, and had they been a million times more numerous, and more formidable, the issue would have been the same, for circumstances are nothing to the living God, and nothing to a living faith. When God fills the vision of the soul, difficulties fade away, and songs of praise break forth from joyful lips.

"And when Jehoshaphat and his people came to take away the spoil of them" (for that was all they had to do) "they found among them in abundance both riches with the dead bodies, and precious jewels, which they stripped off for themselves, more than they could carry away; and they were three days in gathering of the spoil, it was so much. And on the fourth day, they assembled themselves in the valley of Berachah; for there they blessed the Lord."

Such, beloved reader, must ever be the result of a living faith in the living God. More than two thousand five hundred years have rolled away since the occurrence of the event on which we have been dwelling; but the record is as fresh as ever. No change has come over the living God, or over the living faith which ever takes hold of His strength, and counts on His faithfulness. It is as true to-day as it was in the day of Jehoshaphat, that those who believe in the Lord our God shall be established, and shall prosper. They shall be endowed with strength, crowned with victory, clothed with spoils, and filled with songs of praise. May we, then through the gracious energy of the Holy Spirit, ever be enabled to exercise "A LIVING FAITH IN THE LIVING GOD!"

A SCRIPTURAL INQUIRY
AS TO THE TRUE NATURE OF
THE SABBATH, THE LAW, AND CHRISTIAN MINISTRY

THE SABBATH.

If it were merely a question of the observance or non-observance of a day, it might be easily disposed of, inasmuch as the apostle teaches us in Rom. xiv. 5, 6, and also in Col. ii. 16, that such things are not to be made a ground of judgment. But seeing there is a great principle involved in the Sabbath question, we deem it to be of the very last importance to place it upon a clear and Scriptural basis. We shall quote the Fourth Commandment at full length: "Remember the sabbath day, to keep it holy. Six days shalt thou labor, and do all thy work; but the seventh day is the sabbath of the Lord thy God: in it thou shalt not do any work, thou, nor thy son, nor thy daughter, thy manservant, nor thy maidservant, nor thy cattle, nor thy stranger that is within thy gates: for in six days the Lord made heaven and earth, the sea, and all that in them is, and rested the seventh day: wherefore the Lord blessed the sabbath day, and hallowed it" (Ex. xx. 8-11). This same law is repeated in Exodus xxxi. 12-17. And in pursuance thereof we find in Numbers xv. a man stoned for gathering sticks on the sabbath day. All this is plain and absolute enough. Man has no right to alter God's law in reference to the sabbath; no more than he has to alter it in reference to murder, adultery, or theft. This, we presume, will not be called in question. The entire body of old Testament Scripture fixes the seventh day as the sabbath; and the Fourth Commandment lays down the mode in which that sabbath was to be observed. Now where, we ask, is this precedent followed? Where is this command obeyed? Is it not plain that the professing Church neither keeps the right day as the sabbath, nor does she keep it after the Scripture mode? The commandments of God are made of none effect by human traditions, and the glorious truths which hang around "the Lord's day" are lost sight of. The Jew is robbed of his distinctive day and all the privileges therewith connected, which are only suspended for the present, while judicial blindness hangs over that loved and interesting, though now judged and scattered, people. And furthermore, the Church is robbed of her distinctive day and all the glories therewith connected, which if really understood would have the effect of lifting her above earthly things into the sphere which properly belongs to her, as linked by faith to her glorified Head in heaven. In result, we have

- 216 -

neither pure Judaism nor pure Christianity, but an anomalous system arising out of an utterly unscriptural combination of the two.

However, we desire to refrain from all attempt at developing the deeply spiritual doctrine involved in this great question, and confine ourselves to the plain teaching of Scripture on the subject; and in so doing we maintain that if the professing Church quotes the Fourth Commandment and parallel scriptures in defense of keeping the sabbath, then it is evident that in almost every case the law is entirely set aside. Observe, the word is, "Thou shalt not do any work." This ought to be perfectly binding on all who take the Jewish ground. There is no room here for introducing what we deem to be "works of necessity." We may think it necessary to kindle fires, to make servants harness our horses and drive us hither and thither. But the law is stern and absolute, severe and unbending. It will not, it can not, lower its standard to suit our convenience or accommodate itself to our thoughts. The mandate is, "Thou shalt not do *any* work," and that, moreover, on "the seventh day," which answers to our Saturday. We ask for a single passage of Scripture in which the day is changed, or in which the strict observance of the day is in the smallest degree relaxed.

We request the reader of these lines to pause and search out this matter thoroughly in the light of Scripture. Let him not be scared as by some terrible bugbear, but let him, in true Berean nobility of spirit, "search the Scriptures." By so doing he will find that from the second chapter of Genesis down to the very last passage in which the sabbath is named, it means the *seventh* day and none other; and further, that there is not so much as a shadow of divine authority for altering the mode of observing that day. Law is law, and if we are under the law we are bound to keep it or else be cursed; for "it is written, Cursed is every one that continueth not in all things which are written in the book of the law to do them " (Deut. xxvii. 26; Gal. iii. 10).

But it will be said, "We are not under the Mosaic law; we are the subjects of the Christian economy." Granted; most fully, freely and thankfully granted. All true Christians are, according to the teaching of Romans vii. and viii. and Galatians iii. and iv., the happy and privileged subjects of the Christian dispensation. But if so, what is the day which specially characterizes that dispensation? Not "the seventh day," but "the first day of the week"—"THE LORD'S DAY." This is pre-eminently the Christian's day. Let him observe this day with all the sanctity, the sacred reverence, the hallowed retirement, the elevated tone, of which his new nature is capable. We believe the Christian's retirement from all secular things cannot possibly be too profound on the Lord's day. The idea of any one, calling himself a Christian, making the Lord's day a season of what is popularly called recreation, unnecessary traveling, personal convenience, or profit in temporal things, is perfectly shocking. We are of opinion that such acting could not be too severely censured. We can safely assert that we never yet came in contact with a godly, intelligent, right-minded Christian person who did not love and reverence the Lord's day; nor could we have any sympathy with any one who could deliberately desecrate that holy and happy day.

We are aware, alas, that some persons have through ignorance or misguided feelings said things in reference to the Lord's day which we utterly repudiate, and that they have done things on the Lord's day of which we wholly disapprove. We believe that there is a body of New Testament teaching on the important subject of the Lord's day quite sufficient to give that day its proper place in every well-regulated mind. The Lord Jesus rose from the dead on that day (Matt, xxviii. 1-6; Mark xvi. I, 2; Luke xxiv. I; John xx. I). He met His disciples once and again on that day (John xx. 19, 26). The early disciples met to break bread on that day (Acts xx. 7). The apostle, by the Holy Ghost, directs the Corinthians to lay by their contributions for the poor on that day (I Cor. xvi. 2). And finally, the exiled apostle was in the Spirit and received visions of the future on that day (Rev. i. 10). The above scriptures are conclusive. They prove that the Lord's day occupies a place quite unique, quite heavenly, quite divine. But they as fully prove the entire distinctness of the Jewish sabbath and the Lord's day. The two days are spoken of throughout the New Testament with fully as much distinctness as we speak of Saturday and Sunday. The only difference is that the latter are heathen titles, and the former divine. (Comp. Matt. xxviii. I; Acts xiii. 14, xvii. 2, xx. 7; Col. ii. 16).

Having said thus much as to the question of the Jewish sabbath and the Lord's day, we shall suggest the following questions to the reader, namely: Where in the word of God is the sabbath said to be changed to the first day of the week? Where is there any repeal of the law as to the sabbath? Where is the authority for altering the day or the mode of observing it? Where in Scripture have we such an expression as "the Christian sabbath"? Where is the Lord's day ever called the sabbath?[27]

We would not yield to any of our dear brethren in the various denominations around us in the pious observance of the Lord's day. We love and honor it with all our hearts; and were it not that the gracious providence of God has so ordered it in these realms that we can enjoy the rest and retirement of the Lord's day without pecuniary loss, we should feel called upon to abstain from business, and give ourselves wholly up to the worship and service of God on that day—not as a matter of cold legality, but as a holy and happy privilege.

It would be the deepest sorrow to our hearts to think that a true Christian should be found taking common ground with the ungodly, the profane, the thoughtless, and the pleasure-hunting multitude, in desecrating the Lord's day. It would be sad indeed if the children of the kingdom and the children of this world were to meet in an excursion train on the Lord's day. We feel persuaded that any who in any wise profane or treat with lightness the Lord's day act in direct opposition to the Word and Spirit of God.

THE LAW

As regards the law, it is looked at in two ways; first, as a ground of justification; and secondly, as a rule of life. A passage or two of Scripture will suffice to settle both the one and the other: "Therefore by the deeds of the law there shall no flesh be justified in His sight: for by the law is the knowledge of sin" (Rom. iii. 20). "Therefore we conclude that a man is justified by faith without the deeds of the law" (ver. 28). Again: "Knowing that a man is not justified by the works of the law, but by the faith of Jesus Christ, even we have believed in Jesus Christ, that we might be justified by the faith of Christ, and not by the works of the law; for by the works of the law shall no flesh be justified" (Gal. ii. 16).

Then, as to its being a rule of life, we read, "Wherefore, my brethren, ye also are become dead to the law by the body of Christ; that ye should be married to another, even to Him that is raised from the dead, that we should bring forth fruit unto God" (Rom. vii. 4). "But now are we delivered from the law, being dead to that (see margin) wherein we were held: that we should serve in newness of spirit, and not in the oldness of the letter" (ver. 6). Observe in this last-quoted passage two things: first, "we are delivered from the law;" second, not that we may do nature's pleasure, but "that we should *serve* in newness of spirit." Being delivered from bondage, it is our privilege to "serve" in liberty. Again we read, further on in the chapter, "And the commandment which was ordained to life, I found to be *unto death*" (ver. 10). It evidently did not prove as a rule of *life* to him. "I was *alive without the law* once; but *when the commandment came*, sin revived, and *I died*" (ver. 9). Whoever "I" represents in this chapter was alive until the law came, and then he died. Hence, therefore, the law could not have been a rule of life to him; yea, it was the very opposite, even a rule of death.

In a word, then, it is evident that a sinner cannot be justified by the works of the law; and it is equally evident that the law is not the rule of the believer's life. "For as many as are of the works of the law are under the curse" (Gal. iii. 10). The law knows no such thing as a distinction between a regenerated and an unregenerated man: it curses all who attempt to stand before it. It rules and curses a man so long as he lives; nor is there any one who will so fully acknowledge that he cannot keep it as the true believer, and hence no one would be more thoroughly under the curse.

What, therefore, is the ground of our justification? and what is our rule of life? The word of God answers, "We are justified by the faith of Christ," and Christ is our rule of life. He bore all our sins in His own body on the tree; He was made a curse for us; He drained on our behalf the cup of God's righteous wrath; He deprived death of its sting, and the grave of its victory; He gave up His life for us; He went down into death, where we lay, in order that He might bring us up in eternal association with Himself in life, righteousness, favor and glory, before our God and His God, our Father and His Father. (See carefully the following scriptures: John xx. 17; Rom. iv. 25; v. I-10; vi. I-11; vii. *passim*, viii. I-4; I Cor. i. 30, 31; vi. 11; xv. 55-57; 2 Cor. v. 17-21; Gal. iii. 13, 25-29; iv. 31; Eph. i. 19-23; ii. I-6; Col. ii. 10-15; Heb. ii. 14, 15; I Peter i. 23.) If the reader will prayerfully ponder all these passages of Scripture he will see clearly that we are not justified by the works of the law; and not only so, but he will see how we are justified. He will see the deep and solid foundations of the Christian's life, righteousness and peace planned in God's eternal counsels, laid in the finished atonement of Christ, developed by God the Holy Ghost in the Word, and made good in the happy experience of all true believers.

Then, as to the believer's rule of life, the apostle does not say, To me to live is the law; but, "To me to live is Christ" (Phil. i. 21). Christ is our rule, our model, our touchstone, our all. The continual inquiry of the Christian should be, not is this or that according to law? but is it like Christ? The law never could teach me to love, bless and pray for my enemies; but this is exactly what the gospel teaches me to do, and what the divine nature leads me to do. "Love is the fulfilling of the law;" and yet, were I to seek justification by the law, I should be lost; and were I to make the law my standard of action, I should fall far short of my proper mark. We are predestinated to be conformed, not to the law, but to the image of God's Son. We are to be like Him. (See Matt. v. 21-48; Rom. viii. 29; I Cor. xiii. 4-8; Rom. xiii. 8-10; Gal. v. 14-26; Eph. i. 3-5; Phil. iii. 20, 21; ii. 5; iv. 8; Col. iii. I-17.)

It may seem a paradox to some to be told that "the righteousness of the law is fulfilled in us" (Rom. viii. 4), and yet that we cannot be justified by the law, nor make the law our rule of life. Nevertheless, thus it is if we are to form our convictions by the word of God. Nor is there any difficulty to the renewed mind in understanding this blessed doctrine. We are by nature "dead in trespasses and sins," and what can a dead man do? How can a man get life by keeping that which requires life to keep it—a life which he has not? And how do we get life? Christ is our life. We live in Him who died for us; we are blessed in Him who became a curse for us by hanging on a tree; we are righteous in Him who was made sin for us; we are brought nigh in Him who was cast out for us (Rom. v. 6-15; Eph. ii. 4-6; Gal. iii. 13). Having thus life and righteousness in Christ, we are called to walk as He walked, and not merely to walk as a Jew. We are called to purify ourselves even as He is pure; to walk in His footsteps; to show forth His virtues; to manifest His spirit (John xiii. 14, 15; xvii. 14-19; I Peter ii. 21; I John ii. 6, 29; iii. 3).

We shall close our remarks on this head by suggesting two questions to the reader, namely, Would the Ten Commandments without the New Testament be a sufficient rule of life for the believer? Is not the New Testament a sufficient rule without the Ten Commandments? Surely that which is insufficient cannot be our rule of life.

We receive the Ten Commandments as part of the canon of inspiration; and moreover, we believe that the law remains in full force to rule and curse a man as long as he liveth. Let a sinner only try to get life by it, and see where it will put him; and let a believer only shape his way according to it, and see what it will make of him. We are fully convinced that if a man is walking according to the spirit of the gospel, he will not commit murder nor steal; but we are also convinced that a man, confining himself to the standard of the law of Moses would fall very far short of the spirit of the gospel.

The subject of "the law" would demand much more elaborate exposition, but the limits of this paper do not admit of it, and we therefore entreat of the reader to look out the various passages of Scripture referred to and ponder them carefully. In this way we feel assured he will arrive at a sound conclusion, and be independent of all human teaching and influence. He will see how that a man is justified freely by the grace of God through faith in a crucified and risen Christ; that he is made a partaker of divine life, and introduced into a condition of divine and everlasting righteousness, and consequent exemption from all condemnation; that in this holy and elevated position Christ is his object, his theme, his model, his rule, his hope, his joy, his strength, his all; that the hope which is set before him is to be with Jesus where He is, and to be like Him forever. And he will also see that if as a lost sinner he has found pardon and peace at the foot of the cross, he is not, as an accepted and adopted son, sent back to the foot of Mount Sinai, there to be terrified and repulsed by the terrible anathemas of a broken law. The Father could not think of ruling with an iron law the prodigal whom He had received to His bosom in purest, deepest, richest grace. Oh no! "Being justified by faith, we have peace with God through our Lord Jesus Christ; by whom also we have access by faith into this grace wherein we stand, and rejoice in hope of the glory of God" (Rom. v. I, 2). The believer is justified not by works, but by *faith*; he stands not in law, but in *grace*; and he waits not for judgment, but for *glory*.

We come now, in the third place, to treat of the subject of

THE CHRISTIAN MINISTRY

in reference to which we have only to say, that we hold it to be a divine institution: its source, its power, its characteristics, are all divine and heavenly. We believe that the great Head of the Church received in resurrection gifts for His body. He, and not the Church, or any section of the Church, is the reservoir of the gifts. They are vested in Him, and not in the Church. He imparts them as, and to whom, He will. No man, nor body of men, can impart gifts. This is Christ's prerogative, and His alone; and we believe that when He imparts a gift, the man who receives that gift is responsible to exercise the same, whether as an evangelist, a pastor or a teacher, quite independently of all human authority.

We do not by any means believe that all are endowed with the above gifts, though all have some ministry to fulfil. All are not evangelists, pastors, and teachers. Such precious gifts are only administered according to the sovereign will of the divine Head of the Church. Man has no right to interfere with them. Wherever they really exist, it is the place of the assembly to recognize them with devout thankfulness. Christians are exhorted to remember them that are over them in the Lord, to know them that guide them, and those who addict themselves to the ministry of the saints, and those who have spoken to them the word of life. Were they to refuse to do so, they would only be forsaking and rejecting their own mercies, for all things are theirs. (See Rom. xii. 3-8; I Cor. iii. 21-23; xii., xiv., xvi. 15; Gal. i. 11-17; Eph. iv. 7-16; I Thess. v. 12, 13; Heb. xiii. 7, 17; I Peter iv. 10, 11.)

All this is simple enough. We can easily see where a man is divinely qualified for any department of ministry. It is not if a man *say* he has a gift, but if he in reality has it. A man may say he has a gift on the same principle as he may say he has faith (James ii. 14), and it may only be, after all, an empty conceit of his own ill-adjusted mind, which a spiritual assembly could not recognize for a moment. God deals in realities. A divinely-gifted evangelist is a reality; a teacher is a reality; a pastor is a reality; and such will be duly recognized, thankfully received, and counted worthy of all esteem and honor for their work's sake.

Now we hold that unless a man has a *bona fide* gift imparted to him by the Head of the Church, all the instruction, all the education, and all the training that men could impart to him would not constitute him a Christian minister. If a man has a gift, he is responsible to exercise, to cultivate, and to wait upon his gift.

But unless a man has a direct gift from Christ, though he had all the learning of a Newton, all the philosophy of a Bacon, all the eloquence of a Demosthenes, he is not a Christian minister. He may be a very gifted and efficient minister of religion, so called; but a minister of religion and a minister of Christ are two different things. And further, we believe that where the Lord Christ has bestowed a gift, that gift makes the possessor thereof a Christian minister, whom all true Christians are bound to own and receive, quite apart from all human appointment: whereas, though a man had all the human qualifications, human titles and human authority which it is possible to possess, and yet lacked that one grand reality, namely, Christ's gift, he is not a minister of Christ.

We thank God for Christian ministry; and we feel assured that there are many truly gifted servants of Christ in the various denominations around us; but they are ministers of Christ on the ground of possessing His gift, and not, by any means, on the ground of man's ordination. Man cannot add aught to a heaven-bestowed gift. As well might he attempt to add a shade to the rainbow, a tint to the violet, motion to the waves, height to the snow-capped mountains, or daub with a painter's brush the peacock's plumage, as attempt to render more efficient by his puny authority the gift which has come down from the risen and glorified Head of the Church. Ah no! the vine, the olive and the fig-tree, in Jotham's parable (Judges ix.) needed not the appointment of the other trees. God had implanted in each its specific virtue. It was only the worthless bramble which hailed with delight an appointment that raised it from the position of *a real nothing* to be *an official something*. Thus it is with a divinely-gifted man. He has what God has given him: he wants, he asks no more. He rises above the narrow enclosure which man's authority would erect around him, and plants his foot upon that elevated ground where prophets and apostles have stood. He feels that it lies not within the range of the schools and colleges of this world to open to him his proper sphere of action. It appertains not to them to provide a setting for the precious gem which sovereign grace has imparted. The hand which has bestowed the gem can alone provide the proper setting. The grace which has implanted the gift can alone throw open a proper sphere for its exercise. What! can it be possible that those gifts which emanate from the Church's triumphant and glorious Lord are not available for her edification until they are dragged through the mire of a heathen mythology? Alas for the heart that can think so! As well might we say that the fatness of the olive and the pure blood of the grape must be mingled with the contents of a quagmire to render them available for human use.

But it will be asked, "Were there not elders and deacons in the early Church, and ought we not to have such likewise?" Unquestionably there were elders and deacons in the early Church. They were appointed by the apostles, or those whom the apostles deputed: that is to say, they were appointed by the Holy Ghost—the only One who could then, or can now, appoint them. We believe that none but God can make or appoint an elder, and therefore for man to set about such work is but a powerless form, an empty name. Men may, and do, point us to the shadows of their own creation, and call upon us to recognize in those shadows divine realities; but alas! when we examine them in the light of Holy Scripture, we cannot even trace the outline, to say nothing of the living, speaking features of the divine original. We see divinely-appointed elders in the New Testament, and we see humanly-appointed elders in the professing Church; but we can by no means accept the latter as a substitute for the former. We cannot accept a mere shadow in lieu of the substance. Neither do we believe that men have any divine authority for their act when they set about making and appointing elders. We believe that when Paul, or Timothy, or Titus, ordained elders, they did so as acting by the power and under the direct authority of the Holy Ghost; but we deny that any man, or body of men, can so act now. We believe it was the Holy Ghost then, and it must be the Holy Ghost now. Human assumption is perfectly contemptible. If God raises up an elder or a pastor we thankfully own him. He both can and does raise up such. He does raise up men fitted by His Spirit to take the oversight of His flock, and to feed His lambs and sheep. His hand is not shortened that He cannot provide those blessings for His Church even amid its humiliating ruins. The reservoir of spiritual gift in Christ the Head is not so exhausted that He cannot shed forth upon His body all that is needed for the edification thereof. We are of opinion that were it not for our impatient attempts to provide for ourselves by making pastors and elders of our own, we should be far more richly endowed with pastors and teachers after God's own heart. We need not marvel that He leaves us to our own resources when by our unbelief we limit Him in His.

Instead of "proving" Him, we "limit" Him, and therefore we are shorn of our strength and left in barrenness and desolation; or, what is worse, we betake ourselves to the miserable provisions of human expediency. However, we believe it is far better, if we have not God's reality, to remain in the position of real, felt, confessed weakness than to put forth the hollow assumption of strength; we believe it is better to be real in our poverty than to put on the appearance of wealth. It is infinitely better to wait on God for whatever He may be pleased to bestow, than to limit His grace by our unbelief, or hinder His provision for us by making provision for ourselves.

We ask, where is the Church's warrant for calling, making or appointing pastors? Where have we an instance in the New Testament of a Church electing its own pastor? Acts i. 23-26 has been adduced in proof. But the very wording of the passage is sufficient to prove that it furnishes no warrant whatever. Even the eleven apostles could not elect a brother apostle, but had to commit it to higher authority. Their words are, "THOU, LORD, *which knowest the hearts of all,* show whether of these two *Thou hast chosen.*" This is very plain. They did not attempt to choose. God knew the heart. He had formed the vessel. He had put the treasure therein, and He alone could appoint it to its proper place.

It is very evident, therefore, that the case of the eleven apostles calling upon the Lord to choose a man to fill up their number affords no precedent whatever for a congregation electing a pastor: it is entirely against any such practice. God alone can make or appoint an apostle or an elder, an evangelist or a pastor. This is our firm belief, and we ask for Scripture proof of its unsoundness. Human opinion will not avail; tradition will not avail; expediency will not avail. Are we taught from the word of God that the early Church ever elected its own pastors or teachers? We positively affirm that there is not so much as a single line of Scripture in proof of any such custom. If we could only find direction in the word of God to make and appoint pastors, we should at once seek to carry such direction into effect; but in the absence of any divine warrant we could only regard it as a mimicry on our part to attempt any such a thing. Why was not the church at Ephesus, or why were not the churches at Crete, directed to elect or appoint elders? Why was the direction given to Timothy and Titus without the slightest reference to the Church, or to any part of the Church? Because, as we believe, Timothy and Titus acted by the direct power and under the direct authority of God the Holy Ghost, and hence their appointment was to be regarded by the Church as divine.[28]

But where have we anything like this now? Where is the Timothy or the Titus now? Where is there the least intimation in the New Testament that there should be a succession of men invested with the power to ordain elders or pastors? True, the apostle Paul, in his second epistle to Timothy, says, "The things which thou hast heard of me among many witnesses, the same commit thou to faithful men, who shall be able to teach others also" (2 Tim. ii. 2). But there is not a word here about a succession of men having power to ordain elders and pastors. Assuredly teaching is not ordination; still less is it imparting the power to ordain. If the inspired apostle had meant to convey to the mind of Timothy that he was to commit to others authority to ordain, and that such authority was to descend by a regular chain of succession, he could and would have done so; and in that case the passage would have run thus: "The power which has been vested in you, the same do thou vest in faithful men, that they may be able also to ordain others." Such, however, is not the case; and we deny that there is any man or body of men now upon earth possessing power to ordain elders, nor was that power or authority ever committed to the Church. We hold it to be absolutely divine; and therefore, when God sends an elder or a pastor, an evangelist or a teacher, we thankfully hail the heaven-bestowed gift;[29] but we desire to be delivered from all empty pretension. We will have God's reality or nothing. We will have heaven's genuine coin, not earth's counterfeit. Like the Tirshatha of old, who said "that they should not eat of the most holy things till there stood up a priest with Urim and Thummim" (Ezra ii. 63), so would we say, let us rather, if it must be so, remain without office-bearers than substitute for God's realities the shadows of our own creation. Ezra could not accept the pretensions of men. Men might *say* they were priests; but if they could not produce the divine warrant and the divine qualifications, they were utterly rejected. In order for a man to be entitled to approach the altar of the God of Israel, he should not only be descended from Aaron, but also be free from every bodily blemish. (See Lev. xxi. 16-23.) So now, in order for any man to minister in the Church of God, he must be a regenerated man, and he must have the necessary spiritual qualifications. Even St. Paul, in his powerful appeal to the conscience and judgment of the church at Corinth, refers to his spiritual gifts and the fruits of his labor as the indisputable evidences of his apostleship. (See 2 Cor. x., xii.)

Before dismissing the subject of the Christian Ministry, we would offer a remark upon the practise of laying on of hands, which is presented in the New Testament in two ways. First, we find it connected with the communication of a positive gift. "Neglect not the gift that is in thee, which was given thee by prophecy, with the laying on of the hands of the presbytery" (I Tim. iv. 14). This is again referred to in the second epistle: "Wherefore I put thee in remembrance that thou stir up the gift of God which is in thee by the putting on of my hands" (2 Tim. i. 6). This latter passage fixes the import of the expression "presbytery," as used in the first epistle. Both passages prove that the act of laying on of hands in Timothy's case was connected with the imparting of a gift. But secondly, we find the laying on of hands adopted simply for the purpose of expressing full fellowship and identification, as in Acts xiii. 3. It could not possibly mean ordination in this passage, inasmuch as Paul and Barnabas had been in the ministry long before. It simply gave beautiful expression to the full identification of their brethren in that work unto which the Holy Ghost had called them, and to which He alone could send them forth.

Now we believe that the laying on of hands as expressing ordination, if there be not the power to impart a gift, is worth nothing, if indeed it be not mere assumption; but if it be merely adopted as the expression of full fellowship in any special work or mission, we should quite rejoice in it. For example, if two or three brethren felt themselves called of God to go on an evangelistic mission to some foreign land, and that those with whom they were in communion perceived in them the needed gift and grace for such a work, we should deem it exceedingly happy were they to set forth their unqualified approval and their brotherly fellowship by the act of laying on of hands. Beyond this we can see no value whatever in that act.

Having thus, so far as our limits would permit, treated of the questions of the Sabbath, the Law, and the Christian Ministry; having shown that we honor and observe the Lord's day, that we give the Law its divinely appointed place, and finally, that we hold the sacred and precious institution of the Christian Ministry, we might close this paper, did we not feel called upon to present a few other points. In our general teaching and preaching we seek to set forth the fundamental truths of the gospel, such as the doctrine of the Trinity; the eternal Sonship; the personality of the Holy Ghost; the plenary inspiration of Holy Scripture; the eternal counsels of God in reference to His elect; the fullest and freest presentation of His love to a lost world; the solemn responsibility of every one who hears the glad tidings of salvation to accept the same; man's total ruin by nature and by practice; his inability to help himself in thought, word, or deed; the utter corruption of his will; Christ's incarnation, death, and resurrection; His absolute deity and perfect humanity in one person; the perfect efficacy of His blood to cleanse from all sin; perfect justification and sanctification by faith in Christ, through the operation of God the Holy Ghost; the eternal security of all true believers; the entire separation of the Church in calling, standing and hope from this present world.

Then, again, we hold, in common with many of our brethren in the denominations, that the hope of the believer is set forth in these words of Christ: "I will come again and receive you unto myself; that where I am, there ye may be also" (John xiv.

3). We believe that the early Christians were converted to "that blessed hope"—that it was the common hope of Christians in apostolic times. To adduce proofs would swell this paper into a volume.

Furthermore, we believe that all disciples should meet on the first day of the week to break bread (Acts xx. 7); and when so met, they should look to the Head of the Church to furnish the needed gifts, and to the Holy Ghost to guide in the due administration of these gifts.

As to the Scriptural ordinance of baptism, we look upon it as a beautiful exhibition of the truth of the believer's identification with Christ in death. (See Matt. xxviii. 19; Mark xvi. 16; Acts ii. 38, 41; viii. 38; x. 47, 48; xvi. 33; Rom. vi. 3, 4.)

As regards the precious institution of the Lord's Supper, we believe that Christians should celebrate it on every Lord's day, and that in so doing they commemorate the Lord's death until He come. We believe that as baptism sets forth our death with Christ, so the Lord's Supper sets forth Christ's death for us. We do not see any authority in the word of God for regarding the Lord's Supper as "a sacrifice," "a sacrament," or "a covenant." The word is, "This do in remembrance of Me." (See Matt. xxvi. 26-28; Mark xiv. 22-24; Luke xxii. 19, 20; I Cor. xi. 23-26.)

The above is a very brief but explicit statement of what we hold, and preach and practise. We meet in public: our worship meetings, our prayer meetings, our reading meetings, our lectures, our gospel preachings, are all open to the public.

But we have done. We would in this closing line entreat the reader to "search the Scriptures." Let him try everything by that standard. Let him see to it that he has plain Scripture for everything with which he stands connected. "To the law and to the testimony: if they speak not according to this word, it is because there is no light in them" (Isa. viii. 20.).

We can honestly say we love with all our hearts all those who love our Lord Jesus Christ in sincerity; and wherever there is one who preaches a full, free and an everlasting salvation to perishing sinners, through the blood of the Lamb, we wish him godspeed in the name of the Lord.

We now commend the reader to the blessing of the Father, and of the Son, and of the Holy Ghost. If he be a true believer, we pray that in his course down here he may be a bright and faithful witness for his absent Lord. But if he be one who has not yet found peace in Jesus, we would say to him, with solemn emphasis and earnest affection, "BEHOLD THE LAMB OF GOD, WHICH TAKETH AWAY THE SIN OF THE WORLD!" (John i. 29).

C. H. M.

THE MINISTRY OF CHRIST
PAST, PRESENT, AND FUTURE

(Scriptures read before lecture, Exodus xxi. I-6; John xiii. I-10; Luke xii. 37.)

"For even the Son of Man came not to be ministered unto, but to minister, and to give His life a ransom for many." (Mark x. 45.)

It is very necessary, beloved friends, to retire from all thoughts about our service to the Lord, and our work for Him, and to have our hearts occupied with His service toward us. And when I say this, you will not suppose for a moment that it is my desire or thought to weaken in any heart in this assembly, in the smallest degree, the desire to work for Christ, whatever sphere He may open for you, or according to whatever gift He may have bestowed upon you. Quite the reverse; indeed, I would seek in every way to strengthen and intensify that desire. But then one knows, both from experience and observation, that we may be so occupied with *our* work and *our* services that our hearts may lose the sense of what Christ is toward us in His marvelous character as a servant.

And here let me say that my immediate thesis to-night is the Lord Jesus as the servant of His people's necessities. That is the field into which we are introduced by those scriptures which have been read in your hearing. The Lord Jesus is the servant of the soul's necessities in every stage of its history, from first to last,—from the depths of your ruin and degradation as sinners, in all your weakness and failure as saints from day to day, until He plants you in the joys of His own kingdom. And His services will not end there; for, as we read in Luke xii. 37, He will gird Himself, and serve us in the glory. Thus His work as a servant overlaps the whole of the soul's history, past, present, and future. He has served us in the past, He is serving us now, and He will serve us forever.

And here allow me to say that the line of truth which I have to bring before you to-night is of a directly individual character. We were speaking, on this night week, of the truth with respect to our corporate condition and character, and therefore I feel all the more free on this occasion to enter upon what is more directly personal—to speak of truth which bears directly on the soul's individual condition and wants. And I would ask you, my beloved hearers, to place yourselves, so far as through grace you can, in all simplicity and reality, straight in view of this theme—Christ the servant of our necessities.

It is possible there may be souls in this room who want to begin at the very beginning with this most precious theme. They want to know Christ as the One who came into this world to serve them in all their deep and varied need as lost, self-destroyed, guilty, hell-deserving sinners. If there be any such present to-night, I would ask them to ponder deeply that verse which I have read, "The Son of Man is come to serve and to give."

This is a divine reality. Jesus came into this world to meet our need, to serve us in all that in which we need His precious service, and to give His life a ransom for many; to serve us by bearing our sins in His own body on the tree, and working out a full and an eternal salvation. He did not come to get—He did not come to take—He did not come to be ministered to— He did not come to be gazed at—He came to be used; and therefore, while the soul that is exercised may be raising this harassing question, "What can I do for the Lord?" The answer is.

"You must pause and see and believe what the Lord has done for you. You must stand still and see the salvation of God." Remember those words of divine and evangelistic sweetness, "To him that *worketh not*, but believeth on Him that justifieth the ungodly, his faith is counted for righteousness." (Rom. iv. 5.) You can never intelligently or properly serve Christ until you know and believe how He has served you. You must cease your restless doings, and rest in a divinely accomplished work. Then, but not until then, will you be able to start on a career of Christian service. It is most necessary for all anxious souls to understand that all true Christian service begins with the possession of eternal life, and is rendered in the power of the Holy Ghost, the indwelling Spirit, in the light and on the authority of holy Scripture. This is the divine idea of Christian work and service.

Now, though the primary object of this meeting, brethren, is for those who are saints of God, who have set out on their course, still I do not think it would be according to the heart and sympathies of Christ to overlook the fact that there may be some soul in this congregation that wants, as I said, just to begin at the very beginning with this precious mystery—Christ the servant. I say, there may be some here to-night that have never taken the attitude of simple repose in Christ's finished work. They have, it may be, begun to think of their soul's salvation, to think about eternity; but they are occupied with the thought that the Lord is claiming something from them: "I must do this, I must do that, and I must do the other." Now, my beloved friends, if such be here, I repeat, with deepest earnestness, you must cease altogether from your own doings, cease from your own reasonings, cease from your own feelings; because, be assured of it, it is neither feeling nor thinking nor reasoning nor doing at all, but it is pausing and gazing. It is hearing and believing. It is looking off from yourselves and your service to Christ and His service. It is ceasing from your restless and worthless doings, and reposing in full, unquestioning confidence in the one offering of Jesus Christ, which has perfectly satisfied and perfectly glorified God as to the great question of your sin and guilt. Here lies the divine secret of peace—peace in Jesus—peace with God—eternal peace. Nothing will ever be right till you get on this ground. If you are occupied with your doings for Christ, you will never get peace; but if you will only take God at His word, and rest in His Christ, you shall possess a peace which no power of earth or hell can ever disturb.

Now, my beloved hearers, I ask you, before I proceed, this question, Is there a heart in this congregation that has not yet rested here? Is there a heart here to-night that will say, I am not satisfied with Christ's service: I cannot rest in His work? What! The Son of God has stooped to serve you. The One who made you, the One who gave you life and breath and all things, the One to whom all are responsible, He has stooped to become your servant. It is not a question of asking you to do any thing, or asking you to give any thing, because—mark those words—they are words which sweep all through the history of the Son of Man—they are words which, in all their length and breadth and fullness, you can take up and use as if you were the only object of this service in the world—"The Son of Man is come to serve and to give." He is not come to get; He is not come to ask. The legal mind leads you to think that God is an exactor—that He is making demands upon you—that He wants your services in one way or another. But oh remember, I pray you, that your first great business, your primary and all-important work, is to believe in Jesus—to rest sweetly in Him, and in what He has done for you on the cross, and in what He is doing for you on the throne. "This is the work of God, that ye believe on Him whom He hath sent." You remember the interesting question of the Psalmist—a question asked when his eye rested on the magnitude and multitude of Jehovah's benefits—"What shall I render unto the Lord for all His benefits?" What is the reply? "I will take the cup of salvation, and call upon the name of the Lord."

Is this the way to "render unto the Lord"? Yes, this is just the way that gratifies and glorifies Him. If you really want to *render*, you must *take*. Take what? "The cup of salvation"—a full and brimming cup, most surely; and as you drink of that cup, as the glories of God's salvation shine in the vision of your soul, then will streams of living praise flow from your grateful heart. And you know He says, "Whoso offereth praise, glorifieth Me."

In a word, then, you must, first of all, allow your soul to dwell upon the marvelous mystery of Christ's service toward you in all the depth of your need; and the more you dwell upon that, the more will you be in the true attitude to serve Him.

Take another striking illustration. When David, as you remember, in that remarkable passage in the second book of Samuel (chap. vii.), sat in his house of cedar, and looked around at all that God had done for him, he said, "I must rise and build a house." Immediately the prophet was despatched to David to correct him on this point: "You shall not build Me a house, but I will build you a house." You must reverse the matter. God wants you to sit down and gaze yet more fully and intently upon His actings on your behalf. He wants you to look, not only at the past and the present, but to look on into the bright future; to see your entire history overlapped by His own magnificent grace.

And what, let me ask, was the effect of all this upon the heart of David? We have the answer in that one pithy statement: "Then went King David in, and sat before the Lord, and said, 'Who am I?'" Mark the attitude, and ponder the question. They are full of deep meaning. "*He sat.*" This is rest and sweet repose. He wanted to go to work too soon. No, says God, you must sit down and look at my work, and trace my actings on your behalf in the past, the present, and the future.

And then the question, "*Who am I?*" In this we see the blessed fact that self was for the moment lost sight of. It was flung into the shade by the lustre of divine revelation. Self and its poor little actings were set aside by the glory of God and the rich magnificence of His actings on behalf of His servant.

Now, some might have thought that David was an active, useful man when he was rising to take the trowel to build the house; and they might have thought him a good-for-nothing man to be sitting still when there was work to be done. But, brethren, let us remember that God's thoughts are not as our thoughts. He prizes our worship much more highly than our work. Indeed, it is only the true and intelligent worshiper that can be a true and intelligent workman. No doubt God most graciously accepts our poor services, even stamped as they so often are with mistakes of all sorts. But when it becomes a question of the comparative value of service and worship, the former must give place to the latter; and we know that when our brief span of working time shall have expired, our eternity of worship shall begin. Sweet thought!

And let me further remark, ere leaving this part of our subject, that no one need fear in the least that the practical effect of what I have been saying will be to cripple your service, or lead you to fold your arms in culpable idleness or cold indifference. The very reverse is the case, as you may see in the history of David himself. Study at your leisure, I Chronicles xxviii, xxix. There you have a splendid presentation of service—a most triumphant answer to all who would place work before worship. There you see, as it were, King David rising from the attitude of a worshiper into that of a workman, and making ample provision for the building of that very house of which he was not allowed to set one stone upon another. And not only does he make provision according to the claims of holiness, but, as he says, "Because I have set my affection to the house of my God, I have of mine own proper good, of gold and silver, which I have given to the house of my God, *over and above all* that I have prepared for the holy house, even three thousand talents of gold, of the gold of Ophir, and seven thousand talents of refined silver, to overlay the walls of the house." In other words, as we should express it, out of his own private purse, he gave the princely sum of over sixteen millions as a free gift toward the house which was to be reared by the hand of another. This, as he informs us, was "over and above what he had prepared for the holy house," which latter greatly exceeded the amount of England's national debt.

Thus we see that it is the true worshiper that makes the effective servant. It is when we have sat and gazed on the actings of Christ for us that we are enabled in any small degree to act for Him. And then, too, we shall be able to say with David, as he surveyed the untold wealth prepared for the house of God, "It is all Thine, and of Thine own have we given Thee."

I. But we must now turn for a few moments to the opening paragraph of Exodus xxi—"If thou buy a Hebrew servant, six years he shall serve; and in the seventh, he shall go out free for nothing. If he came in by himself, he shall go out by himself: if he were married, then his wife shall go out with him. If his master have given him a wife, and she have borne him sons or daughters; the wife and her children shall be her master's, and he shall go out by himself. And if the servant shall plainly say, I love my master, my wife, and my children; I will not go out free: then his master shall bring him unto the judges; he shall also bring him to the door, or unto the door-post; and his master shall bore his ear through with an awl; and he shall serve him forever."

Here, then, we have one of the shadows of good things to come—a shadow or figure of the True Servant, the Lord Jesus Christ, that blessed One who loved the Church and gave Himself for it. The Hebrew servant, having served the legal time, was perfectly free to go out; but he loved his wife and his children, and that, too, with such a love as led him to surrender his own personal liberty for their sakes. He proved his love for them by sacrificing himself. He might have gone forth and enjoyed his freedom, but what of them? How could he leave them behind? Impossible. He loved them too well for that; and hence he deliberately walked to the door-post, and there, in the presence of the judges, had his ear bored in token of perpetual service.

This was love indeed. There was no mistake about it. The wife and each child, as they gazed ever after on that bored ear, could read the touching and powerful proof of the love of that servant's heart.

Here, beloved, is something for the heart to dwell upon—yea, something over which the heart may well break itself. We see in this Old-Testament type the everlasting Lover of our souls—Jesus, the true servant. You remember that remarkable occasion in our Lord's life when He was setting before His disciples the solemn fact of His approaching cross and passion. You will find it in the eighth chapter of the gospel of Mark: "And He began to teach them that the Son of Man must suffer many things, and be rejected of the elders, and of the chief priests, and scribes, and be killed, and after three days rise again. And He spake that saying openly. And Peter took Him, and began to rebuke Him." Peter would fain, though he knew it not, have interrupted the True Servant in His movement to the door-post. He would have Him pity Himself, and maintain His own personal freedom. But oh, brethren, hearken to the withering rebuke administered to the very man who just before had made such a fine confession of Christ! "But when He had turned about and looked on His disciples, He rebuked Peter, saying, 'Get thee behind Me, Satan; for thou savorest not the things that be of God, but the things that be of men.' "

Mark the action. "He turned and looked on His disciples," as though He would say, If I hearken to your counsel, Peter—if I pity Myself—if I retreat from that cross which lies before Me, then what is to become of these? It is the Hebrew servant saying, "I love my wife, I love my children, I will not go out free."

It is of the very last possible importance for us to see that there was no necessity whatever laid upon the Lord Jesus Christ to walk to the cross; there was no necessity whatever laid upon Him to leave the glory which He had with the Father from all eternity and come down here; and when He had come down into this world, and taken perfect humanity upon Him, there was no necessity laid upon Him that He should have gone to the cross; for at any moment during the whole of His blessed history, from the manger of Bethlehem to the cross of Calvary, He might have gone back to where He came from. Death had no claim upon Him. The prince of this world came and had nothing in Him. He could say, speaking of His life, "No man taketh it from Me, but I lay it down of Myself." (John x. 18.) And on His way from the garden to the cross we hear Him saying, "Thinkest thou that I cannot now pray to My Father, and He shall presently give Me more than twelve legions of angels? But how then shall the Scriptures be fulfilled, that thus it must be?" And may we not say there was much more truth than the utterers were aware of in these accents of mockery which fell on the blessed Saviour's ear as He hung on the cross—"He saved others; Himself He cannot save"? But they might have said, Himself He will not save.

Ah, no! blessed forever be His name! He did not pity or spare Himself, but He pitied us. He beheld us in our hopeless ruin, guilt, misery, and danger. He saw that there was no eye to pity, no arm to save; and—all praise to His matchless name!—He laid aside His glory, came down into this wretched world, became a man, that as a man He might, by the sacrifice of Himself, deliver us from the lake of fire, and associate us with Himself on the new and eternal ground of accomplished redemption, in the power of resurrection-life, according to the eternal counsels of God, and to the praise of His glory.

Now, we cannot possibly overestimate the importance of dwelling upon the fact that there was no necessity whatever laid upon our blessed Lord Jesus Christ to die on the cross, and to endure the wrath of God. Neither in His person, in His nature, nor in His relations was He obnoxious to death. He was God over all, blessed forever. He was the Eternal Son of God. And in His human nature He was pure, spotless, sinless, perfect. He knew no sin. He did always and only the things that pleased God. He glorified Him, and finished His work; and He has saved us in such a way as to glorify God in the most wonderful manner. He was, to use the language of our type, free to go out by Himself; but ah, beloved, had He done so, your place and mine must inevitably have been the lake of fire forever.

To all this the Holy Ghost delights to bear testimony, as one of our own poets has sweetly sung—

"And, Lord, Thy perfect fitnessTo do a Saviour's part,The Holy Ghost doth witnessTo each believer's heart."

Most true; and we might with equal truth say, "His fitness to do a servant's part," because it was the very height of His glory, the very dignity of His person; it was the glory whence He had descended, that enabled Him to stoop down to the very depths of His people's necessities. There is not a necessity—no, not one—in the deepest range of His people's history, or in the lowest depths of their condition, that He has not reached in His marvelous character and His divine ministry as the servant of His people's necessities.

Brethren, let us never forget this. Nay, rather let us constantly cherish in our hearts the most grateful remembrance of it. The more we dwell upon the height of Christ's personal glory, the more fully we shall see the depths of His humiliation. The more profoundly we meditate upon the glory of what He *was*, the more we must be arrested by the grace of what He *became*. "Ye know the grace of our Lord Jesus Christ, that, though He was rich, yet for your sakes He became poor, that ye through His poverty might be rich."

Who can measure the heights and the depths of those two words, "rich" and "poor," in their application to our adorable Lord and Saviour? No created intelligence can fathom them; but most assuredly we should cultivate the habit of dwelling upon the love that shines all along the pathway of the divine Servant as He walked to the cross for us. It is as we dwell upon His love to us that our hearts shall be drawn out by the Holy Ghost in the power of responsive love to Him. "The love of Christ constraineth us; because we thus judge, that if One died for all, then were all dead; and that He died for all, that they which live should not henceforth live unto themselves, but unto Him which died for them, and rose again." (2 Cor. v. 14, 15.)

II. Having thus glanced at our Lord's service toward us in the past, let us look for a few moments at His present service—at what He is now doing for us continually in the presence of God. This we have most blessedly presented to us in that part of John xiii. which I have read for you this evening. The same precious grace shines in this as in all that on which we have been dwelling. If we look back at the past, we behold the Perfect Servant nailed to the cross for us; if we look up to the throne now, we behold Him girded for us, not only according to our present need, but according to the perfect love of His heart—His love to the Father, His love to the Church, His love to each individual believer from the beginning to the end of time.

"Now before the feast of the passover, when Jesus knew that His hour was come that He should depart out of this world unto the Father, having loved His own which were in the world, He loved them unto the end. And during supper [see Greek], the devil having now put into the heart of Judas Iscariot, Simon's son, to betray Him; Jesus knowing that the Father had given all things into His hands, and that He was come from God, and went to God; He riseth from supper, and laid aside His garments; and took a towel, and girded Himself. After that He poureth water into a basin, and began to wash the disciples' feet, and to wipe them with the towel wherewith He was girded."

Here, then, we have a most marvelous presentation of Christ's present service toward "His own which are in the world." There is something peculiarly precious in the expression, "*His own*." It brings us so very near to the heart of Christ. It is so sweet to think that He can look at such poor, feeble, failing creatures as we are, and say, They are Mine. It matters not what others may think about them; they belong to Me, and I must have them in a condition worthy of the place whence I came, and whither I am going.

This, brethren, is ineffably precious and edifying for our souls. It was in the sense of His personal glory, in the consciousness that He had come from God and was going to God, that He could stoop down and wash His people's feet. There was nothing, could be nothing, higher than the place whence Jesus had come; there was nothing, could be nothing, lower than the defiled feet of His disciples: but, blessed and praised forever be His name! He fills up in His own divine person and marvelous service every point between those two extremes. He can lay one hand on the throne of God, and the other on our feet, and be Himself the divine and eternal link between.

Now, there are three things in this scripture which I am anxious to put clearly before you this evening. In the first place, we have the special action of our Lord toward His own in the world; secondly, the spring of that action; and thirdly, the measure of the action:—the action, its spring, and its measure.

(I.) And first, the action itself. You will bear in mind, beloved in the Lord, that what we have presented here is not "the washing of regeneration." That pertains to the first stage of our Lord's service on our behalf. "His own which are in the world"—all who belong to that highly privileged class (and that is simply all who believe in His name) have passed through that great washing, in virtue of which Christ can pronounce them "clean every whit."

There is not a spot or a stain upon the very feeblest of that blessed number whom He calls "His own." "He that is washed needeth not save to wash his feet, but *is clean every whit*: and *ye are clean*, but not all." If a single spot could be detected on one of Christ's own, it would be a dishonor cast upon Him, inasmuch as He has washed us from all our guilt according to the perfection of His work as the Servant of our need, and, far above all, the Servant of the eternal counsels, purposes, and glory of God. He found us clean never a whit, and He has made us "clean every whit."

This is the washing of regeneration, which is never repeated. We have a figure of this in the case of the priests of the Mosaic economy. On the great day of their inauguration they were washed in water. This action was never repeated. But after this, from day to day, in order to fit them for the daily discharge of their priestly functions, they had to wash their hands and their feet in the brazen laver in the tabernacle, or the brazen sea in the temple. This daily washing is the figure of the action in John xiii. The two washings, being distinct, must never be confounded; and being intimately connected, must never be separated. The washing of regeneration is divinely and eternally complete: the washing of sanctification is being divinely and continually carried on. The former is never repeated; the latter is never interrupted. That gives us a part *in* Christ, of which nothing can rob us; and this gives us a part *with* Christ, of which any thing may deprive us. The one is the basis of our eternal life; the other is the ground of our daily communion.

Beloved brethren, see that you understand the meaning of having your feet washed, moment by moment, by the hands of that blessed One who is girded as the divine Servant of your present need. It is utterly impossible for any one to overestimate the importance of this work; but we may at least gather something of its value from our Lord's words to Peter; for Peter, like ourselves, alas! was very far from seizing the full significance of what his Lord was doing. "Then cometh He to Simon

Peter; and Peter saith unto Him, 'Lord, dost Thou wash my feet?' Jesus answered and said unto him, 'What I do thou knowest not now; but thou shalt know hereafter. Peter saith unto Him, 'Thou shalt never wash my feet.' Jesus answered him, 'If I wash thee not, thou hast no part *with* Me.'"

Here is the grand point—"part with Me." The washing of regeneration gives us a part *in* Christ: the daily washing of sanctification gives us a part *with* Christ. In order to full, intelligent, happy communion, we must have a clean conscience, and clean feet. The blood of atonement secures the former; the water of purification maintains the other. But both the blood and the water flowed from a crucified Christ. The death of Christ is the necessary basis of every thing. He died to make us clean; He lives to keep us clean. We are made as clean as His death can make us; we are kept as clean as His life can keep us.

And, be it remembered, this marvelous ministry of Christ on our behalf never ceases. He ever liveth to act *for* us on high, and to act *on* us and *in* us by His Word and Spirit. He speaks to God for us, and He speaks to us for God. He came from God, and traveled down to the profoundest depths of our need. He has gone back to God, to bear us ever on His heart, to meet our daily need, and to maintain us in the integrity of the position and relationship into which He has introduced us.

This is replete with solid comfort for the soul. We are passing through a defiling world, where we are constantly liable to contract evils of one kind or another which, though they cannot touch our eternal life, can very seriously affect our communion. It is impossible for us to tread the sanctuary of the divine presence with soiled feet; and hence the deep and unspeakable blessedness of having One ever in the presence of God for us—One who, having been in this scene, knows its true character; and One who, having come from God, and gone back to Him, knows the full extent of His claims, and all that is needful to fit us for fellowship with Him. The provision is divinely perfect. Sin or uncleanness can never be found in the presence of God. If we can make light of either the one or the other, God cannot and will not. The holiness that shines in the demand for purity is as bright as the grace that provides it. Grace has made the provision, but holiness demands the application thereof. The goodness of God provided a laver for the priests of old, but the holiness of God demanded that the priests should use that laver. The great washing of inauguration introduced them to the office of the priesthood; the washing in the laver fitted them for the duties of that office. How could acceptable priestly service be discharged with unclean hands? Impossible. And we may say it is as impossible that we can walk in the pathway of holiness if our feet are not washed and wiped by that blessed One who has girded Himself to serve us in this matter perpetually.

All this is divinely simple. There are two links in Christianity; namely, the link of eternal life, which can never be snapped by any thing; and the link of personal communion, which can be snapped in a moment by the weight of a feather. Now, it is as our ways are cleansed by the holy action of the Word, through the Holy Ghost, that our communion is maintained in its unbroken integrity. But if I am afraid to face the Word of God, or if I am willfully refusing its action, how can I enjoy communion with God?

I am not speaking now of ignorance of the Word of God. The Lord bears with a wonderful amount of ignorance in us—far more than we could bear with in one another. I do not now refer to the question of ignorance. But suppose a case. A young person entered these walls a few weeks ago, and took her seat on one of these benches. She was dressed out in all the fashion of this world—her head adorned with feathers and flowers, and her fingers with jewels. Her heart full of vanity and folly. Here the grace of God met her in all its fullness and freeness. The arrow of divine conviction entered her soul. She was broken down under the mighty power of the Word, in the hands of the Holy Ghost. She was brought to repentance toward God, and faith in the Lord Jesus Christ. She was saved, there and then, and left the place rejoicing in a full salvation. This joy continued for many days. She was engrossed with her newly found treasure. She never thought about her feathers, her flowers, or her jewels. True, she continued to wear them, simply because she as yet saw nothing wrong in so doing. She knew not as yet that there was so much as a single sentence in the Word of God bearing upon such things.

Brethren, let me just remind you that we should be prepared for such a case as this, and be prepared to meet it. Some of us, I fear, have but little wisdom or patience to deal with cases of this type. We are in undue haste to enter upon what I may call the stripping process. This is a mistake. We must allow time for the hidden virtues of the kingdom of God to develop themselves. We must not attempt to reduce the Christian assembly into a place in which a certain livery is adopted. This will never do. We really cannot reduce all to a dead level. We must allow the Word of God to act on the life which the Spirit of God has implanted. I do nothing but mischief to people if I get them to adopt a certain style of dress merely at my suggestion. The grand thing is to allow the kingdom of God to assert its holy sway over the entire character. This is to His glory and the soul's genuine progress.

Let us pursue our case. Our young friend, in the course of her reading, is arrested by the following pointed passage: "In like manner also, that women adorn themselves in modest apparel, with shamefacedness and sobriety; not with broidered hair, or gold, or pearls, or costly array; but (which becometh women professing godliness) with good works." (I Tim. ii. 9, 10.) And again, "Whose adorning let it not be that outward adorning of plaiting the hair, and of wearing of gold, or of putting on of apparel; but let it be the hidden man of the heart, in that which is not corruptible, even the ornament of a meek and quiet spirit, which is in the sight of God of great price." (I Pet. iii. 3, 4.)

Now, here, brethren, we have illustrated for us the present ministry of Christ—the action of the Word upon the soul—the application of the basin to the feet—the washing of water by the Word. It is Jesus stooping down to wash the feet of this young disciple. The question is, How will she receive the action? Will she resist it, or yield to it? Will she push away the basin? Will she refuse the gracious ministry? "If I wash thee not, thou hast no part *with* Me."

This is very solemn, and it demands our most serious attention. Next in moral importance to having the conscience purged by the blood of Christ stands this cleansing of our ways by the action of the Word, through the power of the Holy Ghost. The former gives us a part *in* Christ; the latter, a part *with* Christ. That is never repeated; this must never be interrupted. If we really desire fellowship with Christ, we must allow Him to wash our feet moment by moment. We cannot tread the pure precincts of the sanctuary of God with defiled feet any more than we can enter them with a defiled conscience.

Hence, therefore, dearly beloved in the Lord, let us look well to it that we have our ways continually submitted to the purifying action of the precious

Word of God. Let us put away every thing which that Word condemns; let us abandon every position and every association and every practice which that Word condemns, that so our holy fellowship with Christ may be maintained in its freshness and integrity. Nothing is more dangerous than to trifle with evil in any shape or form. Ignorance God can and does most graciously bear with, but the willful resistance of His Word in any one point is sure to lead to disastrous results. The heart becomes hardened, the conscience seared, the moral sense blunted, and the whole moral being gets into a most deplorable condition. We get away from the Lord, and make shipwreck of faith and a good conscience. May the Lord keep us near to Himself, walking with Him in tenderness of conscience and uprightness of heart. May His Word ever tell in living formative power upon our souls, that so our way be cleansed according to the claims of the sanctuary of God.

(2.) But let us now inquire for a moment into the spring of this action on which we have been dwelling. This is presented with touching sweetness and power in the first verse of John xiii.—"Having loved His own which were in the world, He loved them unto the end."

Here, then, brethren, we have the mighty spring of Christ's present ministry. It is the changeless love of His heart—a love that was stronger than death, and which many waters could not quench. "Christ loved the Church, and gave Himself for it; that He might sanctify and cleanse it with the washing of water by the Word." (Eph. v. 25, 26.) This is the blessed basis and the motive-spring of that marvelous ministry which our Lord Jesus Christ is now carrying on for us and toward us. He knew what He was undertaking when He uttered those words in the fortieth Psalm, "Lo, I come to do Thy will, O God." He knew what it would cost Him when He took up our case. But His love was and is divinely equal to all. We need not be afraid of exhausting that love which triumphed over all the unutterable horrors of Calvary, and went down under the deep and dark waters of death and judgment. We may at times feel ashamed to have so often to bring our defiled feet to that blessed One to cleanse them; but His love is equal to all, and that love is the spring of His precious and indispensable ministry.

It is a common saying that love is blind, but I look upon it as a libel upon love. Most certainly it does not and could not apply to the love of Christ. He knew all that was in us, and He knows now all our ways and all our weakness and all our follies; but He loves us notwithstanding all, and in the power of that love He acts toward us in order to deliver us from all that He sees in us and about us which would hinder our holy fellowship with the Father and with His Son.

Brethren, of what use, may I ask you, would a blind love be to you or to me? Surely, none whatever. How could we ever repose in a love which only acted toward us in ignorance of our blots and blemishes! Impossible. What we want is a love superior to all our imperfections, and a love that can deliver us from them. This love we have in Christ, blessed be His name! It is a love that, however it may expose us to ourselves, will never expose us to another. It is a love that comes to us with the basin and towel, and stoops down in infinite tenderness and lowly, matchless grace to wash away every soil, and give us the comfortable sense of being "clean every whit." This, brethren, is the love which you and I need, and this is the love which we have found in divine fullness and power in the heart of that perfect Servant who is girded for us ever before the throne. "Having loved *His own* which were in the world, He loved them"—how long? As long as they behaved themselves, and walked with unsoiled feet? Ah, no! this would never do for such as we. "He loved them *unto the end.*" Precious, perfect, divine, everlasting love! a love that overlaps and underlies and outlives all our blots and blemishes, our failings and falterings, our wants and weaknesses, our wanderings and waywardness; a love that has come to us armed with all that our condition could possibly demand; a love that will never cease to act for us and toward us and in us, until it presents us in unblemished perfectness before the throne of God.

(3.) And now one word as to the measure of Christ's present action for us and toward us. This is a point of unspeakable value and importance. It is essential for us to know that, whether it be a question of Christ's service for us in the past or His present service, the measure of both the one and the other is and can be nothing less than the claims of the sanctuary, the throne, and the nature of God. We might suppose that the measure would be our necessities, but this would never do. If we think of Christ's atoning work, we know, and rejoice to know, that precious work has done very much more than meet the deepest measure of our necessities as sinners. Blessed be God! the work of the cross has divinely met all the claims of God. It could never give solid peace to our souls merely to know that the very highest claims of human conscience had been met by the atoning death of Christ. We must be assured on divine authority that the highest claims of the government, the character, the nature, and the glory of God have all been perfectly met by the precious work of Christ.

Thus it is through infinite grace, and here every divinely exercised soul can find settled and eternal peace. Nor is it otherwise in respect to Christ's present work for us. It could never satisfy our souls, brethren, to be told that that work is measured by our very deepest need. That need is met, no doubt; but it is because Christ's present ministry goes far beyond that need, and reaches to, and satisfies the claims of, the sanctuary of God.

Unspeakable mercy! Here we may rest in perfect tranquillity. We have One on high undertaking for us, ever living in the presence of God for us; One who not only knows our necessities, but knows also the claims of God. He knows what this scene is through which we are passing, and He knows what that scene is into which He has entered; and, all praise to His name! He meets in His own perfect ministry both the one and the other. He must needs meet all our claims since He meets all God's claims, for the less must ever be included in the greater.

What solid comfort is here! What unruffled repose! We have One in the presence of God for us, in whose hands all our affairs are perfectly, because divinely, safe. They can never fall through, never go wrong. We may say that ere ever the very weakest of those whom Christ calls "His own in the world" can fail, Christ Himself must fail, and that can be *never*. His own are as safe as Himself.

What a grand reality! With what perfect confidence may we refer every objector, every accuser, every opposer, to this blessed manager! And what folly, on our part, to attempt to answer such ourselves! Oh, beloved brethren, may we learn to lean more confidently on that blessed One who thus presents Himself before our souls as the girded servant of our deep and manifold necessities. May we prize His precious ministry more and more—His ministry for us, His ministry to us. May we repose more sweetly in the assurance that He is speaking to the Father for us, in all our failures, in all our shortcomings, in all our sins. May we remember, for our exceeding comfort, that even before we slip, He has been pleading for us, as He pleaded for Peter. "I have prayed for thee," said the loving One, "that thy faith fail not." Oh, the matchless grace of these words! He did not pray that Peter might not fall, but that, having fallen, his confidence might not give way, his faith might not fail. Thus, too, He pleads for us, and thus we are sustained, and thus we are restored when we fall, else we should very speedily go from bad to worse, and make shipwreck altogether. "He ever liveth to make intercession for us." We are sustained by His precious and powerful ministry every moment. We could not stand for a single hour without Him. Things are continually turning up which would prove destructive of our fellowship, if we had not that blessed One acting for us, whose intervention on our behalf never ceases. He knows not only our need, but He knows what the sanctuary demands; and not only does He know it, but He provides for it, according to His own infinite perfectness and acceptance before God, meeting His people's necessities.

Now, there are some people—I do not know whether there are any here to-night—but there are some people who have got such a one-sided notion of the standing of the believer, that they throw the Lord's priestly ministry overboard altogether. I say it is one-sided, and there is nothing more dangerous than one-sided truth—nothing. I would far rather see a man going through the length and breadth of London publishing palpable error, such as the simplest mind could detect. I would have far less apprehension of the mischievous result of his ministry than of the teaching of a man who takes up one side of a truth, and presses it in such a way as to interfere with some other truth.

Now, there is an adjusting power in the truth of God—an adjusting power in Scripture that constitutes one of its brightest moral glories; and hence we find that while the Word of God most fully and blessedly establishes the truth that the believer stands complete in Christ, justified from all things, accepted in the Beloved, "clean every whit," it, at the same time, with equal clearness and fullness, sets forth the fact that the believer is, in himself, a poor feeble creature, exposed to manifold snares, temptations, and hostile influences; liable at any moment to fall into error and evil; utterly unable to keep himself, or to grapple with the difficulties and dangers which surround him; liable at any moment to contract defilement, which would unfit him for the holy fellowship and worship of the sanctuary.

How, then, are all those things to be met? How is the Christian to be kept in the face of such things? Having an evil nature, a crafty foe, and a hostile world to cope with, how is he to get on? How is he to be kept? How is he to be restored if he wanders? How is he to be lifted up if he falls? The answer to all these questions is found in that ever-precious sentence of inspiration, "He ever liveth to make intercession for us;" and again, "He is able to save to the uttermost;" and again, "We shall be saved by His life;" and again, "Because I live, ye shall live also;" and again, "We have an advocate with the Father."

Brethren, how the heart delights to give forth and to ponder over such utterances as these! They are marrow and fatness to the soul. How can any one, in the face of such passages—to say nothing of his own necessary experiences as to himself and his surroundings—think of calling in question the grand foundation-truth of the priesthood of Christ, in its application to believers now? I can only say, I know not. But alas! alas! there is no accounting for the depths of error into which we may fall, if we allow our minds to work, and get away from the direct authority of holy Scripture. And we may truly say that a most palpable proof of our need of the intercession of Christ is to be found in the sad fact that any of His servants should be found to deny it.

I shall add no more on this point, save to warn all the Lord's dear people against the terrible error of denying our continual need of the priestly ministry, the precious intercession and all-prevailing advocacy of our Lord

Jesus Christ—an error second only to the denial of His atoning work. For most surely our need of His priesthood is second only to our need of His atoning blood.

III. Having then briefly, and, alas! imperfectly, glanced at our Lord's ministry in the past and in the present, we cannot close without a reference to His ministry in the future. Some may feel disposed to say, I do not understand how our Lord can ever be found serving us in the future. I can understand His serving us now on the throne, but how He is to serve us in the kingdom is, I confess, beyond me.

No doubt it is most marvelous, and had we not His own veritable words for it, we might well hesitate in our statement of the fact that our Lord Christ shall serve His people in the very brightness of the glory. But let us hear what He Himself saith to us. Turn for a moment to Luke xii. 35: "Let your loins be girded about, and your lights burning; and ye yourselves like unto men that wait for their lord, when he will return from the wedding; that when he cometh and knocketh, they may open unto him immediately. Blessed are those servants, whom the lord when he cometh shall find watching: verily I say unto you, that *he shall gird himself, and make them to sit down to meat, and will come forth and serve them.*"

This is distinct and unmistakable. Most marvelous, no doubt, but as plain as it is marvelous. Christ will serve us in the kingdom. He will serve us forever. His ministry overlaps our entire history. It reaches down to the very deepest depths of our need as sinners, and up to the very loftiest heights of the glory. It goes back to the past, it covers the present, and it stretches away into the boundless future. Blessed be His name! He loves to serve us, and He gives us the assurance that the very moment, as it were, that He enters upon the glory of name! has given us a whole heart, and nothing can satisfy Him in return but a whole heart from us. His entire service—past, present, and future—is the fruit of His perfect love; and nothing can meet His desire, with respect to us, save a heart responsive in its affections to Him. And where there is this, it will express itself in an anxious, earnest longing for His coming. "Blessed are those servants, whom their lord when he cometh shall find watching."

May the eternal Spirit fill our hearts with genuine love to the Person of our own adorable Lord and Saviour; that so our one grand and undivided purpose may be to live for Him in this scene from which He has been cast out, and to wait for that moment when we shall see Him as He is, and be like Him and with Him forever.

C. H. M.

PRAYER AND THE PRAYER-MEETING •

In considering the deeply important subject of prayer, two things claim our attention; first, the moral basis of prayer; secondly, its moral conditions.

I. The basis of prayer is set forth in such words as the following: "*If ye abide in Me, and My words abide in you*, ye shall ask what ye will, and it shall be done unto you." (John xv. 7.) Again, "Beloved, *if our heart condemn us not*, then have we confidence toward God. And whatsoever we ask, we receive of Him, *because we keep His commandments*, and do those things that are pleasing in His sight." (I John iii. 21, 22.) So also, when the blessed apostle seeks an interest in the prayers of the saints, he sets forth the moral basis of his appeal—"Pray for us; *for we trust we have a good conscience*, in all things willing to live honestly." (Heb. xiii. 18.)

From these passages, and many more of like import, we learn that, in order to effectual prayer, there must be an obedient heart, an upright mind, a good conscience. If the soul be not in communion with God—if it be not abiding in Christ—if it be not ruled by His holy commandments—if the eye be not single, how could we possibly look for answers to our prayers? We should, as the apostle James says, be "asking amiss, that we may consume it upon our lusts." How could God, as a holy Father, grant such petitions? Impossible.

How very needful, therefore, it is to give earnest heed to the moral basis on which our prayers are presented. How could the apostle have asked the brethren to pray for him, if he had not a good conscience, a single eye, an upright mind—the moral persuasion that in all things he really wished to live honestly? We may safely assert, he could do no such thing.

But may we not often detect ourselves in the habit of lightly and formally asking others to pray for us? It is a very common formulary amongst us—"Remember me in your prayers," and most surely nothing can be more blessed or precious than to be borne upon the hearts of God's dear people in their approaches to the mercy-seat; but do we sufficiently attend to the moral basis? When we say, "Brethren pray for us," can we add, as in the presence of the Searcher of hearts, "For we trust we have a good conscience, in all things willing to live honestly"? and when we ourselves bow before the throne of grace, is it with an uncondemning heart—an upright mind—a single eye—a soul really abiding in Christ, and keeping His commandments?

These, beloved reader, are searching questions. They go right to the very centre of the heart—down to the very roots and moral springs of our being. But it is well to be thoroughly searched—searched in reference to every thing, but especially in reference to prayer. There is a terrible amount of unreality in our prayers—a sad lack of the moral basis—a vast amount of "asking amiss."

Hence, the want of power and efficacy in our prayers—hence, the formality—the routine—yea, the positive hypocrisy. The Psalmist says, "If I regard iniquity in my heart, the Lord will not hear me." How solemn this is! Our God will have reality; He desireth truth in the inward parts. He, blessed be His name, is real with us, and He will have us real with Him. He will have us coming before Him as we really are, and with what we really want.

How often, alas! it is otherwise, both in private and in public! How often are our prayers more like orations than petitions—more like statements of doctrine than utterances of need! It seems, at times, as though we meant to explain principles to God, and give Him a large amount of information.

These are the things which cast a withering influence over our prayer-meetings, robbing them of their freshness, their interest, and their value. Those who really know what prayer is—who feel its value, and are conscious of their need of it, attend the prayer-meeting in order to pray, not to hear orations, lectures, and expositions from men on their knees. If they want lectures, they can attend at the lecture-hall or the preaching-room; but when they go to the prayer-meeting, it is to pray. To them, the prayer-meeting is the place of expressed need and expected blessing—the place of expressed weakness and expected power. Such is their idea of "the place where prayer is wont to be made;" and therefore when they flock thither, they are not disposed or prepared to listen to long preaching prayers, which would be deemed barely tolerable if delivered from the desk, but which are absolutely insufferable in the shape of prayer.

We write plainly, because we feel the need of great plainness of speech. We deeply feel our want of reality, sincerity, and truth in our prayers and prayer-meetings. Not unfrequently it happens that what we call prayer is not prayer at all, but the fluent utterance of certain known and acknowledged truths and principles, to which one has listened so often that the reiteration becomes tiresome in the extreme. What can be more painful than to hear a man on his knees explaining principles and unfolding doctrines? The question forces itself upon us, "Is the man speaking to God, or to us?" If to God, surely nothing can be more irreverent or profane than to attempt to explain things to Him; but if to us, then it is not prayer at all, and the sooner we rise from the attitude of prayer the better, inasmuch as the speaker will do better on his legs and we in our seats.

And, having referred to the subject of attitude, we would very lovingly call attention to a matter which, in our judgment, demands a little serious consideration; we allude to the habit of sitting during the holy and solemn exercise of prayer. We are fully aware, of course, that the grand question in prayer is, to have the *heart* in a right attitude. And further, we know, and would ever bear in mind, that many who attend our prayer-meetings are aged, infirm, and delicate people, who could not possibly kneel for any length of time—perhaps not at all. Then again, it often happens that, even where there is not physical weakness, and where there would be real desire to kneel down, as feeling it to be the proper attitude, yet, from actual want of space, it is impossible to change one's position.

All these things must be taken into account; but, allowing as broad a margin as possible in which to insert these modifying clauses, we must still hold to it that there is a very deplorable lack of reverence in many of our public reunions for prayer. We frequently observe young men, who can neither plead physical weakness nor want of space, sitting through an entire prayer-meeting. This, we confess, is offensive, and we cannot but believe it grieves the Spirit of the Lord. We ought to kneel down when we can; it expresses reverence and prostration. The blessed Master "kneeled down and prayed." (Luke xxii. 41.) His apostle did the same, as we read in Acts xx. 36, "When he had thus spoken, he kneeled down and prayed with them all."

And is it not comely and right so to do? Assuredly it is. And can aught be more unseemly than to see a number of people sitting, lolling, lounging, and gaping about while prayer is being offered? We consider it perfectly shocking, and we do here most earnestly beseech all the Lord's people to give this matter their solemn consideration, and to endeavor, in every possible way, both by precept and example, to promote the godly habit of kneeling at our prayer-meetings. No doubt those who take part in the meeting would greatly aid in this matter by short and fervent prayers; but of this, more hereafter.

PART II

We shall now proceed to consider, in the light of holy Scripture, the moral conditions or attributes of prayer. There is nothing like having the authority of the divine Word for every thing in the entire range of our practical Christian life. Scripture must be our one grand and conclusive referee in all our questions. Let us never forget this.

What, then, saith the Scripture as to the necessary moral conditions of prayer? Turn to Matthew xviii. 19—"Again I say unto you, that *if two of you shall agree* on earth as touching any thing that they shall ask, it shall be done for them of My Father which is in heaven."

Here we learn that one necessary condition of our prayers is, *unanimity*—cordial agreement—thorough oneness of mind. The true force of the words is, "If two of you shall symphonize"—shall make one common sound. There must be no jarring note, no discordant element.

If, for example, we come together to pray about the progress of the gospel—the conversion of souls, we must be of one mind in the matter—we must make one common sound before our God. It will not do for each to have some special thought of his own to carry out. We must come before the throne of grace in holy harmony of mind and spirit, else we cannot claim an answer, on the ground of Matthew xviii. 19.

Now, this is a point of immense moral weight. Its importance, as bearing upon the tone and character of our prayer-meetings, cannot possibly be overestimated. It is very questionable indeed whether any of us have given sufficient attention to it. Have we not to deplore the objectless character of our prayer-meetings? Ought we not to come together more with some definite object on our hearts, as to which we are going to wait together upon God? We read in the first chapter of Acts, in reference to the early disciples, "These all continued *with one accord* in prayer and supplication, with the women, and Mary the mother of Jesus, and with His brethren."[30] And again, in the second chapter, we read, "When the day of Pentecost was fully come, they were *all with one accord in one place.*"

They were waiting, according to our Lord's instructions, for the promise of the Father—the gift of the Holy Ghost. They had the sure word of promise. The Comforter was, without fail, to come; but this, so far from dispensing with prayer, was the very ground of its blessed exercise. They prayed; they prayed in one place; they prayed with one accord. They were thoroughly agreed. They all, without exception, had one definite object before their hearts. They were waiting for the promised Spirit; they continued to wait; and they waited with one accord, until He came. Men and women, absorbed with one object, waited in holy concord, in happy symphony—waited on, day after day, earnestly, fervently, harmoniously waited until they were indued with the promised power from on high.

Should not we go and do likewise? Is there not a sad lack of this "one accord," "one place" principle in our midst? True it is, blessed be God, we have not to ask for the Holy Ghost to come,—He has come; we have not to ask for the outpouring of the Spirit,—He has been poured out: but we have to ask for the display of His blessed power in our midst. Supposing our lot is cast in a place where spiritual death and darkness reign. There is not so much as a single breath of life—not a leaf stirring. The heaven above seems like brass; the earth beneath, iron. Such a thing as a conversion is never heard of. A withering formalism seems to have settled down upon the entire place. Powerless profession, dead routine, stupefying mechanical religiousness, are the order of the day. What is to be done? Are we to allow ourselves to fall under the fatal influence of the surrounding malaria? are we to yield to the paralyzing power of the atmosphere that inwraps the place? Assuredly not.

If not, what then? Let us, even if there be but two who really feel the condition of things, get together, with one accord, and pour out our hearts to God. Let us wait on Him, in holy concord, with united, firm purpose, until He send a copious shower of blessing upon the barren spot. Let us not fold our arms and vainly say, "The time is not come." Let us not yield to that pernicious offshoot of a one-sided theology, which is rightly called fatalism, and say, "God is sovereign, and He works according to His own will. We must wait His time. Human effort is in vain. We cannot get up a revival. We must beware of mere excitement."

All this seems very plausible; and the more so because there is a measure of truth in it; indeed it is all true, so far as it goes: but it is only one side of the truth. It is truth, and nothing but the truth; but it is not *the whole truth*. Hence its mischievous tendency. There is nothing more to be dreaded than one-sided truth; it is far more dangerous than positive, palpable error. Many an earnest soul has been stumbled and turned completely out of the way by one-sided or misapplied truth. Many a true-hearted and useful workman has been chilled, repulsed, and driven out of the harvest-field by the injudicious enforcement of certain doctrines having a measure of truth, but not *the* full truth of God.

Nothing, however, can touch the truth, or weaken the force of Matthew xviii. 19. It stands in all its blessed fullness, freeness, and preciousness before the eye of faith; its terms are clear and unmistakable. "If two of you shall agree upon earth, as touching *any thing* that they shall ask, it shall be done for them of My Father which is in heaven." Here is our warrant for coming together to pray for any thing that may be laid on our hearts. Do we mourn over the coldness, barrenness, and death around us? Are we discouraged by the little apparent fruit from the preaching of the gospel—the lack of power in the preaching itself, and the total absence of practical result? Are our souls cast down by the barrenness, dullness, heaviness, and low tone of all our reunions, whether at the table of our Lord, before the mercy-seat, or around the fountain of holy Scripture?

What are we to do? Fold our arms in cold indifference? give up in despair? or give vent to complaining, murmuring, fretfulness, or irritation? God forbid! What then? Come together, "with one accord in one place;" get down on our faces before our God, and pour out our hearts, as the heart of one man, pleading Matthew xviii. 19.

This, we may rest assured, is the grand remedy—the unfailing resource. It is perfectly true that "God is sovereign," and this is the very reason why we should wait on Him; perfectly true that "human effort is in vain," and that is the very reason for seeking divine power; perfectly true that "we cannot get up a revival," and that is the very reason for seeking to get it *down*; perfectly true that "we must beware of mere excitement;" equally true that we must beware of coldness, deadness, and selfish indifference.

The simple fact is, there is no excuse whatever—so long as Christ is at the right hand of God—so long as God the Holy Ghost is in our midst and in our hearts—so long as we have the Word of God in our hands—so long as Matthew xviii. 19 shines before our eyes—there is, we repeat, no excuse whatever for barrenness, deadness, coldness, and indifference—no excuse for heavy and unprofitable meetings—no excuse whatever for lack of freshness in our reunions or of fruitfulness in our service. Let us wait on God, in holy concord, and the blessing is sure to come.

PART III

If we turn to Matthew xxi. 22, we shall find another of the essential conditions of effectual prayer. "And all things whatsoever ye shall ask in prayer, *believing*, ye shall receive." This is a truly marvelous statement. It opens the very treasury of heaven to faith. There is absolutely no limit. Our blessed Lord assures us that we shall receive whatsoever we ask in simple faith.

The apostle James, under the inspiration of the

Holy Ghost, gives us a similar assurance in reference to the matter of asking for wisdom. "If any of you lack wisdom, let him ask of God, that *giveth to all liberally*, and upbraideth not; and it shall be given him. But"— here is the moral condition—"let him ask *in faith, nothing wavering*. For he that wavereth is like a wave of the sea, driven with the wind and tossed. For let not that man think that he shall obtain any thing of the Lord."

From both these passages we learn that if our prayers are to have an answer, they must be prayers of faith. It is one thing to utter words in the form of prayer, and another thing altogether to pray in simple faith, in the full, clear, and settled assurance that we shall have what we are asking for. It is greatly to be feared that many of our so-called prayers never go beyond the ceiling of the room. In order to reach the throne of God, they must be borne on the wings of faith, and proceed from hearts united and minds agreed, in holy purpose, to wait on our God for the things which we really require.

Now, the question is, are not our prayers and prayer-meetings sadly deficient on this point? Is not the deficiency manifest from the fact that we see so little result from our prayers? Ought we not to examine ourselves as to how far we really understand these two conditions of prayer, namely, unanimity and confidence? If it be true—and it is true, for Christ has said it—that two persons agreed to ask in faith can have whatsoever they ask, why do we not see more abundant answers to our prayers? Must not the fault be in us?—are we not deficient in concord and confidence?

Our Lord, in Matthew xviii. 19, comes down, as we say, to the very smallest plurality—the smallest congregation—even to "two;" but of course the promise applies to dozens, scores, or hundreds. The grand point is, to be thoroughly agreed and fully persuaded that we shall get what we are asking for. This would give a different tone and character altogether to our reunions for prayer. It would make them very much more real than our ordinary prayer-meeting, which, alas! alas! is often poor, cold, dead, objectless, and desultory, exhibiting any thing but cordial agreement and unwavering faith.

How vastly different it would be if our prayer-meetings were the result of a cordial agreement on the part of two or more believing souls, to come together and wait upon God for a certain thing, and to persevere in prayer until they receive an answer! How little we see of this! We attend the prayer-meeting from week to week—and very right we should—but ought we not to be exercised before God as to how far we are agreed in reference to the object or objects which are to be laid before the throne? The answer to this question links itself on to another of the moral conditions of prayer.

Let us turn to Luke xi. "And He said unto them, 'Which of you shall have a friend, and shall go unto him at midnight, and say unto him, Friend, lend me three loaves; for a friend of mine in his journey is come to me, and I have nothing to set before him? And he from within shall answer and say, Trouble me not; the door is now shut, and my children are with me in bed; I cannot rise and give thee. I say unto you, though he will not rise and give him because he is his friend, yet because of his *importunity* he will rise and give him as many as he needeth. And I say unto you, Ask, and it shall be given you; seek, and ye shall find; knock, and it shall be opened unto you. For every one that asketh receiveth; and he that seeketh findeth; and to him that knocketh it shall be opened.'" (Ver. 5-10.)

These words are of the very highest possible importance, inasmuch as they contain part of our Lord's reply to the request of His disciples, "Lord, teach us to pray." Let no one imagine for a moment that we would dare to take it upon ourselves to teach people how to pray. God forbid! Nothing is further from our thoughts. We are merely seeking to bring the souls of our readers into direct contact with the Word of God—the veritable sayings of our blessed Lord and Master—so that, in the light of those sayings, they may judge for themselves as to how far our prayers and our prayer-meetings come up to the divine standard.

What, then, do we learn from Luke xi? what are the moral conditions which it sets before us? In the first place, it teaches us to be *definite* in our prayers. "Friend, lend me three loaves." There is a positive need felt and expressed; there is the one thing before the mind and on the heart, and to this one thing he confines himself. It is not a long, rambling, desultory statement about all sorts of things: it is distinct, direct, and pointed,—I want three loaves, I cannot do without them, I must have them, I am shut up, the case is urgent, the time of night—all the circumstances give definiteness and earnestness to the appeal. He cannot wander from the one point, "Friend, lend me three loaves."

No doubt it seems a very untoward time to come—"midnight." Every thing looks discouraging. The friend has retired for the night, the door is shut, his children are with him in bed, he cannot rise. All this is very depressing; but still the definite need is pressed: he must have the three loaves.

Now, we cannot but judge that there is a great practical lesson here which may be applied, with immense profit, to our prayers and our prayer-meetings. Must we not admit that our reunions for prayer suffer sadly from long, rambling, desultory prayers? Do we not frequently give utterance to a whole host of things of which we do not really feel the need, and which we have no notion of waiting for at all? Should we not sometimes be taken very much aback were the Lord to appear to us at the close of our prayer-meeting and ask us, What do you really want Me to give or to do?

We feel most thoroughly persuaded that all this demands our serious consideration. We believe it would impart great earnestness, freshness, glow, depth, reality, and power to our prayer-meetings were we to attend with something definite on our hearts, as to which we could invite the fellowship of our brethren. Some of us seem to think it necessary to make one long prayer about all sorts of things—many of them very right and very good, no doubt—but the mind gets bewildered by the multiplicity of subjects. How much better to bring some one object before the throne, earnestly urge it, and pause, so that the Holy Spirit may lead out others, in like manner, either for the same thing or something else equally definite.

Long prayers are often wearisome; indeed, in many cases, they are a positive infliction. It will perhaps be said that we must not prescribe any time to the Holy Spirit. True indeed;—away from us be the thought! Who would venture upon such a piece of daring blasphemy? We are simply comparing what we find in Scripture (where their brief pointedness is characteristic—see Matt. vi, John xvii., Acts iv. 24-30, Eph. i, iii, etc.) with what we too often—not always, thank God!—find in our prayer-meetings.

Let it, then, be distinctly borne in mind that "long prayers" are not the rule in Scripture. They are referred to in Mark xii. 40, etc., in terms of withering disapproval. Brief, fervent, pointed prayers impart great freshness and interest to the prayer-meeting; but on the other hand, as a general rule, long and desultory prayers exert a most depressing influence upon all.

But there is another very important moral condition set forth in our Lord's teaching in Luke xi, and that is, "*importunity*." He tells us that the man succeeds in gaining his object simply by his importunate earnestness. He is not to be put off; he must get the three loaves. Importunity prevails even where the claims of friendship prove inoperative. The man is bent on his object; he has no alternative. There is a demand, and he has nothing to meet it—"I have nothing to set before my traveling friend." In short, he will not take a refusal.

Now, the question is, how far do we understand this great lesson? It is not, blessed be God, that He will ever answer us "from within." He will never say to us, "Trouble me not"—"I cannot rise and give thee." He is ever our true and ready "Friend"—"a cheerful, liberal, and unupbraiding Giver." All praise to His holy name! Still, He encourages importunity, and we need to ponder His teaching. There is a sad lack of it in our prayer-meetings. Indeed, it will be found that in proportion to the lack of definiteness is the lack of importunity. The two go very much together. Where the thing sought is as definite as the "three loaves," there will generally be the importunate asking for it, and the firm purpose to get it.

The simple fact is, we are too vague and, as a consequence, too indifferent in our prayers and prayer-meetings. We do not seem like people *asking for what they want, and waiting for what they ask*. This is what destroys our prayer-meetings, rendering them pithless, pointless, powerless; turning them into teaching or talking-meetings, rather than deep-toned, earnest prayer-meetings. We feel convinced that the whole Church of God needs to be thoroughly aroused in reference to this great question; and this conviction it is which compels us to offer these hints and suggestions, with which we are not yet done.

PART IV

The more deeply we ponder the subject which has been for some time engaging our attention, and the more we consider the state of the entire Church of God, the more convinced we are of the urgent need of a thorough awakening every where in reference to the question of prayer. We cannot—nor do we desire to—shut our eyes to the fact that deadness, coldness, and barrenness seem, as a rule, to characterize our prayer-meetings. No doubt we may find here and there a pleasing exception, but speaking generally, we do not believe that any sober, spiritual person will call in question the truth of what we state, namely, that the tone of our prayer-meetings is fearfully low, and that it is absolutely imperative upon us to inquire seriously as to the cause.

In the papers already put forth on this great, all-important, and deeply practical subject, we have ventured to offer to our readers a few hints and suggestions. We have briefly glanced at our lack of confidence, our failure in cordial unanimity, the absence of definiteness and importunity. We have referred in plain terms—and we must speak plainly if we are to speak at all—to many things which are felt by all the truly spiritual amongst us to be not only trying and painful, but thoroughly subversive of the real power and blessing of our reunions for prayer. We have spoken of the long, tiresome, desultory, preaching prayers which, in some cases, have become so perfectly intolerable, that the Lord's dear people are scared away from the prayer-meetings altogether. They feel that they are only wearied, grieved, and irritated, instead of being refreshed, comforted, and strengthened; and hence they deem it better to stay away. They judge it to be more profitable, if they have an hour to spare, to spend it in the privacy of their closet, where they can pour out their hearts to God in earnest prayer and supplication, than to attend a so-called prayer-meeting, where they are absolutely wearied out with incessant, powerless, hymn-singing, or long preaching prayers.

Now, we more than question the rightness of such a course. We seriously doubt if this be at all the way to remedy the evils of which we complain. Indeed, we are thoroughly persuaded it is not. If it be right to come together for prayer and supplication—and who will question the rightness?—then surely it is not right for any one to stay away merely because of the feebleness, failure, or even the folly of some who may take part in the meeting. If all the really spiritual members were to stay away on such a ground, what would become of the prayer-meeting? We have very little idea of how much is involved in the elements which compose a meeting. Even though we may not take part audibly in the action, yet if we are there in a right spirit—there really to wait upon God, we marvelously help the tone of a meeting.

Besides, we must remember that we have something more to do in attending a meeting than to think of our own comfort, profit, and blessing. We must think of the Lord's glory; we must seek to do His blessed will, and try to promote the good of others in every possible way; and neither of these ends, we may rest assured, can be attained by our deliberately absenting ourselves from the place where prayer is wont to be made.

We repeat, and with emphasis, the words, "*deliberately* absenting ourselves"—staying away because we are not profited by what takes place there. Many things may crop up to hinder our being present—ill-health, domestic duties, lawful claims upon our time if we are in the employment of others,—all these things have to be taken into account; but we may set it down as a fixed principle that *the one who can designedly absent himself from the prayer-meeting is in a bad state of soul.* The healthy, happy, earnest, diligent soul will be sure to be found at the prayer-meeting.

But all this conducts us, naturally and simply, to another of those moral conditions at which we have been glancing in this series of papers. Let us turn for a moment to the opening lines of Luke xviii. "And He spake a parable unto them to this end, *that men ought always to pray, and not to faint*: saying, 'There was in a city a judge, which feared not God, neither regarded man. And there was a widow in that city, and she came unto him, saying, Avenge me of mine adversary. And he would not for a while; but afterward he said within himself, Though I fear not God, nor regard man, yet, because this widow troubleth me, I will avenge her, lest by her continual coming she weary me.' And the Lord said, 'Hear what the unjust judge saith. And shall not God avenge His own elect, which cry day and night unto Him, though He bear long with them? I tell you that He will avenge them speedily.'" (Ver. I-8.)

Here, then, we have pressed upon our attention the important moral condition of *perseverance*. "Men ought *always* to pray, and *not to faint*." This is intimately connected with the definiteness and importunity to which we have already referred. We want a certain thing; we cannot do without it. We importunately, unitedly, believingly, and perseveringly wait on our God until He graciously send an answer, as He most assuredly will, if the moral basis and the moral conditions be duly maintained.

But we must persevere. We must not faint, and give up, though the answer does not come as speedily as we might expect. It may please God to exercise our souls by keeping us waiting on Him for days, months, or perhaps years. The exercise is good. It is morally healthful; it tends to make us real; it brings us down to the roots of things. Look, for example, at Daniel. He was kept for "three full weeks" waiting on God, in profound exercise of soul. "In those days I Daniel was mourning three full weeks. I ate no pleasant bread, neither came flesh nor wine in my mouth, neither did I anoint myself at all, till three full weeks were fulfilled."

All this was good for Daniel. There was deep blessing in the spiritual exercises through which this beloved and honored servant of God was called to pass during those three weeks. And what is specially worthy of note is, that the answer to Daniel's cry had been despatched from the throne of God at the very beginning of his exercise, as we read at verse 12, "Then said he unto me, 'Fear not Daniel; for *from the first day that thou didst set thine heart to understand, and to chasten thyself before thy God, thy words were heard, and I am come for thy words*. But"—how marvelous and mysterious is this!—"the prince of the kingdom of Persia withstood me one and twenty days; but, lo, Michael, one of the chief princes, came to help me; and I remained there with the kings of Persia. Now I am come to make thee understand what shall befall thy people in the latter days."

All this is full of interest. Here was the beloved servant of God mourning, chastening himself, and waiting upon God. The angelic messenger was on his way with the answer. The enemy was permitted to hinder; but Daniel continued to wait: he prayed, and fainted not; and in due time the answer came.

Is there no lesson here for us? Most assuredly there is. We, too, may have to wait long in the holy attitude of expectancy, and in the spirit of prayer; but we shall find the time of waiting most profitable for our souls. Very often our God, in His wise and faithful dealing with us, sees fit to withhold the answer, simply to prove us as to the reality of our prayers. The grand point for us is, to have an object laid upon our hearts by the Holy Ghost—an object as to which we can lay the finger of faith upon some distinct promise in the Word, and to persevere in prayer until we get what we want. "Praying *always* with all prayer and supplication in the Spirit, and *watching* thereunto *with all perseverance* and supplication for all saints." (Eph. vi. 18.)

All this demands our serious consideration. We are as sadly deficient in perseverance as we are in definiteness and importunity. Hence the feebleness of our prayers and the coldness of our prayer-meetings. We do not come together with a definite object, and hence we are not importunate, and we do not persevere. In short, our prayer-meetings are often nothing but a dull routine—a cold, mechanical service—something to be gone through—a wearisome alternation of hymn and prayer, hymn and prayer, causing the spirit to groan beneath the heavy burden of mere profitless bodily exercise.

We speak plainly and strongly: we speak as we feel. We must be permitted to speak without reserve. We call upon the whole Church of God, far and wide, to look this great question straight in the face—to look to God about it—to judge themselves about it. Do we not feel the lack of power in all our public reunions? Why those barren seasons at the Lord's table? Why the dullness and feebleness in the celebration of that precious feast which ought to stir the very deepest depths of our renewed being? Why the lack of unction, power, and edification in our public readings—the foolish speculations and the silly questions which have been advanced and answered for the last forty years? Why those varied evils on which we have been dwelling, and which are being mourned over almost every where by the truly spiritual? Why the barrenness of our gospel services? Why are souls not smitten down under the Word? Why is there so little gathering-power?

Brethren, beloved in the Lord, let us rouse ourselves to the solemn consideration of these weighty matters. Let us not be satisfied to go on with the present condition of things. We call upon all those who admit the truth of what we have been putting forth in these pages on "Prayer and the Prayer-Meeting," to unite in cordial, earnest, united prayer and supplication. Let us seek to get together according to God; to come as one man and prostrate ourselves before the mercy-seat, and perseveringly wait upon our God for the revival of His work, the progress of His gospel, the ingathering and upbuilding of His beloved people. Let our prayer-meetings be really prayer-meetings, and not occasions for giving out our favorite hymns, and starting our fancy tunes. The prayer-meeting ought to be the place of expressed heed and expected blessing—the place of expressed weakness and expected power—the place where God's people assemble with one accord, to take hold of the very throne of God, to get into the very treasury of heaven, and draw thence all we want for ourselves, for our households, for the Whole Church of God, and for the vineyard of Christ.

Such is the true idea of a prayer-meeting, if we are to be taught by Scripture. May it be more fully realized amongst the Lord's people every where. May the Holy Spirit stir us all up, and press upon our souls the value, importance, and urgent necessity of unanimity, confidence, definiteness, importunity, and perseverance in all our prayers and prayer-meetings.

Yes, there's a power which man can wield,When mortal aid is vain;That eye, that arm, that love to reach,That list'ning ear to gain.

That power is prayer, which soars on high,Through Jesus, to the throne,And moves the hand which moves the worldTo bring deliverance down.

C. H. M.

NOTE.—It may perhaps be useful to notice that in the foregoing most needful pages, the beloved author has been speaking of the *prayer-meeting*, and the moral basis and conditions of prayer in general, not of personal, secret prayer. The importance of it can hardly be overestimated. The lack or neglect of this soon tells in the spiritual life of the Christian. Is not the lack of this the explanation of much leanness of soul, from which knowledge alone is not able to lift us up? It is, as it were, the spiritual gauge of our soul's condition. There, in the secret of the closet, the godly soul ever loves to pour out in its Father's ear its trials, its fears, its desires, its wants, its thanksgivings, in all their details. And what comfort, what joy, what godly strength and purpose, the soul carries from thence! what preparation to go through the daily toil, and testings of the day! Beloved of the Lord, let us wait on God, that we may know more of this secret power, gotten in our closet with Him.

[Ed.]

FOOTNOTES:

[1] The reader should be informed that the word which is rendered "perfect," in the above passage, occurs but this once in the entire New Testament. It is [Greek: artios] (artios) and signifies, ready, complete, well fitted; as an instrument with all its strings, a machine with all its parts, a body with all its limbs, joints, muscles, and sinews. The usual word for "perfect" is [Greek: teleios] (teleios) which signifies the reaching of the moral *end*, in any particular thing.

[2] The reader will distinguish between the expression "in the flesh" as used in Gal. ii. 20, and in Rom. viii. 8, 9. In the former, it simply refers to our condition as in the body. In the latter, it sets forth the principle or ground of our standing. The believer is in the body, as to the fact of his condition; but he is not in the flesh as to the principle of his standing.

[3] ["Thou hast magnified Thy word (or saying) according to all Thy Name," seems more exactly to give the meaning of the passage. ED.]

[4] It is deeply interesting to note that neither the Jews' best Friend nor their worst enemy is once formally named in the book of Esther; but faith could recognize both the one and the other.

[5] When the jailer at Philippi inquired of Paul and Silas, "What must I do to be saved?" they simply replied, "*Believe* on the Lord Jesus Christ and thou shalt be saved, and thy house" (Acts xvi. 30, 31). It would, surely, be well if this method of dealing with an anxious inquirer were more faithfully adopted.

[6] [There are three very distinct aspects of the death of Christ which, to apprehend clearly, is of unspeakable value to the soul.

1st. That which is typified in the blood of the paschal lamb on Israel's doors in Egypt. This is the judgment of God against the sinner in the person of the Substitute provided for him. Rom. iii. 23-27 applies to this.

It brings peace to the soul who believes, for his judgment is passed. Christ has borne it in our stead.

2nd. As revealed at the passage of the Red Sea. There it is fully manifested that God is *for* His people; He has completely overcome their enemy and freed them from his power forever. The prince and his hosts, who ruled over them unto death, are drowned in the sea. God's people have passed out of his dominions, and can now go on with God in perfect freedom. No condemnation remains. Henceforth, to faith, Satan is a vanquished foe. God's people are delivered; they can now, in settled peace, worship, praise, and serve their God. Blessed, holy deliverance and service! Rom. vi.-vii. gives the full teaching of this aspect of the death of Christ.

3rd. As seen in the passage of Jordan. There is no judgment to escape there; no foe pressing behind. It is a question of entering the good land which is just across. It is the death of Christ here as *the ending of His people's history as children of Adam*; that, by resurrection, He may now introduce them, as having died and risen with Him, into the place of glory where He has gone. By this it can be said, "As He is, so are we in this world" (I John iv. 17).

Col. ii. 10-iii. 4, is the New Testament doctrine of this precious truth. ED.]

[7] The reader may here remark that "the old corn of the land of Canaan" is a type of Christ risen and glorified. The manna is a type of Christ in His humiliation. The remembrance of Him in the latter is ineffably precious to the soul. It is sweet to look back and trace His way as the lowly, humble, self-emptied man. This is to feed upon the hidden manna—"Christ, once humbled here." Nevertheless, a risen, ascended and glorified Christ is the true object for the heart of the Christian; but to enjoy Him there, the reproach of this present evil world—all conformity to it— must be rolled away from us by the spiritual application of the circumcision of Christ. He was not conformed to this world, and we must be prepared to identify ourselves with Him in this.

[8] There is a passage in the book of Deuteronomy which, as it may present a difficulty to some minds, should be noticed here. "And the Lord heard the voice of your words, when ye spake unto me; and the Lord said unto me, I have heard the voice of the words of this people which they have spoken unto thee: *they have well said all that they have spoken*" (Deut. v. 28). From this passage, it might seem as though the Lord approved of their making a vow; but if my reader will take the trouble of reading the entire context, from verse 24 to 27, he will see that it has nothing whatever to say to the vow, but that it contains the expression of their terror at the consequences of their vow. They were not able to endure that which was commanded. "If," said they "we hear the voice of the Lord our God any more, then we shall die. For who is there of all flesh that hath heard the voice of the living God speaking out of the midst of the fire, as we have, and lived? Go thou near, and hear all that the Lord our God shall say; and speak thou unto us all that the Lord our God shall speak unto thee; and we will hear it and do it." It was the confession of their own inability to encounter Jehovah in that awful aspect which their proud legality had led Him to assume. It is impossible that the Lord could ever commend an

abandonment of free and changeless grace for a sandy foundation of works of law. (See "Notes on the book of Exodus," page 253. Same publishers.)

[9] [That is, as many as are on that principle—of "law," "works of law." ED.]

[10] [The Greek word translated "show" is more exactly rendered "announce" or "proclaim"—same word as in I Cor. ix. 14. ED.]

[11] It is needful to bear in mind that, while the blood of Christ is that alone which introduces the believer, in holy boldness, into the presence of God, yet it is nowhere set forth as our centre, or bond of union. Truly precious is it for every blood-washed soul to remember, in the secret of the divine presence, that the atoning blood of Jesus has rolled away for ever his heavy burden of sin. Yet the Holy Ghost can only gather us to the person of a risen and glorified Christ, who, having shed the blood of the everlasting covenant, is gone up into heaven in the power of an endless life, to which divine righteousness inseparably attaches. A living Christ, therefore, is our centre and bond of union. The blood having answered for us to God, we gather round our risen and exalted Head in the heavens. "I, if I be lifted up from the earth, will draw all men unto *Me*." We behold in the cup in the Lord's Supper the symbol of shed blood; but we are neither gathered round the cup nor the blood, but round Him who shed it. The blood of the Lamb has put away every obstacle to our fellowship with God; and in proof of this the Holy Ghost has come down to baptize believers into one body, and gather them round the risen and glorified Head. The wine is *the memorial* of a life shed out for sin: the bread is *the memorial* of a body broken for sin: but we are not gathered round a life poured out, nor round a body broken, but round a living Christ, who dieth no more, who cannot have His body broken any more, or His blood shed any more. This makes a serious difference; and when looked at in connection with the discipline of the house of God, the difference is immensely important. Very many are apt to imagine that when any one is put away from or refused communion, the question is raised as to there being a link between his soul and Christ. A moment's consideration of this point in the light of Scripture will be sufficient to prove that no such question is raised. If we look at the case of the "wicked person" in I Cor. v., we see one put away from the communion of the Church on earth who was nevertheless a Christian, as people say. He was not, therefore, put away because he was not a Christian: such a question was never raised; nor should it be in any case. How can we tell whether a man is eternally linked with Christ or not? Have we the custody of the Lamb's book of life? Is the discipline of the Church of God founded upon what we can know, or upon what we *cannot*? Was the man in I Cor. v. linked eternally with Christ, or not? Was the Church told to inquire? Even suppose we could see a man's

name written in the book of life, that would not be the ground of receiving him into the assembly on earth, or retaining him there. That which the Church is held responsible for, is to keep herself pure in doctrine, pure in practice, and pure in association, and all this on the ground of being God's house. "Thy testimonies are very sure; holiness becometh Thy house, O Lord, for ever." When any one was separated, or "cut off," from the congregation of Israel, was it because of not being an Israelite? By no means; but because of some moral or ceremonial defilement which could not be tolerated in God's Assembly. In Achan's case (Josh. vii.), although there were six hundred thousand souls ignorant of his sin, yet God says, "*Israel hath sinned.*" Why? Because they were looked at as God's Assembly, and there was defilement there which, if not judged, all would have been broken up.

[12] Those who are competent to do so can look at the original of this important chapter, where they will see that the word translated "approved" (ver. 19) comes from the same root as that translated "examine himself" (ver. 28). Thus we see that the man who approves himself takes his place amongst the approved, and is the very opposite of those who were amongst the heretics. Now the meaning of a heretic is not merely one who holds false doctrine, though one may be a heretic in so doing, but one who persists in the exercise of *his own will.* The apostle knew that there must be heresies at Corinth, seeing that there were sects: those who were doing their own will were acting in opposition to God's will, and thus producing division; for God's will had reference to the whole body. Those who were acting heretically were despising the Church of God.

[13] It may be well to add a word here for the guidance of any simple-hearted Christian who may find himself placed in circumstances in which he is called upon to decide between the claims of different tables which might seem to be spread upon the same principle. To confirm and encourage such an one in a truthful course of action, I should regard as a most valuable service.

Suppose, then, I find myself in a place where two or more tables have been spread; what am I to do? I believe I am to inquire into the *origin* of these various tables, to see how it became needful to have more than one table. If, for example, a number of Christians meeting together have admitted and retained amongst them any unsound principles, affecting the person of the Son of God, or subversive of the unity of the Church of God on earth; if, I say, such principles be admitted and retained in the assembly, or if persons who hold and teach them be received and acknowledged by the assembly; under such painful and humiliating circumstances the faithful can no longer be there. Why? Because I cannot take my place at it without identifyingmyself with manifestly unchristian principles. The same remark, of course, applies if the case be that of corrupt conduct unjudged by the assembly.

Now, if a number of Christians should find themselves placed in the circumstances above described, they would be called upon to maintain THE PURITY OF THE TRUTH OF GOD while acknowledging as ever the oneness of the body. We have not only to maintain the grace of the Lord's table, but the *holiness* of it also. Truth is not to be sacrificed in order to maintain unity, nor will *true* unity ever be interfered with by the strict maintenance of truth.

It is not to be imagined that the unity of the body of Christ is interfered with when a community based upon unsound principles, or countenancing unsound doctrine or practice, is separated from. The Church of Rome charged the Reformers with schism because they separated from her; but we know that the Church of Rome lay, and still lies, under the charge of schism because she imposes false doctrine upon her members. Let it only be ascertained that the truth of God is called in question by any community, and that, to be a member of that community, I must identify myself with unsound doctrine or corrupt practice, and then it cannot be schism to separate from such a community; nay, I am bound to separate.

[14] It is usual to apply the term "unworthily," in this passage, to *persons* doing the act, whereas it really refers to the *manner* of doing it. The apostle never thought of calling in question the Christianity of the Corinthians; nay, in the opening address of his epistle, he looks at them as "the Church of God which is at Corinth, sanctified in Christ Jesus, called saints" (or saints by calling). How could he use this language in the first chapter, and in the eleventh call in question the worthiness of these saints to take their seat at the Lord's Supper? Impossible. He looked upon them as saints, and as such he exhorted them to celebrate the Lord's Supper in a worthy manner. The question of any but true Christians being there, is never raised; so that it is utterly impossible that the word "unworthily" could apply to *persons*. Its application is entirely to the *manner*. The persons were worthy, but their manner was not; and they were called, as saints, to judge themselves as to their *ways*, else the Lord might judge them in their *persons* as was already the case. In a word, it was as *true* Christians they were called to judge themselves. If they were in doubt as to that, they were utterly unable to judge anything. I never think of setting my child to judge as to whether he is my child or not; but I expect him to judge himself as to his habits, else, if he do not, I may have to do, by chastening, what he ought to do by self-judgment. It is because I look upon him as my child, that I will not allow him to sit at my table with soiled garments and disorderly manners.

[15] The reader will bear in mind that the text does not touch the question of Scriptural discipline. There may be many members of the flock of Christ who could not be received into the Assembly on earth, inasmuch as they may possibly be leavened by false doctrine, or wrong practice. But, though we might not be able to receive them, we do not, by any means, raise the question as to their being in the Lamb's book of life. This is not the province nor the prerogative of the Church of God. "*The Lord* knoweth them that are His; and let every one that nameth the name of Christ depart from iniquity" (2 Tim. ii. 19).

[16] The church of Rome has so entirely departed from the truth set forth in the Lord's Supper, that she professes to offer, in the mass, "an unbloody sacrifice for the sins of the living and the dead." Now, we are taught, in Heb. ix. 22, that "without shedding of blood is no remission;" consequently, the church of Rome has no remission of sins for her members. She robs them of this precious reality, and instead thereof, gives them an anomalous and utterly unscriptural thing, called "an unbloody sacrifice, or mass." This, which, according to her own practice and the testimony of Heb. ix. 22, can never take away sin, she offers day by day, week by week, and year by year. A sacrifice without blood must, if Scripture be true, be a sacrifice without remission. Hence, therefore, the sacrifice of the mass is a positive blind raised by the devil, through the agency of Rome, to hide from the sinner's view the glorious sacrifice of Christ, "*once offered*," and never to be repeated. "Christ, being raised from the dead, dieth no more; death hath no more dominion over Him" (Rom. vi. 9). Every fresh sacrifice of the mass only declares the inefficiency of all the previous sacrifices, so that Rome is only mocking the sinner with an empty shadow. But she is consistent in her wickedness, for she withholds the cup from the laity, and teaches her members that they have body and blood and all in the wafer. But, if the blood be still in the body, it is manifestly not shed, and then we get back to the same gloomy point, namely, "no remission." "Without shedding of blood is no remission."

How totally different is the precious and most refreshing institution of the Lord's Supper, as set before us in the New Testament. There we find the bread broken, and the wine poured out—the significant symbols of a body broken, and of blood shed. The wine is not in the bread, because the blood is not in the body, for, if it were, there would be "no remission." In a word, the Lord's Supper is the distinct memorial of an eternally accomplished sacrifice; and none can communicate thereat, with intelligence or blessing, save those who know the full remission of sins. It is not that we would, by any means, make knowledge a term of communion, for very many of the children of God, through bad teaching, and various other causes, do not know the perfect remission of sins, and were they to be excluded on that ground, it would be making *knowledge* a term of communion, instead of *life* and *obedience*. Still, if I do not know, experimentally, that redemption is an accomplished fact, I shall see but little meaning in the symbols of bread and wine; and, moreover, I shall be in great danger of attaching a species of efficacy to the memorials, which belongs only to the great reality to which they point.

[17] I can only feel myself responsible to present myself in the assembly when it is gathered on proper Church ground, i. e., the ground laid down in the New Testament. People may assemble, and call themselves the Church of God, in any given locality, but if they do not exhibit the characteristic features and principles of the Church of God as set forth in Holy Scripture, I cannot own them. If they refuse, or lack spiritual power, to judge worldliness, carnality, or false doctrine, they are evidently not on proper Church ground: they are merely a religious fraternity, which, in its collective character, I am in no wise responsible before God to own. Hence the child of God needs much spiritual power, and subjection to the Word, to be able to carry himself through all the windings of the professing Church in this peculiarly evil and difficult day.

[18] The same Greek word, *ecclesia*, has been rendered both "church" and "assembly" in our English translation—"assembly" gives the true meaning.

[19] It is of the utmost importance to distinguish between what Christ builds, and what man builds. "The gates of hell" shall assuredly prevail against all that is merely of man; and hence it would be a fatal mistake to apply to man's building words which only apply to Christ's. Man may build with "wood, hay, stubble," alas! he does; but all that our Lord Christ builds shall stand forever. The stamp of eternity is upon every work of His hand. All praise to His glorious name!

[20] There is no such thing in Scripture as being a member of *a* church. Every true believer is a member of *the* Church of God—the body of Christ, and can therefore no more be, properly, a member of anything else, than my arm can be a member of any other body.

The only true ground on which believers can gather is set forth in that grand statement, "There is one body, and one Spirit." And again, "We being many are one loaf, and one body" (Eph. iv. 4; I Cor. x. 17). If God declares that there is but "one body," it must be contrary to His mind to own more than that one.

Now, while it is quite true that no given number of believers in any given place can be called "the body of Christ," or "the assembly of God;" yet they should be gathered on the ground of that body and that assembly, and on no other ground. We call the reader's special attention to this principle. It holds good at all times, in all places, and under all circumstances. The fact of the ruin of the professing Church does not touch it. It has been true since the day of Pentecost; is true at this moment; and shall be true until the Church is taken to meet her Head and Lord in the clouds, that "*there is one body*." All believers belong to that body; and they should meet on that ground, and on no other.

[21] The reader will need to ponder the distinction between the Church viewed as "the body of Christ," and as "the house of God." He may study Eph. i. 22; I Cor. xii. for the former. Eph. ii. 21; I Cor. iii.; I Tim. iii. for the latter. The distinction is as interesting as it is important.

[22] The reader will do well to note the fact that, in Matt. xvi., we have the very earliest allusion to the Church, and there our Lord speaks of it as a future thing. He says, "On this rock I *will* build My Church." He does not say, "I *have* been, or I *am* building." In short the Church had no existence until our Lord Christ was raised from the dead and glorified at the right hand of God. Then, but not until then, the Holy Ghost was sent down to baptize believers, whether Jews or Gentiles, into one body, and unite them to the risen and glorified Head in heaven. This body has been on the earth since the descent of the Holy Ghost; is here still, and shall be until Christ comes to fetch it to Himself. It is a perfectly unique thing. It is not to be found in Old Testament Scripture. Paul expressly tells us it was not revealed in other ages; it was hid in God, and never made known until it was committed to him. (See, carefully, Rom. xvi. 25, 26; Eph. iii. 3-11; Col. i. 24-27.) True it is—most blessedly true—that God had a people in Old Testament times. Not merely the nation of Israel, but a quickened, saved, spiritual people, who lived by faith, went to heaven, and are there "the spirits of just men made perfect." But the Church is never spoken of until Matt. xvi., and there only as a future thing. As to the expression used by Stephen, "The Church in the wilderness" (Acts vii. 38), it is pretty generally known that it simply refers to the congregation of Israel. The *termini* of the Church's earthly history are Pentecost (Acts ii.), and the rapture (I Thess. iv. 16, 17).

[23] Let the reader note this title, "*Son of Man*." It is infinitely precious. It is a title indicating our Lord's rejection as the Messiah, and leading out into that wide, that universal sphere over which He is destined in the counsels of God, to rule. It is far wider than Son of David, or Son of Abraham, and has peculiar charms for us, inasmuch as it places Him before our hearts as the lonely, outcast Stranger, and yet as the One who links Himself in perfect grace with us in all our need—One whose footprints we can trace all across this dreary desert. "The Son of Man hath not where to lay His head." And yet it is as Son of Man that He shall, by-and-by, exercise that

universal dominion reserved for Him according to the eternal counsels of God. See Daniel vii.

[24] The intelligent reader does not need to be told that all believers are priests; and, further, that there is no such thing as a priest upon earth, save in the sense in which all true Christians are priests. The idea of a certain set of men, calling themselves priests in contrast with the people—a certain caste distinguished by title and dress from the body of Christians, is not Christianity at all, but Judaism or intelligently worse. All who read the Bible and bow to its authority will be perfectly clear as to these things.

[25] The reader will notice that in Matthew vi. I, the marginal reading is the correct one: "Take heed that ye do not your *righteousness* before men, to be seen of them." Then we have the three departments of this righteousness, namely, alms-giving (ver. 2); prayer (ver. 3); fasting (ver. 16). These were the very things Cornelius was doing. In short, he feared God, and was working righteousness, according to his measure of light.

[26] [An evangelist will not travel far in our day to find persons who will take him warmly by the hand, and profess lively interest in his work. A moment's intercourse with them, however, will disclose them to be agents of "Christian Science," of "Millennial Dawn" of "Seventh Day Adventism" or of some one or other of like systems—messengers of Satan, all professing Christianity, though in reality destroyers of it; pluming themselves with its name, only to get inside and work destruction the more easily. ED.]

[27] For a fuller exposition of the doctrine of the sabbath, see "Notes on Genesis" (chap. ii.); also, "Notes on Exodus" (chaps. xvi. and xxxi.).

[28] We would here offer a remark in reference to the appointment of deacons in Acts vi. This case has been adduced in proof of the rightness of a congregation electing its own pastor; but the proof fails in every particular. In the first place, the business of those deacons was "to serve tables." Their functions as deacons were temporal, not spiritual. They might possess spiritual gift independently altogether of their deaconship. Stephen did possess such.

But more than this. Although the disciples were called upon to look out for men competent to take charge of their temporal affairs, yet the apostles alone could appoint them. Their words are, "Whom *we* may appoint over this business." In other words, although there is a vast difference between a deacon and a pastor, between taking charge of money and taking the oversight of souls, yet even in the matter of a deacon the appointment in Acts vi. was entirely divine; and hence it affords no warrant for a church electing its own pastor.

We might further add that *office* and *gift* are clearly distinguished in the word of God. There might be, and were, many elders and deacons in any given church, and yet the fullest and freest exercise of gift when the whole church came together into one place. Elders and deacons might or might not have the gift of teaching or exhortation. Such gift was quite independent of their special office. In I Cor. xiv., where it is said, "Ye may all prophesy one by one," and where we have a full view of the public assembly, there is not a word about an elder or a president of any kind whatever.

[29] Let the reader carefully note that *gifts*, as evangelists, pastors, teachers, prophets, being given directly by the Head of the Church for the edification of His people on earth (see Eph. iv. 8-13) were never appointed or "licensed" by apostolic hands or any others. Elders and deacons were to act as guides and to serve in the assemblies in which they had their place. To this position or *office* they were appointed by an apostle, or one sent by him. [ED.]

[30] How interesting to find "Mary the mother of Jesus" named here, as being at the prayer-meeting! What would she have said if any one had told her that millions of professing Christians would yet be praying to her?